Understanding Technology in Education

Understanding Technology in Education

Edited by

Hughie Mackay
Michael Young
and
John Beynon

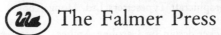 The Falmer Press

(A member of the Taylor & Francis Group)
London · New York · Philadelphia

UK   The Falmer Press, 4 John Street, London WC1N 2ET
USA   The Falmer Press, Taylor & Francis Inc., 1900 Frost Road, Suite 101, Bristol, PA 19007

First published 1991

British Library Cataloguing in Publication Data

Understanding technology in education.
  1. Great Britain. Education. Curriculum subjects. Technology
  I. Mackay, Hughie   II. Young, Michael   III. Beynon, John
  607.41

ISBN 1–85000–887–6
ISBN 1–85000–888–4

Library of Congress Cataloging-in-Publication Data

Understanding technology in education/edited by
  Hughie Mackay, Michael Young & John Beynon.
    Includes bibliographical references.
    ISBN 1–85000–887–6 : ISBN 1–85000–888–4 (pbk.) :
    1. Technology—Study and teaching. I. Mackay, Hughie.
II. Young, Michael F.D. III. Beynon, John.
T65.U35 1990
607.1—dc20   90–40337
                                     CIP

Typeset in 10/12 Garamond by
Graphicraft Typesetters Ltd, Hong Kong

Jacket design by Caroline Archer

Printed in Great Britain by Burgess Science Publishers, Ltd.
Basingstoke

Contents

Contents

Acknowledgments

The editors and publishers are grateful to the following for permission to reproduce copyright material:

Monthly Review Press (New York) for 'Social choice in machine design: the case of automatically controlled machine tools' by David Noble, from Zimbalist, A. (Ed.) (1979) *Case Studies on the Labor Process.*

Pluto Press (London) for 'The gendering of technology', from Cockburn, Cynthia (1985) *Machinery of Dominance: Women, Men and Technical Know-How.*

Ablex (New Jersey) for 'The selling of the new technology', from Webster, Frank and Robins, Kevin (1986) *Information Technology: a Luddite Analysis.*

Polity Press (Cambridge) for 'The information society: ideology or utopia?', from Lyon, David (1988) *The Information Society: Issues and Illusions.*

Pluto Australia for 'Mass production, the Fordist system, and its crisis', from Mathews, John (1989) *Tools of Change: New Technology and the Democratisation of Work.*

The editor and publishers of *Marxism Today* for Murray, Robin 'Life after Henry (Ford)', from the October 1988 issue.

The editor and publishers of *Radical Science* for Linn, Pam 'Microcomputers in education: dead and living labour', from issue 18 (1985).

Technology as an Educational Issue: Social and Political Perspectives

Hughie Mackay

Of all the changes required by the national curriculum, technology is perhaps the most dramatic. Technology's rise to preeminence in recent years — culminating in its status as one of the seven foundation subjects in the national curriculum — provides exciting possibilities for changing educational practices and resolving some key educational dilemmas. As technology is finding its way into the national curriculum, it is, hopefully, becoming redefined: IT was introduced very quickly, with little educational rationale, and with a very narrow definition of computer literacy. Going, however, are the days of IT in schools being about teaching keyboard skills or writing Basic programs, and of IT being a part of mathematics or business studies departments. Going, hopefully, is the approach that technology is a subject only for less academic pupils. Rather, design and technology are to take place across the curriculum, and are seen as encompassing every stage of a product's life cycle — researching, planning, making and evaluating the worth of a product; and IT is to take the form of 'computers across the curriculum'.

We subscribe to a positive view of the educational potential of technology; and see the possibility of radical shifts in what is defined as technology. Teaching may come to be *about* technology — about technology in its social context, as opposed to about abstracted machines. Our interest is in challenging hitherto dominant assumptions and definitions about technology, and showing how it is a key component of social life in the late twentieth century. By taking it on board in this way, technology teaching provides interesting answers to leading questions about vocationalism, relevance and the curriculum; technology opens up some tremendous possibilities.

In itself, of course, the technology has extremely limited consequences — it can be employed to liberate or oppress, to achieve what its designers intended, or for various other purposes. This book is concerned with providing something of a tool-kit — a range of concepts and theories — for investigating how and why technology liberates or oppresses. It aims to provide teachers and educationalists with some key concepts and theories; we hope that these tools will help them to redefine the scope and nature of technology in education; our task is to show, by argument and example, that technology is not to be seen in terms of artefacts alone: technology is much more than that. The book is not like most on technology in education: it is not a cook-book about hardware or software. A tool-kit is made up of the equipment that you need to do a job properly, and we feel that the ideas in the present collection will equip educationalists to understand technology better, and thus to teach about it better.

There has been little opportunity as yet for debate about technology in education. As well as being introduced hastily, IT in education, in particular, was introduced at a time of massive upheaval in the British education system. Perhaps because of the pressure on teachers of recent changes, it has not, generally, been discussed from an educationalist's perspective. Michael Apple, the American sociologist of education, is one of the few exceptions; he cites empirical evidence to support his argument that the growth of IT in education has led to an increase in educational inequality — in relation to class, gender and race. In contrast with the enthusiastic rhetoric of the 'IT into education' lobby, his approach raises some critical points about the technology, in terms of its educational consequences; he sees technology as the latest threat to democratic education. His work is unusual in that, unlike many technologists, he relates technology to the key educational question of equality. Although some technologists may make the mistake of failing to do this, teachers are more likely to be making such educational connections in their work on the technology curriculum. More broadly, Apple argues that education should always be a democratizing movement. As technology moves into the class-room it must be transformed, in order that it does not bring in with it narrow, managerialist views of efficiency; technology in education raises questions not just about what sort of workforce we require, but also about what kind of society.

In contrast to such an educationalist perspective, IT in education has been promoted and received generally uncritically; it is seen as mere artefacts. Artificial intelligence (AI), for example — defined by some as getting machines to do things which, if they were done by people, would be consi-dered 'intelligent' — can provide us with tools for learning. In the form of expert systems, AI has worked within tightly defined domains — medical diagnosis, computer fault diagnosis, etc. To suggest that a machine can behave like a human, however, is to ignore notions of feeling or meaning which are, at least, problematic in relation to a machine. Natural language recognition — machines recognizing human language — is a key component of AI, yet the meaning of any word or phrase is highly dependent on the context in which it is used. For a machine to understand the totality of that context as we humans do would require the codification within the machine of the totality of our cultural knowledge — not a trivial task! AI thus depends on simplistic approaches to human culture.

Yet it is the AI paradigm, rather than a social approach to technology, that has been predominant in discussion of IT in education. The focus has been on the technological artefact, which has been treated as if it can be divorced from its social and cultural context, as if it is a clever machine of which we in education can make use. Technology, we would argue, is much more than that. A range of social theorists have addressed technology, and some of their ideas seem to us highly relevant to achieving an understanding of the nature of technology. If technology is to be a central part of the curriculum, it will become much more than artefacts which can be used.

It seems to us that the technology needs to be viewed in a new way. It needs to be seriously questioned in educationalists' terms — because it is of crucial importance and provides such exciting possibilities. Our aim is to equip educationalists interested in such a project with some key concepts from the sociology of technology; in this field are to be found the concepts and theories for us to make sense of this educational phenomenon, and our aim is to present these in a way which is relevant to the educational endeavour. There has been an emerging sociology of technology in recent years, yet little awareness of this from sociologists of education. In the past, sociology of education has addressed key contemporary questions, but it seems to have missed technology, despite technology's profound impact on schools and the curriculum. We feel that it is possible to develop a better account than the 'mythinformation' and 'technoromanticism' which so pervade the field of technology, particularly IT: there are myths associated with the technology; teachers need to read the myths as adults, appreciating their hidden meanings rather than being taken in by the story. The attractive glitter of new technology must not lead to its unthinking acceptance. Webster and Robins, in their contribution to this volume, document the social forces and organizations which make up the lobby promoting IT, and IT in education; their focus is on the myths which have been associated with IT.

In this introduction I aim to relate some of the broader context of education and technology to contemporary educational developments in technology; in particular, I discuss some crucial changes in the organization of work which have paralleled the introduction of technology into schools. I then go on to to introduce some key ideas from the sociology of technology. The sociology·of technology is itself a recent and emerging discipline and has, as yet, hardly addressed education. It seems, however, to provide some useful aproaches for us in education; we need to develop some of its ideas in relation to schooling.

Education cannot be divorced from the society of which it is a part; and the same applies to understanding technology in education. Unfortunately, all too often technologists have done just this, treating technologies as neutral machines. Technology in education today shares with the whole host of movements for vocationalizing education the premise that (in this case) technology needs to be a part of the school curriculum because of some assumed needs of the labour market. The economic future of the country, many have argued, depends on microelectronics, and most jobs will require IT skills;

hence, schools should be teaching these skills. The heartland nature of microelectronic technology (that it affects every sector, industry and, almost, occupation) means, it is argued, that everyone should become computer literate at school — in the past, through courses with this as an explicit aim, and, more recently or in the future, through pupils' experience with IT across the curriculum. In the same vein, the Terms of Reference of the National Curriculum Working Group for Design and Technology refer to technology as preparation for the world of work:

> the use of computer and information technology in control, simulation and data storage and retrieval is becoming increasingly important in our society.... [This fact] should be reflected in the use of computer and information technology across the curriculum.

There is nothing new in demands for education to serve the needs of industry, and technology can be seen as merely the most recent in a series of innovations in education with this end in mind. However, what it is about technology that is 'relevant' is questionable: that technology presents a labour requirement which is not being met by the education system is at least implicit in the argument of those who advocate the extension of technology in education on the grounds of its prevalence in the workplace; work, it is argued, requires at least the ability to operate technology, and so school leavers must have that knowledge or skill.

The empirical evidence, however, suggests that when technology 'touches' a job, very often it makes the work of the operator *less* skilled, rather than requiring greater skill. Given the market nature of the economy and the strong competition induced, in particular, by international recession, and the fact that greater managerial control over labour will generally reduce worker autonomy over the work process, it would be surprising indeed if this were not often the case. Employers are increasingly reporting their need for transferable skills, rather than narrow technological ones (Wellington, 1989). The labour market demand for technological skills thus seems a somewhat flawed argument for promoting technology in education.

The present era is one of drastic restructuring of capital: worldwide recession and intensified competition have stimulated the demand for new technology — which has been exacerbated in the UK by the introduction of curbs on trade union powers. In particular, we are seeing a shift towards 'flexible specialization' — as in, for example, 'flexible manufacturing systems' (FMS). Piore and Sabel (1984) refer to a 'second industrial divide' which marks the transformation from a system of mass production (Fordism) to one of flexible specialization: the organization of production around large numbers of identical goods is being replaced by the production of smaller batches, required by the increasing segmentation of markets, which is accompanied by greater occupational flexibility (post-Fordism). New technology brings to small-batch production the economies of Fordist production. Mathews' contribution to this volume constitutes an excellent summary of these changes in the organization of production. Considerable debate as to whether 'Fordism', as commonly characterized, has ever been the prevalent mode of organizing production, and as to whether we are witnessing something which is qualitatively different from the so-called Fordist era (Williams *et al.*, 1987; Pollert, 1988, *Science as Culture*, 1990); it is sufficient for us to say that the debate is important and highly relevant to education. Broadening the debate from a narrow focus on *work organization* — as Murray's short paper in this volume does — there has been considerable debate about moves towards a *post-Fordist society* — by which is meant a society characterized not only by flexible and decentralized forms of production, but also the development of new social segmentations which are replacing traditional class divisions. By including Mathews' and Murray's papers, we are not ignoring the; there are changes in the world of work and beyond which have profound consequences for education.

This broader context, of IT being an instrument of capitalist restructuring and thus operating to the detriment of workers, has led some to dismiss IT in education, and to advocate its rejection; Webster and Robins, who are contributors to this volume, take such a stance. Computer literacy and the technologization of education are seen as key components of a policy to vocationalize the education system — with the ideological aim of inculcating people with notions of flexibility and passivity. In the allegedly neutral and inevitable processes of restructuring and automation, pupils are being inculcated with the notion that in their working lives they should expect to be in and out of work, trained and re-trained. Such a path, they argue, is neither inevitable, neutral or desirable (Webster and Robins, 1989).

Critiques of IT in education, it seems to us, should provide some basis for the development of alternatives to prevailing policies; this Webster and Robins singularly fail to do. We feel that in completely rejecting technology in education they are rejecting the *transformative* possibilities of technology — how technology affords opportunities for change, as well as domination, to take place. Developments in technology across the curriculum are not just ways of distracting or duping teachers; they could be part of the progressive development of breaking down of barriers between vocationally relevant and academic forms of education — as vocational education becomes broadened from its traditional, narrow, technical form; and as academic subjects take on board elements of the world of work. Technology thus allows the opportunity to break down an approach to education which is concerned with imparting what is deemed to constitute the body of knowledge of a discipline to 'academic' pupils and a narrow version of vocationalism to the rest. It allows for the breaking down of traditional academic boundaries, the academic division of labour; and for education to become relevant to all pupils' daily experience and future work experience. It also allows the breaking down of the barriers which exist particularly in the British education system between, on the one hand, science and technology subjects and, on the other, the arts and humanities.

The idea that technology is a social phenomenon is the starting point of the sociology of technology, which is concerned with countering notions of technological determinism; many of the contributors to this volume develop critiques of technological determinism. Mackenzie and Wajcman refer to technological determinism as 'the single most influential theory of the relationship between technology and society' (1985, p. 4); it is important because it is the way that most people think of technology.

By technological determinism is meant the notion that technology is autonomous from the society in which it is developed and operated; technology shapes society in a one-way, linear, causal relationship. Technology is somehow outside society, with a momentum of its own; and has effects on society — in other words, technical change causes social change. Clearly such an approach engenders a passivity with regard to technology — it is going to happen anyway; and technological determinism diverts attention from such questions as the relationship of technology to human need. Implicit in technological determinism is that there is no choice about the technology which we have.

The notion of technological determinism is illustrated by the common practice of referring to particular epochs by the name of their characteristic technology: the iron age, the steam age, or the silicon age. The technology, the use of these terms implies, determines the prevailing form of social organization, and can be used as a shorthand for the latter.

Dowling, in his contribution to this volume, explains how and why technology in education is a cultural phenomenon; he argues that technologies are defined by cultures rather than particular cultures defined by their technologies. Technologies are social process, rather than just machines or circuits. The information society thesis is a prevalent contemporary example of technological determinism. Whilst there are many strands of the thesis, and no shortage of those who subscribe to versions of it, they tend to share a belief that the technology is the fundamental determinant of a new, emerging and inevitable social order (which, in turn, is somehow emancipatory for humanity). Stonier's views are among the more preposterous of the school; he sees an era in which

> everyone [is] an aristocrat, everyone a philosopher ... authoritarianism, war and strife will be eliminated.... For the first time in history, the rate at which we solve problems will exceed the rate at which they appear. This will leave us to get on with the real business of the next century. To take care of each other. To fathom what it means to be human.... (1983, p. 214, cited in Webster and Robins, 1989)

Clearly, technology is one of the key issues of late twentieth-century industrial society — from nuclear power to genetic engineering; and it can plausibly be argued that contemporary surveillance technologies, which allow the state to 'see' and know so much about its citizenry, allow the development of a fundamentally different form of society, or of relationship of citizen to state, in which non-conformist actions and thoughts are monitored. The form of our society, however, as Lyon argues in his evaluation of the information society thesis in his contribution to this volume, is not *determined* by the technology, however critical a component the technology may be. Lyon's analysis breaks down the traditional opposing perspectives of technological determinism (new technology is inevitable and beneficial) and social determinism (technology is oppressive and alienating). And provides a balanced account of the role of technology in late twentieth century society.

The sociology of technology has been concerned to counter technological determinism (of which the information society thesis is but one example). Mackenzie and Wajcman (1985) argue the case for addressing the processes whereby technology is socially shaped. In its development and use, a technology is not merely some neutral physical artefact. Technologies are designed for particular purposes, and their design thus comes to embody particular imperatives; to use the terminology of semiotics, they are *encoded* in particular ways. The story of Alan Turing (Hodges, 1985) shows us how technological breakthroughs are social processes, and how the computer as we know it was the outcome (in part) of a complex of social and cultural processes, including one man's search for order; machine cannot be divorced from Turing's biography. Machines do not merely emerge from the inevitable trajectory of 'progress', they have human, social origins. If we apply such an approach to education we can see some of the issues that are thrown up by technology: the computer in the classroom might be useful for effective learning, but such a restricted use or approach does not deal with other key elements of education — for example, equipping pupils with cultural values or for participation in a democratic society. Teachers need technologies that are relevant and sensitive to teaching and learning in the classroom context.

Technologies, argue Mackenzie and Wajcman, do not, in practice, follow some pre-determined, inevitable course of development. The allocation of research and development monies is a remarkably clear way in which one can see that the development of technology is a result of social, political and economic factors, rather than the logical consequence of the nature of existing technology. Further, whilst one would not deny that technologies *do* have effects, or impacts, the nature of these is not built into the technology. Indeed, the same technology can be seen having profoundly different 'effects' in different societies and in different institutions: the laser can be a military or a health technology, and computers can both enable decentralized non-hierarchical organization and meet the needs of multinational corporations. Rather than being fixed, the impact of a technology depends on a broad range of political, economic and social factors. In short, it is argued that sociologists can do more than comment on the effects of technologies. To counter technological determinism, sociologists of technology have sought to show the *choices* which are made in technological development; specifically, they have addressed the *social shaping of technology* (Mackenzie and Wajcman, 1985).

Probably the first writer to develop this approach was Raymond Williams, often seen as the founder of cultural studies. In his seminal *Television Technology and Cultural Form* (1974) he discusses the social history surrounding the conception and development of the television. At the time of its birth, television technology, he argues, was a number of already-existing technologies, which were looking for a social use. Industrialization had led to the twin processes of mobilization and privatization, which created the market for the television. The history of television is thus a history of isolated inventors (e.g., Nipkow, Baird), large corporations (EMI, RCA), and very broad, macro, social processes. Choices were made, and television could have taken a very different form. David Noble's paper in this volume is a similar sort of account: countering the technological-determinist story that numerically-controlled machine tools led to industrial concentration and an increase in managerial control, Noble identifies the social forces at work — the organizations and corporations which promoted it — which were such that N/C (numerical control) took the form it did, and extended managerial control over the workforce. He points to alternative forms which numerically-controlled machine tools *might* have taken.

At least implicit in the social shaping of technology approach is that technology can never be neutral or apolitical. Technologies are commissioned or designed for particular purposes, and in this sense they arise from, and embody elements of, the prevailing social relations; their design embodies particular values and prefers particular uses. This process can be seen as the *encoding* of the technology. Rather than technology resulting from the application of some kind of neutral science (which, in turn, is seen by some as the gradual unfolding to humanity of the natural laws of nature) technologies emerge from particular social situations, or social relations. Technologies embody dead labour, the labour which went into their creation; and this dead labour is brought into use again when employed at a later date by living labour, the labour which is operating the technology today. Taking a particular labour process approach, Linn's contribution to this volume develops these notions, and other related concepts, with regard to the BBC-B microcomputer and the ILEA.

Within sociology, four approaches to the social shaping of technology can be identified; the first two focus on the design and development of technology. The social constructivist approach (Bijker, Hughes and Pinch, 1987) is concerned with writing the history of particular technologies, by examining the groups which were involved in the definition of the problem at various stages, and documenting how the solution which was adopted came to be so. Pinch's work on the bicycle, for example, identifies the *relevant social groups* which were involved in the definition and resolution of a variety of perceived design problems: anti-cyclists (some opposed to women riding bikes), women cyclists, elderly cyclists and sporting young men all had different needs and desires for the bicycle. Through particular definitions of problems, and through processes of *closure* (of debate about possible solutions), the bicycle came to take the form that it did — with pneumatic tyres, for example, because these were fastest, when to many 'relevant social groups' speed was not a critical factor (Pinch and Bijker, 1984). Central to the social constructivist approach is that 'it could have been otherwise'.

The Marxist labour process approach, on the other hand, argues that technological change cannot be fully understood by reference to individual inventions (Russell, 1986). Rather, it is argued, we need to examine how broader socio-economic forces affect the nature of technological problems and solutions; in contrast with the social constructivist approach, it focuses on the broader political and economic context of the technology — specifically, how the social relations of workers and management affect the nature of technologies. Braverman's work on the labour process constitutes the starting-point of recent labour process research (Braverman, 1974). Braverman points to the tendency within capitalism for technology to deskill work and to increase managerial control over the labour process. Labour process work has extended this approach by addressing such issues as the range of managerial strategies which are available in any one situation; and the significance of organizational cultures and control strategies to the design of work.

Most recently, the area of cultural studies has developed work on the cultural nature of technology (Morley and Silverstone, 1990). Haddon, argues that in his paper in this volume, technology can be viewed as a text, encoded with a preferred reading by its originators; but one which is actively decoded by its user. He applies this approach to microcomputing in the home and school. At the same time as embodying imperatives, a technology is not all-constraining; technologies can be appropriated by their users for purposes which differ from the intentions of their inventors (although the scope of such appropriation will always be limited); although much of it is designed for other contexts and purposes, the technology which we have in education provides us with possibilities which differ from those for which the technologies were developed. According to the cultural studies approach, the social nature of technology is not confined to its initial, invention stage: at the marketing stage the nature of a technology is actively constructed; and also at the later consumption stage, where appropriation is of both a use and meaning. Technologies are encoded both in terms of function, in that they embody prefered uses; and symbolically — the consumption of a technology has *meaning* to consumers, and this is taken account of at the earlier stages in the life of a technology, for example by designers. The cultural approach to technology thus treats technology as any other cultural product; it has a history and momentum which to some extent is independent of, rather than determined by, prevailing economic relations. Technologies, in this tradition, can be 'read' as 'texts'.

Any summary of the sociology of technology would be incomplete without reference to the emerging body of feminist work on technology. To conclude with this literature is not to imply its marginality — indeed, much of the critical work on the social nature of technology in recent years is from a feminist perspective. It stands apart from other approaches to the social nature of technology by arguing that these have been fundamentally limited by their tendency to ignore a key element of this social nature of technology, namely the exclusion of women from technology. Most writers in the technology field see the inventor, user, thinker about and reactor to technology as male (Rothschild, 1983). Cockburn in her paper in this volume explains how machines are male territory, and argues that control of technology is one key element of male power; the power of technology thus relates to power in society. Women are largely excluded from the invention, design and control of technology, and largely absent from positions of authority in the powerful institutions which shape technology. Rather, they experience technology as routine assembly or clerical workers, and in the home — where technology has done little to reduce the amount of time women spend on housework (Schwartz Cowan, 1989).

What, one might ask, does this sociology of technology have to do with technology in education? Clearly, technology in schools is moving away from its past, more restricted definitions of, for example, 'the technologist', or 'computer literacy'. Computer literacy, for some time the central plank of DES policy on IT in education, and computer studies, have largely been replaced by 'IT across the curriculum'. IT in education provides opportunities for both good and bad educational practices: independent learning, individually, tailored learning, more active learning, group work, and enhancing social interaction; it has enormous potential, much more than any previous educational technology. Such possible practices depend, however, on teaching philosophies and policies; they are not determined by the technology. On the technology side, we see the possibility of a shift in focus, and of technology becoming a part of the curriculum for *all* pupils. In a second volume we shall be presenting papers which examine the outcome of these developments, in various areas of teaching practice involving technology.

We see the need, more so now than ever before, for a computer or technological literacy. Such a literacy would be far broader than computer literacy as conventionally defined; it would entail, in the language of semiotics, the capacity to 'read' the technology 'text' — to decode the ways in which it has been encoded, and to understand the nature and scope of social relations which it embodies, represents and supports. This would include an understanding of how and by whom a technology is invented, designed, marketed and introduced, what people have to know to use it, how it affects the nature of work and leisure, its symbolic value, its cultural nature, who consumes it, and its effects. Clearly this is a very different programme from the teaching and learning of narrow keyboard skills; the 'information society' is more than a series of machines, and so, too, technological literacy has to be broader than this. This is not an agrument for the teaching of some kind of 'social impact of technology' course alongside (or instead of) the teaching of 'hard' skill; such an approach ignores the essentially social nature of technology — it is not merely a physical artefact which has social impacts. As Mackenzie and Wajcman (1985) point out, a technology is not merely a physical artefact, like the sheds and machines of a steelworks — because for these things to *do* something requires human activity, in this case steelworkers. Further, they argue, there is a third layer to any technology: a steelworks needs human knowledge — to have built it in the first place, to maintain it and to build the next generation of plant. Technology thus encompasses physical artefacts, human activity and human knowledge; it is a very broad phenomenon! From our perspective, technology literacy would involve learning to use the technology to achieve some end, and understanding the capacity and limitations of the technology in that endeavour.

This book was first planned before any of the national curriculum reports. Whether the sort of the technological literacy which we have just outlined will be congruent with the national curriculum remains to be seen. The latter might allow teachers to introduce a variety of exciting teaching practices with and about technology, and could lead to a shift away from narrower conceptions of skill. We and the contributors to this collection are teasing out a set of concepts which can be used to understand technology in education better. These are not sufficient; more are needed, but we want to make a contribution to the debate which is starting. We hope that the present volume will be seen not as a collection of academic papers, but as material which can be drawn on by teachers in their development of the technology curriculum.

References

APPLE, M. (1987) 'Mandating computers', in WALKER, S. (Ed.) *Changing Policies, Changing Teachers: New Directions for Schooling*, Milton Keynes, Open University Press.

BIJKER, W.E., HUGHES, T.P. and PINCH, T.J. (1987) *The Social Construction of Technological Systems: New Directions in the Sociology and History of Technology*, Cambridge, Mass., MIT Press.

BRAVERMAN, H. (1974) *Labor and Monopoly Capital: The Degradation of Work in the Twentieth Century*, New York, Monthly Review Press.

HODGES, A. (1985) *Alan Turing: The Enigma of Intelligence*, London, Unwin Paperbacks.

MACKENZIE, D. and WAJCMAN, J. (Eds) (1985) *The Social Shaping of Technology*, Milton Keynes, Open University Press.

MORLEY, D. and SILVERSTONE, R. (1990) 'Domestic communication — technologies and meanings', *Media, Culture and Society*, 12, 1, pp. 31–55.

PINCH, T.J. and BIJKER, W.E. (1984) 'The social construction of facts and artefacts: or how the sociology of science and the sociology of technology might benefit each other', *Social Studies of Science*, 14, 3, pp. 399–441.

PIORE, M. and SABEL, C. (1984) *The Second Industrial Divide: Possibilities for Prosperity*, New York, Basic Books.

POLLERT, A. (1988) 'The "flexible firm": fixation or fact', *Work, Employment and Society*, 2, 3, pp. 281–316.

ROTHSCHILD, J. (Ed.) (1983) *Machina ex Dea: Feminist Perspectives on Technology*, Oxford, Pergamon.

RUSSELL, S. (1986) 'The social construction of artefacts: a response to Pinch and Bijker', *Social Studies of Science*, 16, 2, pp. 331–46.

SCHWARTZ COWAN, R. (1989) *More Work for Mother: The Ironies of Household Technology from the Open Hearth to the Microwave*, London, Free Association Books, (originally published New York, Basic Books, 1983).

Science as Culture (1990) 8 (special issue on post-Fordism).

STONIER, T. (1983) *The Wealth of Information: A Profile of the Post-industrial Economy*, London, Thames Methuen.

WEBSTER, F. and ROBINS, K. (1989) *The Technical Fix: Education, Computers and Industry*, London, Macmillan.

WELLINGTON, J. (1989) *Education for Employment: The Place of Information Technology*, NFER, Nelson.

WILLIAMS, K., CUTLER, T., WILLIAMS, J. and HASLAM, C. (1987) 'The end of mass production?', *Economy and Society*, 16, 3, pp. 405–39.

WILLIAMS, R. (1974) *Television Technology and Cultural Form*, London, Fontana.

Chapter 1

Social Choice in Machine Design:
The Case of Automatically Controlled
Machine Tools

David Noble

Introduction

Almost everyone would agree that the technology of production and the social relations of production are somehow related. The explanation of this relationship often takes the form of a more or less 'hard' technological determinism: technology is the independent variable which effects changes in social relations; it has its own immanent dynamic and unilinear path of development. Further, it is an irreducible first cause from which social effects automatically follow. These effects are commonly called its 'social impact'.

Social analysts have recently begun to acknowledge that the technology and the social changes it seems to bring about are in reality interdependent, and it has become fashionable to talk about the dialectic between the forces of production and social relations. Nevertheless, most studies of production continue to focus primarily on the ways in which technology affects social relations, and there is precious little effort made to show precisely how technology reflects them. That is, although grantsmanship now demands that people refer to the mutual dependence of technology and society, and although socialists and other radicals now take it for granted that techno-logical development is socially determined, there remains very little concrete, historical analysis that demonstrates the validity of the position. The present essay, a case history of the design, deployment and actual use of automatically controlled machine tools, is meant to be a step in that direction.

Elsewhere I have tried to show that technology is not an autonomous force impinging upon human affairs from the 'outside', but is the product of a social process, a historically specific activity carried on by some people, and not others, for particular purposes (Noble, 1977). Technology thus does not develop in a unilinear fashion; there is always a range of possibilities or alternatives that are delimited over time — as some are selected and others denied — by the social choices of those with the power to choose, choices which reflect their intentions, ideology, social position and relations with other people in society. In short, technology bears the social 'imprint' of its authors. It follows that 'social impacts' issue not so much from the technology of production as from the social choices that technology embodies. Technology, then, is not an irreducible first cause; its social effects follow from the social causes that brought it into being: behind the technology that affects social relations lie the very same social relations. Little wonder, then, that the technology usually tends to reinforce rather than subvert those relations.

Here I want to render this abstract argument concrete by examining a particular technology. Moreover, I want to go a step further and show that the relationship between cause and effect is never automatic — whether the cause is the technology or the social choices that lie behind it — but is always mediated by a complex process whose outcome depends, in the last analysis, upon the relative strengths of the parties involved. As a result, actual effects are often not consonant with the expectations implicit in the original designs. The technology of production is thus twice determined by the social relations of production: first, it is designed and deployed according to the ideology and social power of those who make such decisions; and second, its actual use in production is determined by the realities of the shop-floor struggles between classes.

This essay is divided into six parts. A description and brief history of the technology involved is followed by a two-part section on social choice in design that discusses both the horizontal relations of production (between firms) and the vertical relations of production (between capital and labour). The fourth part examines social choice in the deployment of technology and the fifth looks at shop-floor realities where this technology is being used in the United States today. In the last part some alternative realities, with different social relations, are described.

The technology: automatically controlled machine tools

The focus here is numerically controlled machine tools, a particular production technology of relatively recent vintage. According to many observers, the advent of this new technology has produced something of a revolution in manufacturing, a revolution which, among other things, is leading to increased concentration in the metalworking industry and to a reorganization of the production process in the direction of greater managerial control. These changes in the horizontal and vertical relations of production are seen to follow logically and inevitably from the introduction of the new technology. 'We will see some companies die, but I think we will see other companies grow very rapidly,' a sanguine president of Data Systems Corporation opined (Stephanz, 1971). Less sanguine are the owners of the vast majority of the smaller metalworking firms which, in 1971, constituted 83 per cent of the industry; they have been less able to adopt the new technology because of the very high initial expense of the hardware, and the overheads and difficulties associated with the software (*ibid.*). In addition, within the larger, better endowed shops, where the technology has been introduced, another change in social relations has been taking place. Earl Lundgren, a sociologist who surveyed these shops in the late 1960s, observed a dramatic transfer of planning and control from the shop floor to the office (1969).

For the technological determinist, the story is pretty much told: numerical control leads to industrial concentration and greater managerial control over the production process. The social analyst, having identified the cause, has only to describe the inevitable effects. For the critical observer, however, the problem has merely been defined. This new technology was developed under the auspices of management within the large metalworking firms. Is it just a coincidence that the technology tends to strengthen the market position of these firms and enhance managerial authority in the shop? Why did this new technology take the form that it did, a form which seems to have rendered it accessible only to some firms, and why only this technology? Is there any other way to automate machine tools, a technology, for example, which would lend itself less to managerial control? To answer these questions, let us take a closer look at the technology.

A machine tool (for instance, a lathe or milling machine) is a machine used to cut away surplus material from a piece of metal in order to produce a part with the desired shape, size and finish. Machine tools are really the guts of machine-based industry because they are the means whereby all machinery, including the machine tools themselves, are made. The machine tool has traditionally been operated by a machinist who transmits his skill and purpose to the machine by means of cranks, levers, and handles. Feedback is achieved through hands, ears and eyes. Throughout the nineteenth century, technical advances in machining developed by innovative machinists built some intelligence into the machine tools themselves — automatic feeds, stops, throw-out dogs, mechanical cams — making them partially 'self-acting'. These mechanical devices relieved the machinist of certain manual tasks, but he retained control over the operation of the machine. Together with elaborate tooling — fixtures for holding the workpiece in the proper cutting position and jigs for guiding the path of the cutting tool — these design innovations made it possible for less skilled operators to use the machines to cut parts after they had been properly 'set up' by more skilled men;[1] but the source of the intelligence was still the skilled machinist on the floor.

The 1930s and 1940s saw the development of tracer technology. Here patterns, or templates, were traced by a hydraulic or electronic sensing device which then conveyed the information to a cutting tool which reproduced the pattern in the workpiece. Tracer technology made possible elaborate contour cutting, but it was only a partial form of automation: for instance, different templates were needed for different surfaces on the same workpiece. With the war-spurred development of a whole host of new sensing and measuring devices, as well as precision servomotors which made possible the accurate control of mechanical motion, people began to think about the possibility of completely automating contour machining.

Automating a machine tool is different from automating, say, automotive manufacturing equipment, which is single-purpose, fixed automation, and cost-effective only if high demand makes possible a high product volume. Machine tools are general-purpose, versatile machines, used primarily for small-batch, low-volume production of parts. The challenge of automating machine tools, then, was to render them self-acting while retaining their versatility. The solution was to develop a mechanism that translated electrical signals into machine motion and a medium (film, lines on paper, magnetic or punched paper tape, punched cards) on which the information could be stored and from which the signals could be reproduced.

The automating of machine tools, then, involves two separate processes. You need tape-reading and machine controls, a means of transmitting information from the medium to the machine to make the tables and cutting tool move as desired, and you need a means of getting the information on the medium, the tape, in the first place. The real challenge was the latter. Machine controls were just another step in a known direction, an extension of gunfire control technology developed during the war. The tape preparation was something new. The first viable solution was 'record-playback', a system developed in 1946–47 by General Electric, Gisholt, and a few smaller firms.[2] It involved having a machinist make a part while the motions of the machine under his command were recorded on magnetic tape. After the first piece was made, identical parts could be made automatically by playing back the tape and reproducing the machine motions. John Diebold, a management consultant and one of the first people to write about 'flexible automation', heralded record-playback as 'no small achievement . . . it means that automatic operation of machine tools is possible for the job shop — normally the last place in which anyone would expect even partial automation' (1952, p. 88). But record-playback enjoyed only a brief existence, for reasons we shall explore. (It was nevertheless immortalized as the inspiration for Kurt Vonnegut's *Player Piano*. Vonnegut was a publicist at GE at the time and saw the record-playback lathe which he describes in the novel.)

The second solution to the medium-preparation problem was 'numerical control' (N/C), a name coined by MIT engineers William Pease and James McDonough. Although some trace its history back to the Jacquard loom of 1804, N/C was in fact of more recent vintage; the brainchild of John Parsons, an air force subcontractor in Michigan who manufactured rotor blades for Sikorski and Bell helicopters. In 1949 Parsons successfully sold the air force on his ideas, and then contracted out most of the research work to the Servomechanisms Laboratory at MIT; three years later the first numerically-controlled machine tool, a vertical milling machine, was demonstrated and widely publicized.

Record-playback was, in reality, a multiplier of skill, simply a means of obtaining repeatability. The intelligence of production still came from the machinist who made the tape by producing the first part. Numerical control, however, was based upon an entirely different philosophy of manufacturing. The specifications for a part — the information contained in an engineering blueprint — are first broken down into a mathematical representation of the part, then into a mathematical description of the desired path of the cutting tool along up to five axes, and finally into hundreds or thousands of discrete instructions, translated for economy into a numerical code, which is read and translated into electrical signals for the machine controls. The N/C tape, in short, is a means of formally circumventing the role of the machinist as the source of the intelligence of production. This new approach to machining was heralded by the National Commission on Technology, Automation, and Economic Progress as 'probably the most significant development in manufacturing since the introduction of the moving assembly line' (Lynn, Roseberry and Babich, 1966, p. 89).

Choice in design: horizontal relations of production

This short history of the automation of machine tools describes the evolution of new technology as if it were simply a technical, and thus logical, development. Hence it tells us very little about why the technology took the form that it did, why N/C was developed while record-playback was not, or why N/C as it was designed proved difficult for the metalworking industry as a whole to absorb. Answers to questions such as these require a closer look at the social context in which the N/C technology was developed. In this section we will look at the ways in which the design of the N/C technology reflected the horizontal relations of production, those between firms. In the following section, we will explore why N/C was chosen over record-playback by looking at the vertical relations of production, those between labour and management.

To begin with, we must examine the nature of the machine-tool industry itself. This tiny industry which produces capital goods for the nation's manufacturers is a boom-or-bust industry that is very sensitive to fluctuations in the business cycle, experiencing an exaggerated impact of good times — when everybody buys new equipment — and bad times — when nobody buys. Moreover, there is an emphasis on the production of 'special' machines, essentially custom-made for users. These two factors explain much of the cost of machine tools: manufacturers devote their attention to the requirements of the larger users so that they can cash in on the demand for high-performance specialized machinery, which is very expensive due to high labour costs and the relatively inefficient low-volume production methods (see Rosenberg, 1963; Wagoner, 1968; Brown and Rosenberg, 1961; Melman, 1959). The development of N/C exaggerated these tendencies. John Parsons conceived of the new technology while trying to figure out a way of cutting the difficult contours of helicopter rotor-blade templates to close tolerances; since he was using a computer to calculate the points for drilling holes (which were then filed together to make the contour) he began to think of having the computer control the actual positioning of the drill itself. He extended this idea to three-axis milling when he examined the specification for a wing panel for a new combat fighter. The new high-performance, high-speed aircraft demanded a great deal of difficult and expensive machining to produce airfoils (wing surfaces, jet engine blades), integrally stiffened wing sections for greater tensile strength and less weight, and variable thickness skins. Parsons took his idea, christened 'Cardomatic' after the IBM cards he used, to Wright Patterson Air Force Base and convinced people at the Air Material Command that the air force should underwrite the development of this potent new technology. When Parsons got the contract, he subcontracted with MIT's Servomechanism Laboratory, which had experience in gunfire control systems.[3] Between the signing of the initial contract in 1949 and 1959, when the air force ceased its formal support for the development of software, the military spent at least $62 million on the research, development, and transfer of N/C. Up until 1953, the Air Force and MIT mounted a large campaign to interest machine-tool builders and the aircraft industry in the new technology, but only one company, Giddings and Lewis, was sufficiently interested to put their own money into it. Then, in 1955, N/C promoters succeeded in having the specifications in the Air Material Command budget allocation for the stockpiling of machine tools changed from tracer-controlled machines to N/C machines. At that time, the only fully N/C machine in existence was in the Servomechanism Lab. The Air Force undertook to pay for the purchase, installation, and maintenance of over 100 N/C machines in factories of prime subcontractors; the contractors, aircraft manufacturers, and their suppliers would also be paid to learn to use the new technology. In short, the Air Force created a market for N/C. Not surprisingly, machine-tool builders got into action, and research and development expenditure in the industry multiplied eightfold between 1951 and 1957.

The point is that what made N/C possible — massive Air Force support — also helped determine the shape the technology would take. While criteria for the design of machinery normally includes cost to the user, here this was not a major consideration; machine-tool builders were simply competing to meet performance and 'competence' specifications for government-funded users in the aircraft industry. They had little concern with cost-effectiveness and absolutely no incentive to produce less expensive machinery for the commercial market.

But the development of the machinery itself is only part of the story; there was also the separate evolution of the software. Here, too, Air Force requirements dictated the shape of the technology. At the outset, no one fully appreciated the difficulty of getting the intelligence of production on tape, least of all the MIT engineers on the N/C project, few of whom had had any machining experience before becoming involved in the project. Although they were primarily control engineers and mathematicians, they had sufficient hubris to believe that they could readily synthesize the skill of a machinist. It did not take them long to discover their error. Once it was clear that tape preparation was the stumbling-block to N/C's economic viability, programming became the major focus of the project. The first programs were prepared manually, a tedious, time-consuming operation performed by graduate students, but thereafter efforts were made to enlist the aid of Whirlwind, MIT's first digital computer. The earliest programs were essentially subroutines for particular geometric surfaces which were compiled by an executive program. In 1956, after MIT had received another air force contract for software development, a young engineer and mathematician named Douglas Ross came up with a new approach to programming. Rather than treating each separate problem with a separate subroutine, the new system, called APT (Automatically Programmed Tools), was essentially a skeleton program — a 'systematized solution', as it was called — for moving a cutting tool through space; this skeleton was to be 'fleshed out' for every particular application. The APT system was flexible and fundamental; equally important, it met air force specifications that the language must have a capacity for up to five-axis control. The air force loved APT because of its flexibility; it seemed to allow for rapid mobilization, for rapid design change, and for interchangeability between machines within a plant, between users and vendors, and between contractors and subcontractors throughout the country (presumably of 'strategic importance' in case of enemy attack). With these ends in mind, the air force pushed for standardization of the APT system, the Air Material Command cooperated with the Aircraft Industries Association Committee on Numerical Control to make APT the industry standard, and the machine-tool and control manufacturers followed suit, developing 'postprocessors' to adapt each particular system for use with APT.

Before long the APT computer language had become the industry standard, despite initial resistance within aircraft company plants. Many of these companies had developed their own languages to program their N/C equipment, and these in-house languages, while less flexible than APT, were nevertheless proven, relatively simple to use and suited to the needs of the company. APT was something else entirely. For all its advantages — indeed, because of them — the APT system had decided disadvantages. The more fundamental a system is, the more cumbersome it is, and the more complex it is, the more skilled a programmer must be, and the bigger a computer must be to handle the larger amount of information. In addition, the greater the amount of information, the greater the chance for error. But initial resistance was overcome by higher level management, who had come to believe it necessary to learn how to use the new system 'for business reasons' (cost-plus contracts with the air force). The exclusive use of APT was enforced. Thus began what Douglas Ross himself has described as 'the tremendous turmoil of practicalities of the APT system development'; the system remained 'erratic and unreliable', and a major headache for the aircraft industry for a long time.

The standardization of APT, at the behest of the air force, had two other interrelated consequences. First, it inhibited for a decade the development of alternative, simpler languages, such as the strictly numerical language

NUFORM (created by A.S. Thomas, Inc.), which might have rendered contour programming more accessible to smaller shops. Second, it forced those who ventured into N/C into a dependence on those who controlled the development of APT,[4] on large computers and mathematically sophisticated programmers. The aircraft companies, for all their headaches, could afford to grapple with APT because of the air force subsidy, but commercial users were not so lucky. Companies that wanted military contracts were compelled to adopt the APT system, and those who could not afford the system, with its training requirements, its computer demands and its headaches, were thus deprived of government jobs. The point here is that the software system which became the *de facto* standard in industry had been designed with a user, the air force, in mind. As Ross explained, 'the universal factor throughout the design process is the economics involved. The advantage to be derived from a given aspect of the language must be balanced against the difficulties in incorporating that aspect into a complete and working system' (Ross, 1978, p. 13). APT served the Air Force and the aircraft industry well, but at the expense of less endowed competitors.

Choice in design: vertical relations of production

Thus far we have talked only about the form of N/C, its hardware and software, and how these reflected the horizontal relations of production. But what about the precursor to N/C, record-playback? Here was a technology that was apparently perfectly suited to the small shop: tapes could be prepared by recording the motions of a machine tool, guided by a machinist or a tracer template, without programmers, mathematics, languages, or computers.[5] Yet this technology was abandoned in favor of N/C by the aircraft industry and by the control manufacturers. Small firms never saw it. The Gisholt system, designed by Hans Trechsel to be fully accessible to machinists on the floor, was shelved once that company was bought by Giddings and Lewis, one of the major N/C manufacturers. The GE record-playback system was never really marketed since demonstrations of the system for potential customers in the machine-tool and aircraft companies elicited little enthusiasm. Giddings and Lewis did in fact purchase a record-playback control for a large profile 'skin mill' at Lockheed but switched over to a modified N/C system before regular production got under way. GE's magnetic tape control system, the most popular system in the 1950s and 1960s, was initially described in sales literature as having a 'record-playback option', but mention of this feature soon disappeared from the manuals, even though the system retained the record-playback capacity.[6]

Why was there so little interest in this technology? The answer to this question is complicated. First, air force performance specifications for four- and five-axis machining of complex parts, often out of difficult materials, were simply beyond the capacity of either record-playback or manual methods. In terms of expected cost reductions, moreover, neither of these methods appeared to make possible as much of a reduction in the manufacturing and storage costs of jigs, fixtures, and templates as did N/C. Along the same lines, N/C also promised to reduce more significantly the labour costs for toolmakers, machinists and patternmakers. And, of course, the very large air force subsidization of N/C technology lured most manufacturers and users to where the action was. Yet there were still other, less practical, reasons for the adoption of N/C and the abandonment of record-playback, reasons that have more to do with the ideology of engineering than with economic calculations. However useful as a production technology, record-playback was considered quaint from the start, especially with the advent of N/C. N/C was always more than a technology for cutting metals, especially in the eyes of its MIT designers, who knew little about metalcutting: it was a symbol of the computer age, of mathematical elegance of power, order, and predictability, of continuous flow, of remote control, of the automatic factory. Record-playback, on the other hand, however much it represented a significant advance on manual methods, retained a vestige of traditional human skills; as such, in the eyes of the future (and engineers always confuse the present and the future) it was obsolete.

The drive for total automation which N/C represented, like the drive to substitute capital for labour, is not always altogether rational. This is not to say that the profit motive is insignificant — hardly. But economic explanations are not the whole story, especially in cases where ample government financing renders cost-minimization less of an imperative. Here the ideology of control emerges most clearly as a motivating force, an ideology in which the distrust of the human agency is paramount, in which human judgment is construed as 'human error'. But this ideology is itself a reflection of something else: the reality of the capitalist mode of production. The distrust of human beings by engineers is a manifestation of capital's distrust of labour. The elimination of human error and uncertainty is the engineering expression of capital's attempt to minimize its dependence upon labour by increasing its control over production. The ideology of engineering, in short, mirrors the antagonistic social relations of capitalist production. Insofar as the design of machinery, like machine tools, is informed by this ideology, it reflects the social relations of production.[7] Here we will emphasize this aspect of the explanation — why N/C was developed and record-playback was not — primarily because it is the aspect most often left out of such stories.

Ever since the nineteenth century, labour-intensive machine shops have been a bastion of skilled labour and the locus of considerable shop-floor struggle. Frederick Taylor introduced his system of scientific management in part to try to put a stop to what he called 'systematic soldiering' (now called 'pacing'). Workers practiced pacing for many reasons: to keep some time for themselves, to exercise authority over their own work, to avoid killing 'gravy' piece-rate jobs by overproducing and risking a rate cut, to stretch out available work for fear of lay-offs, to exercise their creativity and ingenuity in order to 'make out' on 'stinkers' (poorly rated jobs), and, of course, to express hostility to management (see Roy 1951–2, 1953; Mathewson, 1969). Aside from collective cooperation and labour-prescribed norms of behaviour, the chief vehicle available to machinists for achieving shop-floor control over production was their control over the machines. Machining is not a handicraft skill but a machine-based skill; the possession of this skill, together with control over the speeds, feeds, and motions of the machines, enables machinists alone to produce finished parts to tolerance (Montgomery, 1976b). But the very same skills and shop-floor control that made production possible also make pacing possible. Taylor therefore tried to eliminate soldiering by changing the process of production itself, transferring skills from the hands of machinists to the handbooks of management; this, he thought, would enable management, not labour, to prescribe the details of production tasks. He was not altogether successful. For one thing, there is still no absolute science of metal-cutting and methods engineers, time-study people, and Method Time Measurement (MTM) specialists — however much they may have changed the formal processes of machine-shop practice — have not succeeded in putting a stop to shop-floor control over production.[8]

Thus, when sociologist Donald Roy went to work in a machine shop in the 1940s, he found pacing alive and well. He recounts an incident that demonstrates how traditional patterns of authority rather than scientific management still reigned supreme:

> 'I want 25 or 30 of those by 11 o'clock,' Steve the superintendent said sharply, a couple of minutes after the 7:15 whistle blew. I [Roy] smiled at him agreeably. 'I mean it,' said Steve, half smiling himself, as McCann and Smith, who were standing near us, laughed aloud. Steve had to grin in spite of himself and walked away. 'What he wants and what he is going to get are two different things,' said McCann. (Roy, 1953, p. 513)

Thirty years later, sociologist Michael Burawoy returned to the same shop and concluded, in his own study of shop-floor relations, that 'in a machine shop, the nature of the relationship of workers to their machines rules out coercion as a means of extracting surplus' (1976).

This was the larger context in which the automation of machine tools took place; it should be seen, therefore, as a further managerial attempt to wrest control over production from the shop-floor workforce. As Peter Drucker once observed, 'What is today called automation is conceptually a logical extension of Taylor's scientific management' (1967, p. 26). Thus it is not surprising that when Parsons began to develop his N/C 'Cardomatic' system, he took care not to tell the union (the UAW) in his shop in Traverse City about his exciting new venture. At GE (Schenectady), a decade of work-stoppages over lay-offs, rate cuts, speed-ups and the replacement of machinists with less skilled apprentices and women during the war, culminated in 1946 in the biggest strike in the company's history, led by machinists in the United Electrical Workers (UE) and bitterly opposed by the GE Engineers' Association. GE's machine-tool automation project, launched by these engineers soon afterwards, was secret, and although the project had strong management support, publicist Vonnegut recalled, with characteristic understatement, that 'they wanted no publicity this time.'[9]

During the first decade of machine-tool automation development, the aircraft industry — the major user of automatic machine tools — also experienced serious labour trouble as the machinists and auto workers competed to organize the plants. The post-war depression had created discontent among workers faced with lay-offs, company claims of inability to pay, and massive downward reclassifications (Allen and Schneider, 1956). Major strikes took place at Boeing, Bell Aircraft (Parsons' prime contractor), McDonnell Douglas, Wright Aeronautical, GE (Evandale) (jet engines), North American Aviation, and Republic Aircraft. It is not difficult, then, to explain the popularity among management and technical men of a November 1946 *Fortune* article entitled 'Machines Without Men'. Surveying the technological fruits of the war (sensing and measuring devices, servomechanisms, computers, etc.), two Canadian physicists promised that 'these devices are not subject to any human limitations. They do not mind working around the clock. They never feel hunger or fatigue. They are always satisfied with working conditions, and never demand higher wages based on the company's ability to pay.' In short, 'they cause much less trouble than humans doing comparable work' (Leaver and Brown, 1946, p. 203).

One of the people who was inspired by this article was Lowell Holmes, the young electrical engineer who directed the GE automation project. However, in record-playback, he developed a system for replacing machinists that ultimately retained machinist and shop-floor control over production because of the method of tape preparation.[10] This 'defect' was recognized immediately by those who attended the demonstration of the system; they showed little interest in the technology. 'Give us something that will do what we say, not what we do,' one of them said. The defects of record-playback were conceptual, not technical; the system simply did not meet the needs of the larger firms for managerial control over production. N/C did. 'Managers like N/C because it means they can sit in their offices, write down what they want, and give it to someone and say, "do it,"' the chief GE consulting engineer on both the record-playback and N/C projects explained. 'With N/C there is no need to get your hands dirty, or argue' (personal interview). Another consulting engineer, head of the Industrial Applications Group which served as intermediary between the research department and sales department at GE (Schenectady) and a key figure in the development of both technologies, explained the shift from record-playback to N/C: 'Look, with record-playback the control of the machine remains with the machinist — control of feeds, speeds, number of cuts, output; with N/C there is a shift of control to management. Management is no longer dependent upon the operator and can thus optimize the use of their machines. With N/C, control over the process is placed firmly in the hands of management — and why shouldn't we have it?' (personal interview). It is no wonder that at GE, N/C was often referred to as a management system, not as a technology of cutting metals.[11]

Numerical control dovetailed nicely with larger efforts to computerize company operations, which also entailed concentrating the intelligence of manufacturing in a centralized office. In the intensely anti-Communist 1950s, moreover, as one former machine-tool design engineer has suggested, N/C looked like a solution to security problems, enabling management to remove blueprints from the floor so that subversives and spies couldn't get their hands on them. N/C also appeared to minimize the need for costly tooling and it made possible the cutting of complex shapes that defied manual and tracer methods, and reduced actual chip-cutting time. Equally important, however, N/C replaced problematic time-study methods with 'tape time' — using the time it takes to run a cycle as the base for calculating rates — replaced troublesome skilled machinists with more tractable 'button-pushers', and eliminated once and for all the problem of pacing. If, with hindsight, N/C seems to have led to organizational changes in the factory, changes which enhanced managerial control over production, it is because the technology was chosen, in part, for just that purpose. This becomes even clearer when we look at how the chosen technology was deployed.

Choice in deployment: managerial intentions

There is no question but that management saw in N/C the potential to enhance their authority over production and seized upon it, despite questionable cost-effectiveness.[12] Machine-tool builders and control manufacturers, of course, also promoted their wares along these lines; well attuned to the needs of their customers, they promised an end to traditional managerial problems. Thus the president of the Landis Machine Company, in a trade journal article entitled 'How Can New Machines Cut Costs?' stressed the fact that 'with modern automatic controls, the production pace is set by the machine, not by the operator' (Stickell, 1960, p. 61). The advertising copy of the MOOG Machine Company of Buffalo, New York, similarly described how their new machining centre 'has allowed management to plan and schedule jobs more effectively', while pointing out, benevolently, that 'operators are no longer faced with making critical production decisions' (MOOG Hydra-Point News, 1975).

Machine-tool and control system manufacturers peddled their wares and the trade journals, forever in search of advertisements, echoed their pitch. Initially, potential customers believed the hype; they very much wanted to. Earl Lundgren, the sociologist who surveyed N/C user plants in the 1960s, concluded that the 'prime interest in each subject company was the transfer of as much planning and control from the shop to the office as possible' and that management believed that 'under numerical control the operator is no longer required to take part in planning activities' (Lundgren, 1969).

In my own survey (1977–78) of twenty-five plants in the Midwest and New England — including manufacturers of machine tools, farm implements, heavy construction equipment, jet engines and aircraft parts, and specialized industrial machinery — I observed the same phenomenon. Everywhere, management initially believed in the promises of N/C promoters and attempted to remove all decision-making from the floor and assign unskilled people to N/C machines; to substitute 'tape time' for problematic time studies to set base rates for piecework and measure output quotas; and to tighten up authority by concentrating all mental activity in the office and otherwise to extend detail control over all aspects of the production process.

This is not to say, however, that I drew the same conclusions that Lundgren did in his earlier survey. Characteristically, for an industrial sociologist, he viewed such changes as requirements of the new technology, whereas, in reality, they reflected simply the possibilities of the technology which were 'seized upon' (to use Harry Braverman's phrase) by management to realize particular objectives, social as well as technical. There is nothing inherent in N/C technology, however, that makes it necessary to assign programming and machine tending to different people (that is, to management and workers, respectively); the technology merely makes it possible (Braverman, 1974, p. 199). Management philosophy and motives — reflecting the social relations of the capitalist mode of production in general and a historically specific economic and political context in particular — make it necessary that the technology be deployed in this way.

One illustration of managerial choice in machine deployment is provided by the experience of a large manufacturing firm near Boston. In 1968, owing to low worker morale, turnover, absenteeism, and the general unreliability of programming and machinery, the company faced what it termed a 'bottleneck' in its N/C lathe section. Plant managers were frantic to figure out a way to achieve the expected output from this expensive equipment. In that prosperous and reform-minded period, they decided upon a job enlargement/enrichment experiment wherein machine operators would be organized into groups and their individual tasks extended. Although it was the hope of the company that such a reorganization would boost the morale of the men on the floor and motivate them to 'optimize the utilization' of the machinery, the union was at first reluctant to cooperate, fearing a speed-up. The company was thus hard pressed to secure union support for their program and instituted a bonus for all participants. At one of the earliest management-union meetings on the new programme, the company spokesman began his discussion of the job-enlargement issue with the question (and thinly veiled threat), 'Should we make the hourly people button-pushers or responsible people?'

Given the new technology, management believed they now had the choice, and, given the pressure of unusual circumstances, they were prepared to exercise it in what they understood to be an atypical way.[13]

A second illustration of the managerial imperative behind technological determinism is provided in an interview I had with two shop managers in a plant in Connecticut. Here, as elsewhere, much of the N/C programming is relatively simple and I asked the men why the operators couldn't do their own programming. At first they dismissed the suggestion as ridiculous, arguing that the operators would have to know how to set feeds and speeds, that is, be industrial engineers. I pointed out that the same people probably set the feeds and speeds on conventional machinery, routinely making adjustments on the process sheet provided by the methods engineers in order to make out. They nodded. They then said that the operators couldn't understand the programming language. This time I pointed out that the operators could often be seen reading the mylar tape — twice-removed information describing the machining being done — in order to know what was coming (for instance, to anticipate programming errors that could mess things up). Again, they nodded. Finally they looked at each other, smiled, and one of them leaned over and confided, 'We don't want them to.' Here is the reality behind technological determinism in deployment.

Reality on the shop floor

Although the evolution of a technology follows from the social choices that inform it, choices which mirror the social relations of production, it would be an error to assume that in having exposed the choices, we can simply deduce the rest of reality from them. Reality cannot be extrapolated from the intentions that underlie the technology any more than from the technology itself.[14] Desire is not identical to satisfaction.

'In the conflict between the employer and employed,' John G. Brooks observed in 1903, 'the "storm centre" is largely at this point where science and invention are applied to industry.'[15] It is here that the reality of N/C was hammered out, where those who chose the technology finally came face-to-face with those who did not.

The introduction of N/C was not uneventful, especially in plants where the machinists' unions had a long history. Work stoppages and strikes over rates for the new machines were common in the 1960s, as they still are today. At GE, for example, there were strikes at several large plants and the entire Lynn, Massachusetts plant was shut down for a month during the winter of 1965. There are also less overt indications that management dreams of automatic machinery and a docile, disciplined workforce, but they have tended to remain just that.[16] Here we will examine briefly three of management's expectations: the use of 'tape time' to set rates; the deskilling of machine operators; and the elimination of pacing.

Early dreams of using tape time to set base rates and measure performance and output proved fanciful. As one N/C operator observed, while rates
on manual machines were sometimes too high, they were usually within a
reasonable range, whereas the rates on N/C were 'out of all relation to reality
— ridiculously high; N/C's were supposed to be like magic but all you can
do automatically on them is produce scrap.' The machines, contrary to their
advertisements, could not be used to produce parts to tolerance without the
repeated manual intervention of the operator in order to make tool offset
adjustments, correct for tool wear and rough castings, and correct programming errors (not to mention machine malfunctions, such as 'random holes' in
drills and 'plunges' in milling machines, often attributable to overheating). As
the N/C operator just quoted explained, in a response to a *New York Times*
article on the wonders of computer-based metalworking,

> Cutting metals to critical tolerances means maintaining constant con-
> trol of a continually changing set of stubborn, elusive details. Drills
> run. End mills walk. Machines creep. Seemingly rigid metal castings
> become elastic when clamped to be cut, and spring back when re-
> leased so that a flat cut becomes curved, and holes bored precisely on
> location move somewhere else. Tungsten carbide cutters impercept-
> ibly wear down, making the size of a critical slot half a thousandth
> too small. Any change in any one of many variables can turn the
> perfect part you're making into a candidate for a modern sculpture
> garden, in seconds. Out of generations of dealing with the persistent,
> ornery problems of metal cutting comes the First Law of Machining:
> 'Don't mess with success.' (Tulin, 1978)

In reality, N/C machines do not run by themselves — as the United
Electrical Workers argued in its 1960 *Guide to Automation*, the new equipment, like the old, requires a spectrum of manual intervention and careful
attention to detail, depending upon the machine, the product, and so on. The
fiction that the time necessary to do a job could be determined by simply
adding a standard factor or two (for set-up, breaks, etc.) to the tape (cycle)
time, was exploded early on, and with it hope of using the tape to measure
performance (although some methods people still try).

The deskilling of machine operators has also, on the whole, not taken
place as expected, for two reasons. First, as mentioned earlier, the assigning of
labour grades and thus rates to the new machinery was, and is, a hotly
contested and unresolved issue in union shops. Second, in union and non-
union shops alike, the determination of skill requirements for N/C must take
into account the actual degree of automation and reliability of the machinery.
Management has thus had to have people on the machines who know what
they are doing simply because the machines (and programming) are not
totally reliable; they do not run by themselves and produce good finished

parts. Also, the machinery is still very expensive (even without micro-processors) and thus so is a machine smash-up. Hence, while it is true that many manufacturers initially tried to put unskilled people on the new equipment, they rather quickly saw their error and upgraded the classification. (In some places the most skilled people were put on the N/C machines and given a premium but the lower formal classifications were retained, presumably in the hope that some day the skill requirements would actually drop to match the classification — and the union would be decertified.) The point is that the intelligence of production has neither been built entirely into the machinery nor been taken off the shop floor. It remains in the possession of the workforce.[17]

This brings, us, once again, to the question of shop-floor control. In theory, the programmer prepares the tape (and thus sets feeds and speeds, thereby determining the rate of production), proofs it out on the machine, and then turns the show over to the operator, who from then on simply presses start and stop buttons and loads and unloads the machine (using standard fixtures). This rarely happens in reality, as was pointed out above. Machining to tolerances generally requires close attention to the details of the operation and frequent manual intervention through manual feed and speed overrides. This aspect of the technology, of course, reintroduces the control problem for management. Just as in the conventional shop, where operators are able to modify the settings specified on the worksheet (prepared by the methods engineer) in order to restrict output or otherwise 'make out' (by running the machine harder), so in the N/C shop the operators are able to adjust feeds and speeds for similar purposes.

Thus, if you walk into a shop you will often find feed-rate override dials set uniformly at, say, 70 or 80 per cent of tape-determined feed rate. In some places this is called the '70 per cent syndrome'; everywhere it is known as pacing. To combat it, management sometimes programmes the machines at 130 per cent, and sometimes actually locks the overrides altogether to keep the operators out of the 'planning process'. This in turn gets management into serious trouble since the interventions are required to get the parts out of the front door.

It is difficult to assess to what extent the considerable amount of intervention is attributable to the inherent unreliability of the complex equipment itself, but it is certainly true that the technology develops shortcomings once it is placed on the shop floor, whether or not they were there in the original designs. Machines often do not do what they are supposed to do and down time is still excessive. Technical defects, human errors, and negligence are acknowledged problems, and so is sabotage. 'I don't care how many computers you have, they'll still have a thousand ways to beat you,' lamented one manager of N/C equipment in a Connecticut plant. 'When you put a guy on an N/C machine, he gets temperamental,' another manager in Rhode Island complained. 'And then, through a process of osmosis, the machine gets temperamental.'

On the shop floor, it is not only the choices of management that have an effect. The same antagonistic social relations that, in their reflection in the minds of designers, gave issue to the new technology, now subvert it. This contradiction of capitalist production presents itself to management as a problem of 'worker motivation', and management's acceptance of the challenge is its own tacit acknowledgment that it does not have shop-floor control over production, that it is still dependent upon the workforce to turn a profit.

Thus, in evaluating the work of those whose intentions to wrest control over production from the work force informed the design and deployment of N/C, we must take into account an article written by two industrial engineers in 1971 entitled 'A Case for Wage Incentives in the N.C. Age'. It makes it quite clear that the contradiction of capitalist production has not been eclipsed — computers or no computers:

> Under automation, it is argued, the machine basically controls the manufacturing cycle, and therefore the worker's role diminishes in importance. The fallacy in this reasoning is that if the operator malingers or fails to service the machine for a variety of reasons both utilization and subsequent return on investment suffer drastically.
>
> Basic premises underlying the design and development of N.C. machines aim at providing the capability of machining configurations beyond the scope of conventional machines. Additionally, they 'de-skill' the operator. Surprisingly, however, the human element continues to be a major factor in the realization of optimum utilization or yield of these machines. This poses a continuing problem for management, because a maximum level of utilization is necessary to assure a satisfactory return on investment. (Doring and Saling, 1971, p. 31)

The motivation problem boils down to this: What will a machine operator, 'skilled' or 'unskilled', do when he sees a $250,000 milling machine heading for a smash-up? He could rush to the machine and press the panic button, retracting the workpiece from the cutter or shutting the whole thing down, or he could remain seated and think to himself, 'Oh, look, no work tomorrow.' For management, the situation poses the dilemma faced by every capitalist, a contradiction succinctly, if inadvertently, expressed by another plant manager in Connecticut. With a colleague chiming in, he proudly described the elaborate procedure they had developed whereby every production change, even the most minor, had to be okayed by an industrial engineer. 'We want absolutely no decision made on the floor,' he insisted; no operator was to make any change from the process sheets without the written authorization of a supervisor. A moment later, however, looking out onto the floor from his glass-enclosed office, he reflected upon the reliability of the machinery, and the expense of parts and equipment, and emphasized, with equal conviction, that 'We need guys out there who can think.'

Alternative realities

Shop-floor realities are determined by the social relations, as well as the technology, of production and, as we have seen, the latter is shaped by the former no less than the reverse. But thus far we have examined only the ways in which managerial intentions, introduced in the form of new technology, are subverted in practice; this is only part of the story, the part defined, in a restricted way, by social relations which assign to labour a 'negative' role. Having had to adopt a defensive posture against a far more powerful adversary, the American trade union movement opted out of certain struggles (for instance, for the right to make production decisions, now an exclusive 'management prerogative') in order to concentrate on and gain advantage in others (for example, job security, wages, benefits). Accordingly, when confronted with changing technology, labour has generally limited its response to *post hoc* resistance. This has meant, of course, that labour's choices have not been registered in the actual design and deployment stages and that, therefore, the technology does not reflect its interest. A more forward-looking and sophisticated labour movement, however, facing an intensified management drive toward rationalization and automation, could transcend this passive role and begin to act positively, demanding, and preparing itself for, a voice in design and deployment decisions. As one American N/C machine operator has argued:

> The introduction of automation means that our skills are being downgraded, and instead of having the prospect of moving up to a more interesting job, we now have the prospect of either unemployment or a dead-end job. [But] there are alternatives that the union can explore. We have to establish the position that the fruits of technological change can be divided up — some to the workers, not all to the management, as is the case today. We must demand that the machinist rise with the complexity of the machine. Thus, rather than dividing his job up, the machinist should be trained to program and repair his new equipment — a task well within the grasp of most people in the industry.
>
> Demands such as these strike at the heart of most management prerogative clauses which are in many collective-bargaining contracts. Thus, to deal with automation effectively, one has to strike another prime ingredient of business unionism: the idea of 'let the management run the business'. The introduction of N.C. equipment makes it imperative that we fight such ideas. (Emspak, unpublished)

The real potential of this challenge can perhaps best be illustrated by the existing variations in deployment of the latest generation of N/C machines, called Computer Numerical Control (CNC) systems. CNC machines come equipped with a small minicomputer control unit. With this addition, made feasible by the advent of microprocessors, it becomes possible to store the information from a dozen or so tapes right on the machine itself and then simply retrieve the right program to make a part. More important, the information from the tape can be manipulated and edited: the sequence of operations can be changed, and operations can be added or subtracted. After the changes are made and the parts are run, the machine can produce a 'corrected' tape for permanent storage in the company library. With this technology, it becomes possible not only to edit tapes on the shop floor but to create them from scratch; in some systems, programs for even rather complex contours can be made right at the machine by either punching in the required information at a keyboard on the console (so-called manual data input — MDI) or by moving the machine itself to make the first part and entering the information after each operation. (This feature, of course, reintroduces the record-playback concept in an updated digitized form.)

Made possible by the revolution in microelectronics and introduced by machine-tool manufacturers in order to penetrate the vast job market (because it eliminates the overhead requirements of software preparation — the major obstacle for the job shop) and by large metalworking plants in order to get around insurmountable software programming problems (because it allows for easy tape correcting and editing), the new CNC technology lends N/C as never before to total shop-floor control.

Although the large metalworking plants in the United States are steadily introducing CNC equipment, the potential for shop-floor control is far from being realized. The GE plant in Lynn, Massachusetts, is a typical example. Here machine operators are not permitted to edit programs — much less to make their own — on the new CNC machines; quite often the controls are locked. Only supervisory staff and programmers are allowed to edit the programs. Managers are afraid of losing shop-floor control or confusing their tidy labour classification and wage system; programmers are afraid that operators lack the training and experience required for programming — an argument that has convinced at least some operators that these functions are beyond their intellectual grasp. The shortcomings of this system for the operators are obvious. Less obvious are the shortcomings for management: lower quality production and excessive machine down time. If the programs are faulty and the operator cannot (or is not allowed to) make the necessary adjustments, the parts produced will be faulty. If a machine goes down because of programming problems on the second and third shifts, when the programmers are not around, it is likely to be down for the night, with a corresponding loss in productivity.

The situation is quite different in the state-owned weapons factory in Kongsberg, Norway, a plant with roughly the same number of employees, a similar line of products (aircraft parts and turbines), a similar mix of commercial and military customers, and, most important, the same types of CNC machinery (although here they tend to be European-made rather than Japanese) as at GE.[18] But in Norway the operators routinely do all of the editing, according to their own criteria of safety, efficiency, quality, and convenience; they change the sequence of operations, add or subtract operations, and sometimes alter the entire structure of the program to suit themselves. When they are satisfied with a program and have finished producing a batch of parts, they press a button to generate a corrected tape which, after being approved by a programmer, is put into the library for permanent storage.

All operators are trained in N/C programming and, as a consequence, their conflicts with the programmers are reduced. One programmer — who, like most of his colleagues, had received his training in programming while still a machine operator — justified having any programmers at all by the fact that the programmer was a specialist and was thus more proficient (he also dealt directly with customers and did most of the APT programming of highly complex aircraft parts). Yet when asked if it bothered him to have his well-worked programs tampered with by the operators, he replied, without hesitation, that 'the operator knows best; he's the one who has to actually make the part and is more intimately familiar with the particular safety and convenience factors; also, he usually best knows how to optimize the program for his machine.'

This situation, it should be pointed out, is unusual even for Norway. It is the result of many factors. The Iron and Metalworkers' Union in Norway is the most powerful industrial union in the country and the local 'club' in Kongsberg is a potent force in the industrial, political and social life of Kongsberg, representing a cohesive and rather homogeneous working-class community. The factory is important in state policy, as a holding company in electronics, and is an important centre of high-technology engineering. Also, social democratic legislation in Norway has encouraged worker participation in matters pertaining to working conditions and has given unions the right to information. Most important, however, the local 'club' has been involved for the last seven years in what has been called the 'trade union participation project', an important development in workers' control which focuses upon the introduction of computer-based manufacturing technology.

In 1971, the Iron and Metalworkers' Union, faced with an unprecedented challenge of new computer-based information and control systems (for production, scheduling, inventory, etc., as well as machining), took steps to learn how to meet it. They succeeded in hiring, on a single-party basis (that is, without management collaboration), the government-run Norwegian Computing Centre to research the new technology for them. As the direct result of this unprecedented effort, computer technology was demystified for the union, and the union — and labour in general — was demystified for the computer scientists at the Centre; the union became more sophisticated about the technology and the technical people became more attuned to the needs and disciplines of trade unionists. In practical terms, the study resulted in the production of a number of textbooks on the new technology written by and for shop stewards, the creation of a new union position, the 'data shop steward', and, in time, the establishment of formal 'data agreements' (between individual companies and their local 'clubs' and between the national union and the employers' federation) which outlined the union's right to participate in decisions about technology.

The Kongsberg plant was the first site of such trade union participation. Here the data shop steward, a former assembly worker, is responsible for keeping abreast of and critically scrutinizing all new systems; another man is assigned the job of supervising the activity of the data shop steward to ensure that he doesn't become a 'technical man', that is, captive either of the technology or of management and out of touch with the interests of the people on the shop floor. The responsibilities are enormous: this is not a situation in which union and management cooperate harmoniously, nor is it a management-devised job-enlargement scheme to motivate workers. The task of the data shop steward, and the union in general, is to engage, as effectively as possible, in a struggle over information and control, a struggle engaged in, with equal sophistication and earnestness, by the other side.

When management plans to introduce a new computerbased production system, for example, the union must assume as a matter of course (based upon long experience) that the proposed design reflects purposes that are not necessarily consonant with the interests of the workers. The data shop steward and his colleagues must learn about the system early enough, and investigate it thoroughly enough, to ensure that it contains no features that make possible, for example, the measurement of individual performance or any monitoring of shop-floor activities that would restrict worker freedom or control. As it turns out, all new systems invariably contain such features (since they are often camouflaged attempts to introduce control mechanisms that have been successfully resisted by the workers in other forms), and it is up to the union to identify them and demand that they be eliminated. It is the union's responsibility to its members, in short, to struggle to 'recondition' the system so that it meets their own, as well as management's, specifications. At Kongsberg, for example, after a long battle, the union has succeeded in securing for all of the people on the shop floor complete access to the computer-based production and inventory systems. Just as CNC has made automatic machining more accessible to shop-floor control, so computer-integrated production systems have made it possible to eliminate certain managerial functions by simply extending the reach of the people on the shop floor. How this technology will actually be employed in a plant depends less upon any inherent nature of the technology than upon the particular manufacturing processes involved, the political and economic setting, and the relative power and sophistication of the parties engaged in the struggle over control of production.

The social relations of production shape the technology of production as much as the other way around. Given different social relations, one sees different designs, different deployment. Of course, these relations are themselves shaped by larger conditions — the political, economic, and cultural climate, the labour market, trade union traditions and strengths, international competition and the flow of investment capital. These factors always influence the conditions for struggle, define its constraints. But whatever the constraints, whatever the social conditions, the technological possibilities remain.

Notes

1   The use of jigs and fixtures in metalworking dates back to the early nineteenth century and was the heart of interchangeable parts manufacture, as Merritt Roe Smith has shown (1976). Eventually, in the closing decades of the century, the 'toolmaker' as such became a specialized trade, distinguished from the machinist. The new function was a product of modern management, which aimed to shift the locus of skill and control from the production floor, and the operators, to the toolroom. But however much the new tools allowed management to employ less skilled, and thus cheaper, machine operators, they were nevertheless very expensive to manufacture and store and they lent to manufacture a heavy burden of inflexibility, shortcomings which one Taylorite, Sterling Bunnell, warned about as early as 1914 (cited in David Montgomery, Forthcoming). The cost-savings that resulted from the use of cheaper labour were thus partially offset by the expense of tooling. Numerical control, as we will see, was developed in part to eliminate the cost and inflexibility of jigs and fixtures and, equally important, to take skill, and the control of it, off the floor altogether. Here again, however, the expense of the solution was equal to or greater than the problem. It is interesting to note that in both cases expensive new technologies were introduced to make it possible to hire cheaper labour, and the tab for the conversion was picked up by the state — the Ordnance Department in the early nineteenth century, the Departments of the Army and Navy in World War I, and the Air Force in the second half of the twentieth century.

2   The discussion of the record-playback technology is based upon extensive interviews and correspondence with the engineers who participated in the projects at General Electric (Schenectady) and Gisholt (Madison, Wisconsin), and the trade journal and technical literature.

3   This brief history of the origins of N/C is based upon interviews with Parsons and MIT personnel, as well as the use of Parsons' personal files and the project records of the Servomechanism Laboratory.

4   The Air Force funded development of APT was centred initially at MIT. In 1961 the effort was shifted to the Illinois Institute of Technology Research Institute (IITRI) where it has been carried on under the direction of a consortium composed of the Air Force, the Aircraft Industries Association (AIA), and major manufacturers of machine tools and electronic controls. Membership in the consortium has always been expensive, beyond the financial means of the vast majority of firms in the metalworking industry. APT system use, therefore, has tended to be restricted to those who enjoyed privileged access to information about the system's development. Moreover, the APT system has been treated as proprietary information within user plants; programmers have had to sign out for manuals and have been forbid-

den from taking them home or talking about their contents with people outside the company.

5   Technically, record-playback was as reliable as N/C, if not more so — since all the programming was done at the machine, errors could be eliminated during the programming process, before production began. Moreover, it could be used to reproduce parts to within a tolerance of a thousandth of an inch, just like N/C. (It is a common mistake to assume that if an N/C control system generates discrete pulses corresponding to increments of half a thousandth, the machine can produce parts to within the same tolerances. In reality, the limits of accuracy are set by the machine itself — not to mention the weather — rather than by the electrical signals.)

6   This history is based upon interviews with Hans Trechsel, designer of Gisholt's 'Factrol' system, and interviews and correspondence with participating engineering and sales personnel at GE (Schenectady), as well as articles in various engineering and trade journals.

7   It could be argued that control in the capitalist mode of production is not an independent factor (a manifestation of class conflict), but merely a means to an economic end (the accumulation of capital). Technology introduced to increase managerial control over the workforce and eliminate pacing is, in this view, introduced simply to increase profits. Such reductionism, which collapses control and class questions into economistic ones, renders impossible any explanation of technological development in terms of social relations or any careful distinction between productive technology which directly increases output per person-hour and technology which does so only indirectly by reducing worker resistance or restriction of output. Finally, it makes it hard to distinguish a technology that reduces pacing from a gun in the service of union-busting company agents; both investments ultimately have the same effect and the economic results look the same on the balance sheet. As Jeremy Brecher reminds us, 'The critical historian must go behind the economic category of cost-minimization to discover the social relations that it embodies (and conceals)' (1978).

8   The setting of rates on jobs in machine shops is still more of a guess than a scientific determination. This fact is not lost on machinists, as their typical descriptions of the methods-men suggests: 'They ask their wives, they don't know; they ask their children, they don't know; so they ask their friends.' Of course, this apparent and acknowledged lack of scientific certainty comes into play during bargaining sessions over rates, when 'fairness' and power, not science, determine the outcome.

9   Kurt Vonnegut, letter to author, February, 1977.

10 The fact that record-playback lends itself to shop-floor control of production more readily than N/C is borne out by a study of N/C in the United Kingdom done by Erik Christiansen in 1968. Only in those cases where record-playback or plugboard controls were in use (he found six British-made record-playback jig borers) did the machinist keep the same pay scale as with conventional equipment and retain control over the entire machining process. In Christiansen's words, record-playback (and plugboard programming) 'mean that the shop floor retains control of the work cycle through the skill of the man who first programmed the machine' (1968, pp. 27, 31).

11 GE Company, 1958. See also Forrester *et al.*, 1955.

12　The cost-effectiveness of N/C depends upon many factors, including training costs, programming costs, computer costs, and the like, beyond mere time saved in actual chip-cutting or reduction in direct labour costs. The MIT staff who conducted the early studies on the economics of N/C focused on the savings in cutting time and waxed eloquent about the new revolution. At the same time, however, they warned that the key to the economic viability of N/C was a reduction in programming (software) costs. Machine-tool company salesmen were not disposed to emphasize these potential drawbacks, though, and numerous users went bankrupt because they believed what they were told. In the early days, however, most users were buffered against such tragedy by state subsidy. Today, potential users are somewhat more cautious, and machine-tool builders are more restrained in their advertising, tempering their promise of economic success with qualifiers about proper use, the right lot and batch size, sufficient training, etc.

For the independent investigator, it is extremely difficult to assess the economic viability of such a technology. There are many reasons for this. First, the data is rarely available or accessible. Whatever the motivation — technical fascination, keeping up with competitors, etc. — the purchase of new capital equipment must be justified in economic terms. But justifications are not too difficult to come by if the item is desired enough by the right people. They are self-interested anticipations and thus usually optimistic ones. More important, firms rarely conduct post-audits on their purchases, to see if their justifications were warranted. Nobody wants to document his errors and if the machinery is fixed in its foundation, that is where it will stay, whatever a post-audit reveals; you learn to live with it. The point here is that the economics of capital equipment is not nearly so tidy as economists would sometimes have us believe. The invisible hand has to do quite a bit of sweeping up after the fact.

If the data does exist, it is very difficult to get hold of. Companies have a proprietary interest in the information and are wary about disclosing it for fear of revealing (and thus jeopardizing) their position vis-à-vis labour unions (wages), competitors (prices), and government (regulations and taxes). Moreover, the data, if it were accessible, is not all tabulated and in a drawer somewhere. It is distributed among departments, with separate budgets, and the costs to one are the hidden costs to the others. Also, there is every reason to believe that the data that does exist is self-serving information provided by each operating unit to enhance its position in the firm. And, finally, there is the tricky question of how 'viability' is defined in the first place. Sometimes, machines make money for a company whether they were used productively or not.

The purpose of this aside is to emphasize the fact that 'bottom-line' explanations for complex historical developments, like the introduction of new capital equipment, are never in themselves sufficient, nor necessarily to be trusted. If a company wants to introduce something new, it must justify it in terms of making a profit. This is not to say, however, that profit-making was its real (or, if so, its only) motive or that a profit was ever made. In the case of automation, steps are taken less out of careful calculation than on the faith that it is always good to replace capital with labour, a faith kindled deep in the soul of manufacturing engineers and managers (as economist Michael

Piore, among others, has shown: see, for example, Piore, 1968). Thus, automation is driven forward, not simply by the profit motive, but by the ideology of automation itself, which reflects the social relations of production.

13   This experiment was relatively successful, but short-lived. Attracted to the programme by the bonus, the reorganized work groups soon grew accustomed to the new conditions: no foremen or punch clock, their own tool crib, their own scheduling of parts through the shop, and even some training in programming. Morale improved and turnover, absenteeism, and the scraprate declined accordingly. However, managerial enthusiasm for the experiment soon waned and, after only a few half-hearted years, it was unilaterally called off. The company claimed that the union's desire to extend the experiment to other areas of the shop and to other plants within the same corporation threatened to make the program too expensive since an extension of the experiment meant also an extension of the bonus. The union business agent, formerly a shop steward in the experimental programme and one of its staunchest supporters, explained the termination in another way: the company was losing control over the workforce.

14   This is an error that Braverman tended to make in discussing N/C.

15   Cited in D. Montgomery (Forthcoming), Ch. 4, p. 1.

16   Perhaps the single most important, and difficult, task confronting the critical student of such rapidly evolving technologies as N/C is to try to disentangle dreams from realities, a hoped-for future from an actual present. The two realms are probably nowhere more confused than in the work of technologists. Thus, criticism of existing, or past, realities are typically countered with allusions to a less problematic future; the present is always the 'debugging phase', the transition, at the beginning of the 'learning curve' — merely a prelude to the future. As such, it is immune from scrutiny and criticism. To argue, as we do here, that N/C machinery does not run by itself or that mere 'button-pushers' cannot produce good parts consistently on N/C, invites the rebuffs of those in the know, who refer to the automatic loading of N/C machines by the Unimate robots, to Flexible Manufacturing Systems (FMS) that tie any number of machines together with an automatic transfer line, to adaptive controls with sensors that automatically correct for tool wear and rough castings and the like, or to Direct Numerical Control (DNC) systems which centralize control over a whole plant of N/C equipment through one computer. Three important things must be kept in mind when dealing with such counter-arguments.

First, technical people, it must be remembered, always have their eyes on the future — it is their job; they live in the state-of-the-art world which often has very little connection with industrial reality. Thus, it is hardly surprising that technical forecasters of the late 1950s predicted that by now at least 75 per cent of machine tools in the USA would be N/C (it is less than 2 per cent), and that we would be seeing fully automatic metalworking factories (there are none). There is no better reason to believe the engineering and trade journals today, much less the self-serving forecasts of manufacturing engineers. All too often, social analysts merely echo these prophets, extrapolating wonderful or woeful consequences of projected technological changes without paying the slightest attention to the mundane vicissitudes of historical experience, or industrial practice. To them, the critic must respond: look again.

Second, judging from past experience, there is little reason simply to assume that the new experimental or demonstration systems will actually function on the shop floor as intended, much less perform economically. This author has visited four plants in the United States with FMS systems and found their economic justifications suspect, their down time excessive, and their reliability heavily dependent upon a highly skilled force of computer operators, system attendants, and maintenance men; there was also little sign of further development. Adaptive systems, under development at Cincinnati Milacron, are still in an experimental stage; when placed on the shop floor, these even more complex and sensitive pieces of machinery are bound to produce more maintenance problems than they solve. DNC is simply another name for the automatic factory, the supreme fantasy of the industrial technocrats, now heralded by self-serving computer jocks, supported by beleaguered corporate managers (whose far-sightedness is more rhetorical than real), and, as usual, funded by the military (in this case, the air force ICAM program).

Third, the ultimate viability of these technologies under the present mode of production depends, in the final analysis, upon the political and economic conditions that prevail and upon the relative strengths of the classes in their struggle over the control of production. To assume simply that the future will be what the designers and/or promoters of these technologies think it will be would be to beg all of the questions being raised here, to ratify, out of hand, a form of technological determinism. Further, it would be to deny the realm of freedom that is being described, a freedom which could result not only in the delaying or subverting of these technologies (and thus the purposes they embody) — allowing for more time to struggle for greater freedom — but also in the fundamental reshaping of their design and use to meet ends other than simple capital accumulation and the extension of managerial and corporate power. See, for example, the discussion of Computer Numerical Control (CNC) in the final section on 'alternative realities' below.

In short, a facile reference to the future is the educated habit of technical people in our society, people who are quite often seriously (and sometimes dangerously) ignorant of the past and mistaken about the present. To adopt their habit would be to suspend judgment (or, rather, yield to their judgment), to forego the critical, concrete, historical examination and assessment of the present situation, which alone can guide us intelligently into the still clouded future.

17 The shortage of skilled manpower has always been cited by managers and technical people as a justification for the introduction of labour-saving technologies like N/C. Rarely, however, is the shortage actually demonstrated or explained in any compelling way; it remains a necessary and unquestioned ideological prop. For a manpower shortage is a relative thing; relative to new Air Force and aircraft industry requirements in the cold war, there was a perceived shortage. But, given that shortages are only perceived in relation to a present or future need, they are predictable; they are not natural phenomena but socially created ones, remediable through training programs and sufficient monetary and other incentives. (This author remembers, for exam-

ple, that not so long ago he went to college on loan programs created to deal with a recognized shortage of college teachers, relative to a vastly expanding educational system.) Thus, when managers introduce N/C because of the impending retirement of the last generation of skilled machinists, we must ask, where are their replacements? Why have apprenticeship programs been eliminated or shortened? Why do vocational courses habituate young people to 'semi-skilled' work in the name of training for a craft? The answer is that the shortage is, in reality, created to complement the new technology, not the other way around. Fortunately for capital, however, the skill is not entirely eliminated, however 'unskilled' the classification; passed on informally and on the job, it remains on the shop floor. If it wasn't there, finished parts would never make it out of the door.

18   The following discussion of the situation in Kongsberg, Norway, is based upon correspondence and personal contact with participants in the trade union participation project and a research visit to Scandinavia in October 1978.

References

ALLEN, A. and SCHNEIDER, B. (1956) *Industrial Relations in the California Aircraft Industry*, Berkeley, Institute of Industrial Relations, University of California.

BRAVERMAN, H. (1974) *Labor and Monopoly Capital: The Degradation of Work in the Twentieth Century*, New York, Monthly Review Press.

BRECHER, J. (1978) 'Beyond technological determinism: some comments', talk presented at the Organization of American Historians Convention, April.

BROWN, M. and ROSENBERG, N. (1961) 'Patents, research and technology in the machine tool industry', *The Patent, Trademark and Copyright Journal of Research and Education*, 5 (Spring).

BURAWOY, M. (1976) 'The organization of consent: changing patterns of conflict on the shop floor, 1945–1975', unpublished doctoral dissertation, University of Chicago.

CHRISTIANSEN, E. (1968) *Automation and the Workers*, London, Labour Research Development Publications, Ltd.

DIEBOLD, J. (1952) *Automation*, New York, Nostrand.

DORING, M. and SALLING, R. (1971) 'A case for wage incentives in the N.C. age', *Manufacturing, Engineering and Management*, 66, 6.

DRUCKER, P.F. (1967) 'Technology and society in the twentieth century', in KRANZBERG AND PURSELL, *Technology in Western Civilization*, (Eds) New York, Oxford University Press.

EMSPAK, F. (n.d.) 'Crisis and authority in the seventies', unpublished manuscript.

FORRESTER, J. et al. (1955) *Strengthening Management for the New Technology*, American Management Association.

GE COMPANY MANAGEMENT CONSULTING SERVICES DIVISION (1958) *Next Steps in Management — An Appraisal of Cybernetics*.

LEAVER, E.W. and BROWN, J.J. (1946) 'Machines without men', *Fortune*, November.

LUNDGREN, E. (1969) 'Effects of N/C on organizational structure', *Automation*, 16 (January).

LYNN, F., ROSEBERRY, T. and BABICH, V. (1966) 'A history of recent technological innovations', in National Commission of Technology, Automation and Economic Progress, *The Employment Impact of Technological change*, Appendix, Vol. II *Technology and the American Economy* Washington, DC, Government Printing Office.

MATHEWSON, S.B. (1969, originally 1931), *Restriction of Output Among Unorganized Workers*, Carbondale, Ill., Southern Illinois University Press.

MELMAN, S. (1959) 'Report on the productivity of operations in the machine tool industry in western Europe', European Productivity Agency Project No. 420.

MONTGOMERY, D. (1976a) 'Whose standards? Workers and reorganization of production in the United States, 1900–1920', unpublished manuscript, University of Pittsburgh.

MONTGOMERY, D. (1976b) 'Workers' control of machine production in the nineteenth century', *Labor History*, 17 (Fall), pp. 486–509.

MONTGOMERY, D. (forthcoming) *The Fall of the House of Labor*.

NOBLE, D.F. (1977) *America By Design: Science, Technology and the Rise of Corporate Capitalism*, New York, Alfred A. Knopf.

PIORE, M. (1968) 'The impact of the labor market upon the design and selection of productive techniques within the manufacturing plant', *Quarterly Journal of Economics*, 82.

ROSENBERG, N. (1963) 'Technical change in the machine tool industry, 1840–1910', *Journal of Economic History*, 23, pp. 414–43.

ROSS, D. (1978) 'Origins of APT language for automatically programmed tools', Softech, Inc.

ROY, D.F. (1951–1952) 'Quota restriction and goldbricking in a machine shop', *American Journal of Sociology*, 57.

ROY, D.F. (1953) 'Work satisfaction and social reward in quota achievement: an analysis of piecework incentive', *American Sociological Review*, 18.

ROY, D.F. (1954–1955) 'Efficiency and "the fix": informal inter-group relations in a piecework machine shop', *American Journal of Sociology*, 60.

SMITH, M.R. (1976) *Harpers Armory and the New Technology*, Ithaca, New York, Cornell University Press.

STEPHANZ, K. (1971) 'Statement of Kenneth Stephanz', in *Introduction to Numerical Control and Its Impact on Small Business*, Hearing before the Subcommittee on Science and Technology of the Select Committee on Small Business, US Senate, 92nd Congress, 1st session (June 24, 1971).

STICKELL, G. (1960) 'How can new machines cut costs?', *Tooling and Production*, August.

TULIN, R. (1978) 'Machine tools', *New York Times*, 2 April, p. 16.

WAGONER, H. (1968) *The United States Machine Tool Industry from 1900 to 1950*, Cambridge, Massachusetts, MIT Press.

Chapter 2

The Gendering of Technology

Cynthia Cockburn

It is a fact known to the youngest school child that women and men 'do different jobs'. A sexual division of labour is one of the most marked and persistent of the patterns that characterize human society everywhere. In Britain, men and women cluster in different industries. For example, while women are only 14.8 per cent of the labour force in the industrial group called the 'mechanical engineering industry', they are 70.3 per cent of the labour force in 'footwear and clothing' (Department of Employment, 1983).[1] Within any one industry, of course, there will be people doing many different kinds of job. So a large proportion of that female 14.8 per cent in 'mechanical engineering' is in fact doing traditional women's work in the offices and canteens of engineering firms. The closer we look, the more differences we find between what women do and what men do. Using 'occupational' in place of 'industrial' statistics — what we actually work at rather than the type of firm we work in — we find that 76.7 per cent of the clerical labour force is women. On the other hand, only 4.8 per cent of people in processing, making and repairing jobs in connection with metal or electrical products are women (Department of Employment, 1983).

Women are clustered into relatively few occupations. Of women manual workers, 85 per cent work in three broad occupational groups: catering, cleaning, hairdressing and other personal services; painting, repetitive assembling, product inspecting, packaging and similar occupations; and making and repairing jobs (excluding those in metal and electrical work). Of women non-manual workers, no less than 91 per cent are to be found within three categories: selling; clerical jobs; and professional and related work in education, welfare and health services (Department of Employment, 1983).

Men, by contrast, are engaged in a far wider range of activities and there are few from which they are entirely absent. More importantly, they monopolize the higher ranks of most. It is useful to distinguish 'horizontal' segregation of occupations, whereby men and women engage in different *kinds* of work, from 'vertical' segregation, whereby the sexes attain different *levels* of seniority in their occupations. The statistics show that men occupy a disproportionate number of higher-grade positions and women are concentrated in the lower grades of the rather limited range of work they do (Hakim, 1979).

Studies of individual industries or firms show that when one gets down to workplace level the divisions between women and men are yet more pronounced. An occupational category such as 'warehouse hand' is likely to conceal a situation in which heavy work like pushing goods around is done by men, sedentary work like checking delivery notes is done by women. In particular, sex divisions nearly always break cleanly along the line of skill. Jobs formally classified as skilled are done by men. Women are found in jobs that are considered unskilled and semi-skilled (Coyle, 1982; Cavendish, 1982; Pollert, 1981; Westwood, 1984).

A recent British survey involving over 3,000 women obtained an even closer look at segregation by sex. Working women reported in 63 per cent of cases that they worked in 'women-only' jobs. The occupational segregation was higher still if the professions and office work were weeded out. For instance, of semi-skilled factory workers no less than 73 per cent were working only with women in their particular job. Even more of men's work is exclusively male. Of the smaller number of husbands interviewed in this same survey, 81 per cent of those working with other people worked only with men, and 98 per cent had male supervisors (Martin and Roberts, 1984).

Surprisingly, there has been little lessening of occupational segregation by sex during this century. Catherine Hakim used a number of different measures to find out whether a change had occurred between 1901 and 1971. She found that the proportion of occupations without any women workers at all was relatively constant at around 9 per cent between 1901 and 1961, but an improvement had been detectable by 1971, as a few women pioneers penetrated male fields in the forward-looking decade of the 1960s. The proportion of all occupations in which women were at least as well represented as men in the labour force as a whole, however, remained virtually constant over the seventy-year period, at the low level of 25 per cent of the total. Typically male occupations remained at a fairly constant high level of 73 per cent of all occupations listed. The proportion of occupations in which women were greatly overrepresented (at 70 per cent or more of the workforce) actually *increased* slightly, from 9 per cent to 12 per cent. In addition, Hakim's data indicated a trend towards greater vertical segregation over the period. Men, not women, were climbing. She summarized: 'Occupational concentration and occupational segregation have remained relatively unchanged in Britain over seven decades' (1979, p. 43).

It seems that the phenomenon of sex segregation is not limited to Britain. Reports from the USA (Gross, 1968) and European countries (OECD, 1980) show a similar situation. In Third World countries, though the actual occupations done by women and by men may vary widely, the existence of a clear sexual division of labour of some kind characterizes them all (Boserup, 1971). Even in the USSR, where the ideology of the 1917 revolution and the shortage of skilled labour in the period that followed gave a boost to women's entry into non-traditional work, the return of a measure of normalcy was accompanied by an increase in occupational segregation by sex. Though more women than in Britain are scientists, engineers and technicians, they tend to be in the lower-ranking branches and grades of the fields in which they work. The 1970 census in the USSR showed that men were not taking their place alongside women in traditionally female jobs. Ninety-eight per cent of nurses and nursery school personnel, 99 per cent of stenographers and 91 per cent of catering employees were female (Lapidus, 1976; Sacks, 1976)

Divided by technology

Technology has an important position in this widespread sexual division of labour. Technological knowledge at the professional level, and technological know-how at the practical level, are sharp differentiators of men and women. Taking occupational categories, for instance: in 1983 in Britain, women were only 8.6 per cent of the professionals in science, engineering and technology, and 4.8 per cent of the labour force who process, make and repair metal and electrical goods (Department of Employment, 1975, 1983). The former figures show a slight gain (of 1.5 per cent) since 1975, the latter a slight fall (1.1 per cent).

More detailed information is obtainable from the statistics of education and training. These, besides, are a better pointer to the future. Again, a difference is observable between the educational levels. Girls and boys start out on their different routes while still at school. If we take maths, physics, computer studies and technical drawing as indicators of future technological career choices, we find females already disadvantaged at 16 years of age. At GCE 'O' level, for instance, though the percentages have been slowly rising since 1970, girls still had only 43.6 per cent of the passes in maths, 27.9 per cent in physics, 27.3 per cent in the relatively new subject of computer studies, and 4.6 per cent in technical drawing in 1983. The disadvantage is confirmed and deepened by 18 years of age. At 'A' level these percentages fall to 31.1, 21.0, 19.6 and 2.9 per cent respectively.[2]

If we move up the age range to vocational training, we find, in 1982–83, women representing only a negligible 1 per cent of those entering for the craft engineering exams of the City and Guilds of London Institute, the body officially responsible for qualifying craft workers.[3] The situation is hardly better on the courses leading to the somewhat higher level of engineering technician exams, which are certified by the Business and Technical Education Council: a little over 2 per cent of those entering were women in 1982–83.[4] Among students of English polytechnics enrolling on advanced 'engineering and technology' courses in 1983 there were 720 full-time female students to 7,125 male (9.2 per cent). Against 1,172 female 'sandwich' students there were 17,917 males (6.1 per cent), and only 419 young women were getting day release to attend these courses as against 10,798 young men (3.7 per cent).[5]

Finally, among full-time university undergraduates in 'engineering and technology', women represented 9.1 per cent in 1983. This proportion had, however, doubled since 1975.[6] The picture is of an overwhelmingly male field of work into which a few women pioneers are making their way. It is a little easier for those who make it over the 'A'-level threshhold and can follow the professional route, unremittingly hard for those young women who must take the manual, vocational route. At all levels, while the pioneers have a little more female company each year, pioneers they remain.

The effect on women as people and as workers of their exclusion from the skills needed to govern the technologies of production will gradually become clear in the course of this book. One point is worth making here, however. It is costing women money. The Equal Pay Act of 1970, operational in 1975, promised to bring women's pay up to the level of men's. Yet while women's average gross hourly earnings as a proportion of men's were boosted, partly by the new legislation, from 63 per cent to 75 per cent between 1970 and 1977 they then slipped and stood at 73.5 per cent in 1984 (Department of Employment, 1984). If we consider average gross weekly earnings, which include the fact that men have access to more overtime possibilities than women, we find that women's pay packets look even thinner. They earned 54.5 per cent of what men earned in 1974 and had only crept up to 65.8 per cent of men's weekly earnings by 1984 (Department of Employment, 1984).

It is by now widely accepted that the reason the Equal Pay legislation of the 1970s failed to achieve equal pay for women is that the majority of women are segregated into fields of employment in which they are unable to compare themselves with men for purposes of grading and pay (Snell, Glucklich and Povall, 1981). Skilled manual work pays more than unskilled; professional jobs pay more than office work. In technology, as in other fields, women are not on the career paths that offer pay and prospects. In the engineering industry, for example, of a total of 2.3 million employed in 1982, 22 per cent, or around half a million, were women. Yet their share of the industry's wage bill was certainly not proportional to their numbers, since 45 per cent were in relatively low-paid operator jobs and almost all the remainder in equally ill-rewarded clerical work. Only 2.5 per cent of the women working in the engineering industry were in managerial, scientific, technological or technician occupations (EITB, 1984). It is the men in the industry who earn the skilled wages and the professional salaries. And the same technological division of labour by sex, with the same pecuniary effects, applies outside as within the engineering industry proper.

Men's appropriation of technology

To understand the different relation the sexes have to technology today we need to recognize the relevance of technology to power and to the emergence of power systems in the past. Despite the stereotype of the stone-age caveman dragging 'his' woman along by the hair and wielding a club (technology?) in his free hand, the evidence of archaeology does not point to any 'natural' distance between women and technology.[7] Today, when explaining the emergence of human societies, the emphasis has shifted from Man The Hunter to Woman The Gatherer (Slocum, 1975). It is suggested that females, not males, were the first technologists. Under pressure of nutritional stress, caring for both self and young, females are the more likely sex to have invented the digging stick, the carrying sling or bag, the reaping knife and sickle, pestles and pounders, methods of winnowing, washing, detoxifying and preserving food (Tanner and Zihlman, 1976; Tanner, 1981). It is well established that women were the first horticulturalists, purposefully growing selected plants in and around their settlements (Martin and Voorhies, 1975). They may well have invented and used the hoe, spade, shovel and scratch-plough (Stanley, 1981). Whether hunting animals (large or small), or herding, gardening and farming, a simple division of labour may have occurred. We need not suppose, however, that it gave one sex a marked monopoly of technological skills.[8]

As human societies have developed in different parts of the world at different times, they have tended to pass through broadly similar phases. Often these are designated by archaeologists according to the material of the dominant technology: stone age, bronze age, iron age. Associated with the technologies are successive stages in social organization. Women appear to have been central to the organization of social life until the late neolithic age. As the neolithic ceded to the bronze age, however, in many cultures of which a record exists it is possible to see a shift towards male dominance.[9] A relatively egalitarian and peaceful community of woman-centred kinship clans gave way to an increasingly centralized society divided into hierarchical classes, based on agriculture, warfare and slavery. As this occurred, it seems, women were actively subjugated by men, excluded from many crafts and trades and displaced from their positions of political and religious authority.[10] The rise of class society is associated with a shift to patrilineality (determining descent through the male blood line) and to patrilocality (a wife moving to the domain of her husband's family on marriage).[11] It is also associated with an increasing division of labour, the emergence of specific crafts and trades.

In particular, the new occupations surrounding metallurgy were highly significant. The importance of metals and of the skills of smelter, founder and smith to the military and agricultural exploits of rulers and ruling classes can be in no doubt. It seems that in male-dominated societies these occupations are seen as male. Technological skills are a source of power and where men were in possession of all other vehicles of power, from state organization to marriage, it would have been surprising to find women in possession of mechanical powers. The 'mighty five' devices — lever, wedge, screw, wheel and inclined plane — that made it possible to move mountains and build pyramids were the technical armoury of men.

It was not in the cradles of 'civilization', however, but in the western extremities of Europe that technology would explode in the eighteenth and nineteenth centuries AD, and it is of interest to trace the technological division of labour by sex as it progressed there. As the use of iron was rapidly expanded in the eighth and ninth centuries,[12] it is clear that women's role in production, though of prime importance then as it has continued to be ever since ('two-thirds of the world's work hours'), was nonetheless confined to particular activities associated with domestic consumption. Apart from food preparation and childcare, women were responsible for 'spinning, dyeing, weaving, tending the garden, raising livestock and . . . cultivating land' (Wemple, 1981, p. 70). It was men who were the goldsmith, weapon-smith and blacksmith, 'making ploughshare and coulter, goad and fish-hook, awl and needle', and the carpenter, 'responsible not only for various tools and utensils but for houses and ships' (Whitelock, 1952, p. 106).

In the later Middle Ages again we find rural women involved with 'dairy work, gardening, food preparation and the textile crafts of carding, slubbing, spinning and weaving', while their male equivalents 'worked the land, reared livestock, repaired hedges, ditches and tools' (Chaytor and Lewis, 1982).[13] Among these tools were more and more made of iron. Iron was rapidly becoming the basis of the dominant technology. 'It is the consensus among historians of agriculture that the medieval peasantry used an amount of iron which would have seemed inconceivable to any earlier rural population and that the smithy became integral to every village' (White, 1962, p. 41). And there were few trades more associated with manliness than that of smith.

The towns, which grew rapidly in importance in the thirteenth and fourteenth centuries, were the centres of specialized handicrafts. Under the authority of the feudal state, the craft and merchant guilds laid down the rules by which apprentices might be recruited and trained and business carried on. The guilds covered certain skilled techniques producing goods for consumption, such as printing. But they also included those that produced tools and implements: carpenter, wright and various kinds of smith. The guilds were male in character (Wilkinson, 1969; Postan, 1975). Women engaged extensively in economic life in the towns, but mainly in sex-specific areas that had by long tradition been female. They were domestic servants, washerwomen, bakers, brewers and innkeepers, roles that were extensions into trade of the concerns of domestic life: food, drink and textiles, goods and services for domestic consumption.

The sexual division of labour was not absolutely total at this period, however. Women appear listed alongside men as engaging in certain kinds of production (shoemaking for instance) and in certain fields of commerce (as drapers, chandlers and even ironmongers). The pattern that we have seen to exist today, however, whereby women cluster in a few occupations and men spread across many, is evident in the Middle Ages. Poll tax returns for Oxford in 1380, for instance, mention six trades followed by women, six in which both women and men were employed, and no fewer than eighty-one that were followed exclusively by men. Alice Clark concluded from her study of medieval trades that, though women followed some skilled and semi-skilled occupations, 'no traces can be found of any organisation existing' within them.[14] Certainly women were not considered a threat to male occupational rights. A statute of Edward III expressly exempted women from the ordinance that men should not follow more than a single craft. 'But the intent of the King and his Council,' it reads, 'is that Women, that is to say Brewers, Bakers, Carders and Spinners and Workers as well of Wool as of Linen Cloth and of Silk, Brawdesters and Breakers of Wool and all other that do use and work all Handy Works may freely use and work as they have done before this time . . .' (quoted in Hutchins, 1978).

The role of the guilds extended beyond an immediate trade to social organization within the town. A woman therefore might be a member of a guild without actually plying its trade. A daughter might take up right of patrimony in her father's guild for the civic advantages it afforded. Some are known to have become apprenticed to a master in his guild so as to work as a domestic servant to his wife. Widows frequently inherited their husbands' enterprises. Widows are therefore sometimes named even as farriers and smiths. An exceptional woman might have broken the convention to carry out this work herself, but a commoner practice was for a widow to manage the business while hired journeymen and apprentices carried out the skilled practical aspects of the work.

Tools that make tools

In this account of early divisions of labour we can distinguish certain skills which were of special significance in production and which yielded, as a consequence, greater influence to those who possessed them than was yielded by ordinary productive abilities. They are the skills that were required for making tools, implements and weapons. In other words, *they involved competence in the production or adaptation of other producers' instruments of labour.* Eventually we will see these skills evolve into those that make machinery and later still into those that build computer systems.

Why should these abilities afford greater power than others: than the knowledge needed to nurture children, for instance, or to weave cloth or plough the land? The answer is, first, related to systems of class power. Those who own the means of production, whether slave-owning emperors, land-owning feudal nobles or factory-owning capitalists, depend for the making of their wealth on a yoking in tandem of labour and tools, labour and machinery. They may be expected therefore to pay well, in cash or food, freedom or status, for the skills they need to effect this linkage and continually to improve its productivity. Other talents could, in another world, have been valued more highly. But from the onset of male-dominated class-structured societies, the priority has been supremacy in a struggle for ownership and control of disposable surpluses. That priority has forced the development of technology in a certain direction. The forcing-house has often been warfare.

Secondly, however, those who possessed these skills had a source of power over everyone who did not. Such men rendered other people dependent on them for the maintenance of their own environment and instruments of labour. They were in a position to impede or enhance, direct or redirect other producers' labour processes. They acquired a degree of authority among other men of those classes who worked manually. It will be clear also that the skills enhanced men's power over women. Not only were women firmly subordinated to men in the patriarchal family, but they were also dependent on them for certain important practical processes of everyday life. The technological skills, defined as male property, were therefore both a cause and an effect of male supremacy.

Meanwhile, technological knowledge was evolving. By the early fourteenth century Europe had made considerable progress towards substituting water and wind power for human labour in apparatus of many different kinds. Applications of the new sources of power were advancing in step: the cam in the eleventh and twelfth centuries; the spring and treadle in the thirteenth; complex forms of gearing in the fourteenth. In the fifteenth century the crank, connecting-rod and governor were coming into widespread use, aiding the very significant step of converting reciprocating to continuous rotary motion. By the sixteenth century, 'Europe was equipped not only with sources of power far more diversified than those known to any previous culture, but also with an arsenal of technical means for grasping, guiding and utilizing such energies which was immeasurably more varied and skilful than any people of the past had possessed or than was known to any contemporary society' (White, 1962, p. 128).

The history of invention represents the inventors of antiquity, the Middle Ages and the Renaissance, as invariably male. A hefty and comprehensive 'history of the machine' published in 1979 encompasses technological development from the Cro-Magnon anvil to the space rocket. Among approximately 450 men named in connection with invention in this book there is one woman, Ada Lady Lovelace, mathematician (Strandh, 1979). The question of what part women did or did not play in technological invention is a knotty one. Women have almost always been 'hidden from history' when the historians were men. Autumn Stanley's work (1983) reaffirms women's creativeness. She suggests that we should be sceptical of the male historians of technology and look for the hidden women. We should, besides, give greater emphasis to the activities to which women notably *have* contributed their ideas: preparing food, healing, making garments, caring for children. After all, the significance ascribed to any productive practice has been largely a male choice.

Stanley proposes that 'all else being equal' we may assume that those who work in a process invent the tools by which it is carried on. While this is likely to be true for very early periods of human history, it is to miss a crucial characteristic of subsequent patriarchal and class societies. Women were systematically excluded from all sources of power, including the technologies that held sway over their own female areas of production. The development of textile technology, for instance, has been a male, not a female, project. The following discussion by Lynn White Jr of the technology of the spinning wheel makes clear how differentiated were the considerations of *mechanics* from the consideration of spinning thread:

> The spinning wheel is mechanically interesting not only because it is the first instance of the belt transmission of power and a notably early example of the flywheel principle, but because it focussed attention upon the problem of producing and controlling the various rates of speed in different moving parts of the same machine. One turn of the great wheel sent the spindle twirling many times; but not content with this, by *c*. 1480 crafts*men* [my emphasis] has developed a U-shaped flyer rotating around the spindle and permitting the operations of both spinning and winding the thread on a bobbin to proceed simultaneously. To accomplish this, spindle and flyer had to rotate at different speeds, each driven by a separate belt from the large wheel, which, of course, revolved at a third speed. Finally, by 1524, the crank, connecting-rod and treadle had been added to the spinning wheel. (1962, p. 119)

Was White being sexist in assuming that these developments originated with men? I think not. Leonardo da Vinci is credited with the invention of the flyer for the spindle in 1490. Johann Jurgen, a woodcarver of Brunswick, invented a partly automatic spinning wheel employing a flyer around 1530 (Mumford, 1934, p. 144).[15] The way of thinking that would have enabled such innovations arose not in the main from the spinning of thread but from a familiarity with other kinds of apparatus and technique. The matter of differential speeds, for instance, was being explored in clockmaking at this time; the notion of the fly-wheel and the transmission belt were used in the development of grinding mills. Technological knowledge is essentially a *transferable* knowledge, profitably carried from one kind of production to another. It is a field of its own. We will see this in the contemporary studies that follow: computer-aided design and cutting systems built for use with metals are adapted for use with cloth; a robot developed for use in the car industry stimulates developments that will solve management problems in warehousing. Men move from industry to industry carrying know-how across the boundaries of firm and sector. Then, as now, it was men and not women who had mobility (intellectual, occupational and physical mobility) and the overview it afforded. Later of course it would be other men — Hargreave, Arkwright, Crompton, Kay — who would adapt the domestic textile apparatus for factory and mechanized use.

What is at issue here is not women's inventiveness. There is no doubt that women have the ability to be as imaginative and innovative as men. Women have frequently 'had ideas' for the improvement of tools and machinery with which they worked. They have seldom had the craft skills to effect in wood or metal the improvements they conceived. Besides, despite the frequent adulation by historians of male inventors, technological development is not in reality a series of brainwaves. A materialist understanding of history gives the personal less significance than the social. In tracing technological change, therefore, the focus needs to be 'not upon individuals, however heroic, but upon a collective, social process in which the institutional and economic environments play major roles' (Rosenberg, 1982, p. 35). The social process of technological development has been overwhelmingly a male process. It is women's lack of social and economic power that holds them 'down' to the role of producer of goods for immediate consumption. Since the bronze age, women have worked *for* men, whether the man was head of household, slave-owner or feudal lord. It is clear that they also produced *by means of* man-made technologies. They were subject to that particular form of material control that comes of men as a sex having appropriated the role of toolmaker to the world.

Machines that make machines

The departure that was about to change the world dramatically for both women and men, however, was not a technical invention. It was capitalism: an entirely new set of social relationships that would find the organizational means to bring science and technology together and harness them for production. During the sixteenth and seventeenth centuries the peasant economy of the countryside and the craft economy of the towns, both essentially home-based domestic forms of production, changed their character. From among the yeoman farmers and the guild masters emerged a new stratum of large-scale producers. The merchant class also grew in number and in influence. Wealth, accumulated through trade in England and overseas, sought new ways of making more wealth. Independent craft production gave way to 'manufacture' as merchants became entrepreneurs, no longer simply buying from but actively employing the producers.

At first the new capitalist class 'put out' the material to scattered producers to work on in their homes, and in this way the domestic system continued for a while within the new mode of production. Much of women's production continued to be carried on under the authority of father or husband. Eventually, however, entrepreneurs saw advantage in gathering producers into workshops and factories where an employer could enjoy economies of scale and supervise production more closely.

As the restraints of the guild system were shrugged off, the new class of employers found it possible and profitable to introduce a subdivision of the work process. Merchandise that had once been produced by a single craftsman undertaking all the varied parts of the process was now the product of a series of manual workers, each of whom repeated a part of the task over and over again with a single tool. Some of the detail tasks were more skill-demanding than others. The workforce could be differentiated: some remained relatively skilled and costly, but others could now be less skilled, and a new cheap category of entirely unskilled 'hands' was called into play. Often these were women or children, many of whom were drawn from the surplus population thrown off the land by the agrarian revolution.

A significant change began to occur in the relationship between producers and 'their' technologies. The craftsman had owned his own tools. This included the tools owned by those men who made the tools that other producers used. The craftsman guarded the 'mystery' of how to use them. As Marx put it, 'the labourer and his means of production remained closely united, like the snail with its shell' (1954, p. 339).[16] Now the snail had to be prised from its shell if capitalism was to fulfil its potential: in the new factories the employer owned the instruments of labour and put the worker to work on them. For many artisans who had once purchased materials with their own money, worked with their own tools and sold to their own customers, the change was historic. Now what they sold, all they had to sell, was their labour power.

So, as the capitalist initiative (which was also, it must be noted, a masculine initiative) drew into existence this new class of wage workers, unknown in the feudal world, men of the two classes were drawn into endemic conflict. Capital might own the instruments of production but working men alone had the craft know-how to use them. How and by whom, for how long and for what reward, the tools and techniques were to be used became the basis of the struggle that has been the prime mover of history in the intervening 200 or 300 years.

The process, however, had a long way yet to go. Technology would not only set in opposition the interests of the employing class and the working class. It would also be instrumental in forming the new working class as a stratified and divided one. As the general-purpose tools of the craftsmen were put to use in a subdivided production process, the tools too were altered — simplified and multiplied — to suit the new detail tasks. Simple tools, combined and associated with a power source and a transmitting mechanism, resulted in a machine. The machine was soon associated with others in a factory system that itself had the characteristics of a machine. The groundwork was laid for vast new possibilities of accumulation for the owner of the new mechanical means of production.

Machinery offered men as a sex opportunities that were not open to women. Already certain technologies of which men had exclusive tenure had a special significance in production; now they took on an amplified importance. Those who had traditionally worked the materials from which tools were made would now adapt their skills to the new machine age. What capital needed in place of smiths and wrights were 'mechanics' and 'engineers'. It was only men, inevitably, who had the tradition, the confidence and in many cases also the transferable skills to make the leap. It was therefore exclusively men who became the maintenance mechanics and the production engineers in the new factories, governing capital's new forces of production.

Marx singled out these key employees in the new 'machinofacture'. He noted the essential division between the operators, who are actually employed on the machines, and their unskilled attendants. But, he wrote, in addition a historically new worker appears, a 'class of persons, whose occupation it is to look after the whole of the machinery and repair it from time to time; such as engineers, mechanics, joiners etc. This is a superior class of workmen, some of them scientifically educated, others brought up to a trade; it is distinct from the factory operative class and merely aggregated to it. This division of labour is purely technical' (1954, p. 396). These technical men were the one category of worker whose earning power was not reduced by the introduction of machinery. If one mechanic, together with a handful of unskilled, low-paid machine operators, can put out of work many craftsmen, capital could (and as we shall see later still can) afford to pay the technical newcomer relatively well.

The old-style smith and wright, new-style mechanic and engineer, however, were also to play another part in production history. Machinery was crippled in its complete development so long as machine-building itself remained a handicraft affair. As Marx noted: 'The expansion of industries carried on by means of machinery, and the invasion by machinery of fresh branches of production, were dependent on the growth of a class of workmen who, owing to the almost artistic nature of their employment, could increase their numbers only gradually and not by leaps and bounds' (1954, p. 361). Besides, because of the increasing size of the prime movers and the use of iron and steel — as Marx put it, 'a more refractory material', huge masses of which had now 'to be forged, to be welded, to be cut, to be bored and to be shaped' — it was inevitable that machines had to be invented with which to build machines (1954, pp. 362–3).

Skills, however, were still needed to design, develop and build these machines that were to make machines to do the work of men and women. While one kind of skilled man, therefore, had become the mechanic and engineer of the 'downstream' processes of what Marx called Department II, where they supervised the machines that produced the means of consumption, his brother now moved 'upstream' to become the mechanic and engineer of Department I, the influential machine-building or capital goods industry producing the means of production for others.[17]

The struggle over technical skills

The Combination Acts, which had outlawed collective organization by workers, were repealed in 1824–25. After this, journeymen from many of the male crafts formed trade unions. At first there existed a variety of societies, local or regional in scope, representing millwrights machinists and other categories of technical skill. The strongest of these was the Steam Engine Makers, founded in 1826, and later known as the 'Old Mechanics'. In 1851, many of the smaller societies joined together to form a new union, the Amalgamated Society of Engineers, Machinists, Smiths, Millwrights and Pattern-Makers. It was an exclusive, skilled union, characterized by high membership subscriptions and generous benefits, and it became a model for other skilled unions. Not all metalworkers belonged to it: the Old Mechanics among other societies kept apart; later the United Pattern-Makers, a highly elite section, would break away. But the ASE nonetheless quickly became one of the largest unions in the country and had a membership of 72,000 by 1891 (Pelling, 1976; Jefferys, 1946).

Meanwhile the scope of the industry itself was expanding to encompass different kinds of metal-work: the heavy sectors of ship and locomotive building, the machine tool industry and eventually lighter sectors producing consumer goods such as bicycles. In the 1870s the employers organized themselves into the Iron Trades Employers' Association, the better to fight back against the unions. The employers, by repeated cycles of technological innovation, attempted to deskill the work of the engineering industry and divest themselves of dependence on the craft engineers. The skilled workers of the ASE and other engineering unions on the contrary struggled to maintain craft regulation of work, including an agreed ratio of apprentices to journeymen, and to prevent the employers fragmenting the labour process and using unskilled handymen on the machines (Zeitlin, 1979).

> Pattern-making foundry work, blacksmiths' work and boilermaking all saw the appearance of minor labour-saving devices; but the most fundamental and rapid changes were taking place in the machine shop, which with its fitters and turners, was the heart of the Engineers' empire. About 1890 came the capstan and turret lathe, the vertical, horizontal and later the universal milling machine, the external and surface grinder, the vertical borer, and the radial drill. Work on these specialist machines did not require the all-round competence of the craftsman and many of the men put onto them, at wage rates below craft standards, had neither served an apprenticeship nor picked up a broad experience on the shop floor. (Clegg, Fox and Thompson, 1964, p. 138)

Instrumental in bringing about this subdivision of work and the deskilling of craft engineers was a new breed of formally educated professional engineers. Civil engineers — men like Isambard Kingdom Brunel — had already achieved status and acclaim as architects of the era of canal, road and rail. Now, towards the end of the nineteenth century, the new high-status industrial engineer was interposing himself between the mechanic and the employer in science-based manufacture. Entire new industries such as electrical and chemical engineering grew up, which had no craft basis. In these the engineer was not only key employee but also often manager (Noble, 1979).

The engineering employers were in perpetual struggle with the craft engineering unions and took the offensive in a nationwide lockout in 1897. Bitterness lay in the fact that while the capitalist and the skilled men needed each other, they did not need each other equally. As David Noble points out, technological innovation was often achieved by their combined efforts. The skilled man saw in new scientific knowledge about the nature of the material world the basis for new or refined methods of production; the capitalist recognized the potential for enhancing profitability. Often, 'these two visions took shape as one in a single mind: the capitalist was frequently an inventor of sorts, while the inventive craftsman shared not a little of the entrepreneurial spirit of the capitalist' (Noble, 1979, p. 5). The difference was that the capitalist would readily turn the skilled man's own inventions against him, with the help of other brands of engineer.

From this history it will be clear that the technically knowledgeable and skilled fraternity is by no means simply a 'superior class of workman', as Marx put it. It is varied, it is hierarchically stratified and its component parts are continually shifting in relative status. Technological skills are forced by capital to adapt and change. They do not only act on others' skills, they are also acted upon. The skilled men respond by demarcating and defending areas of competence. As a result the unions at one moment join forces, at another split apart. Some categories of technical men are always ahead of 'the state of the art', and consequently in demand. Some are running to keep up, fearful of technological redundancy, the obsolescence of their knowledge, the demise of the process they are accustomed to work at. The challenge for all of them is to keep abreast of technology, maintain marketable skills and retain a governing role over the machinery on which other people produce, at the point both of its manufacture and of its application. Those technologists who succeed, 'do well' by themselves. Their role develops more and more from control of machinery to control of labour processes and so to control of people:

> They are entrusted not only with planning the labour process and with keeping production up to pre-established technical standards, but also, and mainly, with maintaining the hierarchical structure of the labour force and with perpetuating capitalist social relations, that is with keeping the producers separated (alienated) from the product of their collective labour and from the production process. (Gorz, 1976, p. 169)

The advent of powered machinery was, then, profoundly contradictory for men as a sex. On the one hand, many men could view it only with hatred. It was the enemy. It enabled capital to dispense with the skills of the skilled man and the muscle power of the labourer. On the other hand, mechanical skills were the property of men as a sex, much as machinery itself was the property of the dominant class. Men's power over women could only be enhanced by advances in technology.

The vested interests of men with technical skills led them into an ambiguous class position. Technological change can be seen as class warfare. 'It would be possible to write quite a history of the inventions, made since 1830, for the sole purpose of supplying capital with weapons against the revolts of the working class,' wrote Marx (1954, p. 411). And who designs and uses those weapons in class struggle if not the mechanics and engineers? Some are working-class men. Others are drawn from the ranks of the bourgeoisie. Either way they play an equivocal role in the struggle between the workforce and the employer. David Noble noted that 'as those charged with supervision of the industrial labour force, engineers found labour organizations difficult and disagreeable, and as professionals, they viewed unions as a measure of mediocrity' (Noble, 1979, p. 41). So, whether they were members of elite unions, whether they were non-unionized and actively anti-union, the technologists' close identification with the machinery and those that owned it was always in danger of standing between them and other workers. Women workers, whether in industries producing consumer goods or, as increasingly occurred in the twentieth century, in the capital goods industries, were always among the 'others'. Men's power over women continued to exert itself, in this way and in others, within the changing relations of capitalism.

Women's relationship to the machine

The preferential place that men have carved for themselves in production has survived from the earliest days and through several revolutions in economic organization. Perhaps most striking of all, men maintained their unique grasp of technological skills when capitalism exploded apart the ownership of the instruments of production from the skills they entailed and unleashed an unprecedented epoch of technological development. We now have a kind of genealogy for the maintenance technician, the systems technologist, technical manager and professional engineer as we will encounter them in the 'new technology' workplaces of the 1980s.

We also have the beginnings of a similar genealogy for the women 'operators' we are going to encounter. We know that women have continuously contributed a large proportion of total production and that a very sizeable part of that has been in food and clothing, whether for immediate consumption or for sale. In addition, of course, women have been the ones to perform almost all the 'reproductive' tasks associated with childcare and housekeeping that are not normally classed as work.

Women were also employed, particularly when single, in the heaviest types of manual labour, were exploited as domestic servants, as 'servants in husbandry' working in the fields, and even carrying coal, washing lead and breaking ore in the mines. More women were forced into labouring (or pauperism) as the break-up of the old feudal relationships dispossessed the least secure. Female cottagers who had scratched a living from vegetable patch and grazing rights on the commons were made landless by the enclosure movement that 'rationalized' the land into large-scale farms. More and more of the women working as independent or family producers in towns lost their livelihood as competition from outwork and factory work organized on capitalist lines in the rural areas destroyed urban craft production. At first many women, like men, became outworkers in their own homes. As indus-trialization advanced they followed the work to the factories. Women were unpractised in craft organization and many had the docility that results from subordination within the home. The new class of male employers could benefit by this — in a sense they stole a march on men of the working class (Pinchbeck, 1981; Hutchins, 1978; Neff, 1966; Kessler-Harris, 1982; Baker, 1964).

The effect of the industrial revolution and the special uses of women, as perceived by the new captains of industry, were contradictory for women themselves. Some results were clearly adverse. Women and children were terribly exploited and abused in the frenzy of capitalist production. Industrial methods wiped out women's small businesses — bleaching and brewing, for instance. Women's types of production were brought more firmly under the sway of a male principle. Making clothing, food and drink, for instance, as it was socialized and mechanized, became more institutionally subject to men's special knowledge of machinery than women's domestic production had been subject to individual men's knowledge of tools.

As industrialization increased and more and more women were drawn into work, a powerful adaptation of the old ideology of 'a woman's place' evolved to ensure that women's relationship to work and earning was no more than provisional. A basic theme of this ideology was the assumption that woman's proper role was that of wife and mother. 'Remaining in the home was central to the maintenance of a woman's sexual purity and respec-tability.' The theme of this ideal Victorian lady, says Sarah Eisenstein, 'developed in some complexity and with uneasy insistence, in the early nineteenth century, in literature, popular magazines, religious tracts and pub-lic debate'. As she points out, these were middle-class ideas that had little real relevance to the situation of working-class women, yet 'they informed the ideology of the period so thoroughly that they dominated prevailing attitudes towards working women and shaped the terms in which those women inter-preted their own experience' (Eisenstein, 1983, pp. 55–7). Women, as a con-sequence, worked but could not aspire to the great achievements dreamed of by many Victorian men.

More positively, however, the development of a female industrial labour force did bring practical opportunities for women to evade both this gender ideology and the more material aspects of male dominance. First, it meant coming out of the enclosed sphere of the patriarchal family into the more public sphere of the patriarchal firm. This is not so simple a move as it sounds. The feudal and the early capitalist domestic system of manufacture had made the home a far from private place. In a sense the home became truly a private sphere only once production had left it. The constitution of 'home and work', the 'private and public' as we know them was in many ways a cultural artefact of the industrial revolution. The more significant factor was that an increasing number of husbands and fathers lost some of their control over their daughters and wives, as they came to depend in part on an income earned by these womenfolk in the domain of another man.

Second, many women started to earn an independent wage. Though often enough it was quickly subsumed into household income for the disposition of the head of the household, nonetheless it increasingly gave some women independent means. The population of women was greater than that of men throughout the nineteenth century, and the surplus increased from 1851 to 1901 (Hutchins, 1978, p. 75). Not all women would be able to marry and many would be widowed. By 1911, 54 per cent of single women would be working for a wage (Hutchins, 1978, p. 90).

Writing in 1915, and looking back over the previous century, Elizabeth Leigh Hutchins concluded:

> the working woman does not appear to me to be sliding downwards ... rather is she painfully, though perhaps for the most part unconsciously, working her way upwards out of more or less servile conditions of poverty and ignorance into a relatively civilised state, existing at present in a merely rudimentary form. She has attained at least to the position of earning her own living and controlling her own earnings, such as they are. She has statutory rights against her employer, and a certain measure of administrative protection in enforcing them. The right to a living wage, fair conditions of work, and a voice in the collective control over industry are not yet fully recognised, but are being claimed more and more articulately and can less and less be silenced and put aside.... Among much that is sad, tragic and disgraceful in the industrial exploitation of women, there is emerging this fact, fraught with deepest consolation: the woman herself is beginning to think. (Hutchins, 1978, p. xviii)

The third change was that women were not only following their own traditional kinds of work into the factories. They were also diversifying their roles in production. Though they were found in their greatest numbers in the spinning and weaving mills, and in jam-making, confectionery and other forms of large-scale food production, soon they were also producing other kinds of commodity. Even in the early 'domestic' years of capitalist production women had begun to do 'unskilled', heavy and dirty work in metallurgy, making nails, nuts, bolts, screws, buckles, locks, bits and stirrups. Defoe wrote of the West Midlands area in 1769 that 'every Farm has one Forge or more' (Defoe, 1796, cited by Pinchbeck, 1981, p.272), and these forges were producing not for farm consumption but for capitalists. When these 'small iron trades' began to be organized into a factory system, women followed. In 1841 the number of women in the Birmingham district employed in metal manufacture was estimated at 10,000. Twenty-five years later there were 2,050 females returned as employed in Birmingham pen-works and others were employed in the light chain trade, in lacquering brass, and making files and pins (Hutchins, 1978).

Women, then, were spreading into new spheres of production as production industrialized. What now became significant, however, was the particular role they played *within* these new industries. Women clustered within three types of occupation. Hutchins noted, from visits to non-textile factories early in this century, 'that men and women are usually doing, not the same, but different kinds of work and that the work done by women seems to fall roughly into three classes'(1978, pp. 66–7). Her first class was 'rough hard work preparing and collecting the material, or transporting it from one part of the factory to another'. A second was finishing and preparing goods for sale: examining, folding, wrapping and packing. It is the third group of jobs, however, that is the most interesting for us. They are the routine production jobs on machines that we shall see women doing in the 1980s. This work is 'done on machines with or without power, and this includes a whole host of employments and an endless variety of problems. Machine tending, press-work, stamp-work, metal-cutting, printing, various processes of brasswork, pen-making, machine ironing in laundries, the making of hollow-ware or tin pots and buckets of various kinds.' Hutchins did not of course note that the mechanics who kept these machines going were *not* women. It could be taken as given that those jobs belonged to men.

The response of male workers

The final significant effect of the industrial revolution on women was that it threw them, in many cases, into direct competition with men for work. Some of the new machine-based occupations of the late eighteenth and early nineteenth centuries, while they demanded great stamina, no longer called for sheer muscle. Employers could and often did replace men with women and children. Whereas the craft guilds had been organized mainly in exclusion of other men — the exclusion of women being more or less taken for granted — the skilled trade unions were obliged to direct their energies to keeping women out. Men could do little to prevent capital engaging women to work in the new industries. Men's efforts therefore had to be geared to segregating women and maintaining sexual divisions *within* the factory. Consciously and actively, male workers hedged women into unskilled and low-paid occupations. In printing, for instance, the male compositors and machine-minders confined women to book-binding and other print-finishing operations where they were severely exploited by employers.

It is the most damning indictment of skilled working-class men and their unions that they excluded women from membership and prevented them gaining competences that could have secured them a decent living. Virginia Penny wrote in 1869 that women's lot would be greatly improved if only women might enter the trades and professions monopolized by men. 'Apprentice ten thousand women to watchmakers,' she said. 'Put some thousands in the electric telegraph offices all over the country; educate one thousand lecturers for mechanics' institutes ... then the distressed needle-woman will vanish, the decayed gentlewoman and broken-down governessses cease to exist' (Penny, 1869, cited by Meyer, 1972, p. 286). Men were not misled in perceiving women as a weapon in employers' hands by which their own wages could be kept down. Where they were misled was in their response. Instead of helping women to acquire skills and to organize their strength, they weakened women (and in the long run the entire working class) by continuing to exploit women domestically and helping the employer to exploit them as a secondary labour market. Not only were women barred from men's areas of skill but women's particular skills came to be universally undervalued in comparison: undervalued and underpaid. 'There is no reason, save custom and lack of organization, why a nursery-maid should be paid less than a coal-miner. He is not one whit more capable of taking her place than she is of taking his,' wrote Elizabeth Hutchins (1978, p. 201).

So great a gulf had men in earlier centuries fixed between women and technology, however, that the ASE was not obliged to see women as a threat to the engineer throughout the nineteenth century. The kinds of semi-skilled work brought into being by the mechanization of engineering (in the main, machining metal) were not seen by employers as appropriate areas in which to try to substitute women for men. The stratum of 'handymen' infiltrated by the employer into engineering works was just that: men. The Victorian and Edwardian women's movements did not include in their demands technical skills for women. It was not until the First World War, when they were brought into munitions and other heavy industries to release men for the Front, that women began to approach the masculine sphere of technical skill and consequently to be feared for the first time as 'dilutees'.

The *Labour Gazette* in 1917 estimated that one out of three working women was replacing a man (Braybon, 1981). Women went into a number of industries besides munitions:

> They planed, moulded, mortised and dovetailed in sawmills; drove trucks in flour and oil and cake mills; made upholstery and tyre tubes; bottled beer and manufactured furniture; worked in cement factories, foundries and tanneries, in jute mills and wool mills; broke limestone and loaded bricks in steel works and worked as riveters in

shipbuilding yards. They could be found in car factories, in quarrying and surface mining and brickmaking ... only underground mining, stevedoring and steel and iron smelting were still all male. (Solden, 1978, p. 102)

Women, says this author, shattered the myth that they were incapable of skilled work.

A serious challenge was made to male exclusiveness in the ASE by the radical shop stewards' movement of the war and post-war years. Progressiveness on the woman question was a logical position for the shop stewards, whose aim was to turn the ASE from a craft union into an all-grades industrial union (Hinton, 1981; Frow and Frow, 1982). Nonetheless, the pledge the government had given the union to lay off dilutees at the end of the war was honoured. Many thousands of women were ejected from their jobs. High unemployment among women resulted, made worse by the slump of 1920.

The ASE became the Amalgamated Engineering Union in 1922, but still did not admit women members. Meanwhile women's role in the engineering industry expanded fast in the inter-war years, as they became the characteristic semi-skilled assembly-line labour force in the industries producing the new electrical consumer goods (Gluckman, 1984). In the Second World War women again replaced men in many engineering jobs, both unskilled and skilled. This time the situation for the traditionalist men in the union was past saving. Women were, with bad grace on the part of many members, finally accepted into the union on 1 January 1943. The women's section had 139,000 members by 1944 (Solden, 1978, pp. 152–3).

Acceptance into the union, however, did not mean that those women who had acceded to skilled jobs in the war were able to consider them theirs for keeps. After the war, women were once more expected to retire gracefully to domestic life, and for the most part they did so. Those who stayed were reduced to unskilled or semi-skilled work. Women found themselves addressed by an intense ideology of 'femininity' and 'domesticity'. The media, advertising, fiction and film all ludicrously reinforced gender differences, flying in the face of women's lived experiences. The ideology identified men with work and earning, women with home and caring. To associate women with technological competence now seemed as ridiculous as it had ever seemed.

Yet the situation of women was to change once again in the 1950s and 60s as the economic boom caused a demand for their labour and women themselves, even married women now, began to aspire to independence, work and careers in greater numbers than ever before. By the time the recession of the late 1970s hit the British economy, women had grown to be 42 per cent of the labour force (EOC, 1983). Statements by Conservative ministers to the effect that women were expected to do the decent thing and return home, leaving the shrinking supply of jobs to men, were this time ignored by women. Women's consciousness had changed radically since the post-war period and this had influenced 'public opinion' more generally. Supportive legislation of the early 1970s had strengthened women's hand. This time they held on to work, though it was often part-time and low-paid. While the number of male employees in employment fell by 14 per cent between 1971 and 1983, the number of women rose by 7 per cent. The recession, and its handling by the government, has caused a dramatic increase in unemployment during the 1980s, but women have experienced it less acutely than men to date (EOC, 1983).

The way out of the recession for British capital, fervently promoted by a monetarist government, is by shedding labour, reducing the wages of the remainder and investing in super-productive new electronic technology. In such a situation, with men objectively weakened in the labour market, employers indifferent to or even positive towards employing women, and women themselves showing a new confidence in their right to work, we might expect to see women entering technical training and skilled occupations in new technology in equal numbers with men. If, as is becoming apparent, this is not happening, it should alert us to ask more penetrating questions about how male dominance is renegotiated and how the sexual division of labour continues to be reproduced over time.

Notes

1 Figures relate to Great Britain and show women as a percentage of the occupational and industrial labour forces.
2 Department of Education and Science (1970–83) cited in Equal Opportunities Commission (1984). Figures relate to England and Wales, Summer examinations.
3 Figures obtained from City and Guilds of London Institute during 1984.
4 Figures obtained from the Business and Technical Education Council during 1984.
5 Department of Education and Science (1981), Table 22, and the Welsh Office. Figures relate to England and Wales and are cited in Equal Opportunities Commission (1984).
6 Statistics published by the Department of Education and Science (*Statistics of education: universities*) and the University Grants Committee (*University statistics*) and cited in Equal Opportunities Commission (1984).
7 The stereotype caveman reflects scientific theories as they were developed, almost entirely by men, in the patriarchal and ethnocentric societies of western Europe in the nineteenth and early twentieth century. It has been pointed out that it would not be surprising if these men had looked for and found a replica of themselves in prehistory. Nancy Makepeace Tanner suggests that these scientists in effect produced a modern 'origin myth' (1981, p. 3). The effect of male bias among anthropologists on the study of societies in early stages of development is demonstrated by Ruby Rohrlich-Leavitt, Barbara Sykes and Elizabeth Weatherford (1975).

8   Leacock (1981) illustrates this point by reference to the sex-egalitarian gathering and hunting community of the Montagnais-Naskapi of Canada in the period immediately preceding their conversion to Christianity by Jesuit missionaries.

9   Çatal Huyuk, a settlement of *c.* 6,000 BC, represents the transition from neolithic village to bronze-age town. James Mellaart's excavations revealed a society based on cattle breeding and irrigation agriculture, supplemented by gathering, hunting and fishing (Mellaart, 1967). House design and burial arrangements, evidence of female deities and female priests, lead to the conclusion that women were socially pre-eminent at Çatal Huyuk (Rohrlich-Leavitt, 1980).

10 A well-authenticated instance of this, explicit in epic poetry, laws and codes, occurred in the Middle East between the fourth and second millennia BC (Rohrlich-Leavitt, 1980). The process was theorized by Frederick Engels (1972) in the nineteenth century. A material factor that may have enabled men to subjugate women is proposed by Autumn Stanley. Drawing on evidence from foraging societies that have adopted a sedentary agricultural existence and a grain-based diet, she suggests that this change precipitates an increase in body fat, earlier puberty in women and regular ovulation, all tending to a dramatic increase in fertility. It could have been excessive childbearing that, in neolithic agricultural communities, first put women at a physical and economic disadvantage relative to men (Stanley, 1981).

11 Whether fully matriarchal societies ever existed is doubtful. There is, however, evidence of matrilineal and matrilocal societies which would certainly have ensured a centrality for women, and also of societies existing in the more recent past in which the sexes were very much more equal than our own (Leacock, 1981). In place of 'patriarchy', therefore, as a timeless trans-historical expression, it is helpful to use the concept of a 'sex/gender system', as proposed by Rubin (1975, p. 159). This enables us to conceptualize changes over historical periods in the relative power of men and women as sexes, variations in the 'set of arrangements by which a society transforms biological sexuality into products of human activity and in which these transformed sexual needs are satisfied'.

12 See White (1962), who suggests that the iron age proper began for Europe in the ninth century AD (p. 40).

13 Chaytor and Lewis are referring to rural life in the pre-capitalist period.

14 This and other information in this and the succeeding paragraph is drawn from Clark (1919). In Chapter V she traces the position of women in craft and trade in the fourteenth to sixteenth centuries (pp. 150–70).

15 The electrification of kitchen equipment, which began in the last decade of the nineteenth century, was the work of electrical engineers, not housewives.

16 Much of the account of the development of industrial capitalism in this chapter is drawn from Chapters XIII–XV of this volume of *Capital*.

17 'The total production of society may be divided into two major departments. . . .

   I Means of Production — commodities having a form in which they must, or at least may, pass into productive consumption.

   II Articles of Consumption — commodities having a form in which they pass into... individual consumption.' (Marx, 1954, p. 399)

References

BAKER, E.F. (1964) *Technology and Women's Work*, USA, Columbia University Press.

BOSERUP, E. (1971) *Women's Role in Economic Development*, London, George Allen and Unwin.

BRAYBON, G. (1981) *Women Workers in the First World War*, Beckenham, Croom Helm.

CAVENDISH, R. (1982) *Women on the Line*, London, Routledge and Kegan Paul.

CHAYTOR, M. and LEWIS, J. (1982) 'Introduction' in Clark, *Working Life of Women in the Seventeenth Century*, (first published 1919), London, Routledge and Kegan Paul.

CLARK, A. (1919) *Working Life of Women in the Seventeenth Century*, reprinted London, Routledge and Kegan Paul, 1982.

CLEGG, H.A., FOX, A. and THOMPSON, A.F. (1964) *A History of British Trade Unions since 1869*, Vol. 1, Oxford.

COYLE, A. (1982) 'Sex and skill in the clothing industry', in WEST, J. (Ed.) *Work, Women and the Labour Market*, London, Routledge and Kegan Paul.

DEFOE, D. (1796) *Tour*, cited in Pinchbeck (1981).

DEPARTMENT OF EDUCATION AND SCIENCE (1970–83) *Statistics of Education and Statistics of School Leavers*, London, HMSO.

DEPARTMENT OF EDUCATION AND SCIENCE (1981) *Statistics of Education: Further Education*, London, HMSO.

DEPARTMENT OF EMPLOYMENT (1975) *New Earnings Survey*, London, HMSO.

DEPARTMENT OF EMPLOYMENT (1983) *New Earnings Survey*, London, HMSO.

DEPARTMENT OF EMPLOYMENT (1984) *New Earnings Survey, 1970–84*, London, HMSO.

EITB (1984) *Women in Engineering*, Occasional paper No. 11.

EISENSTEIN, S. (1983) *Give Us Bread But Give Us Roses*, London, Routledge and Kegan Paul.

ENGELS, F. (1972) *Origins of the Family, Private Property and the State*, Pathfinder Press.

EQUAL OPPORTUNITIES COMMISSION (1983) *Annual Report*.

EQUAL OPPORTUNITIES COMMISSION (1984) *9th Annual Report*.

FROW, E. and FROW, R., (1982) *Engineering Struggles*, Working Class Movement Library.

GLUCKMAN, M. (1984) 'Women and the "new industries": changes in class relations in the 1930s', paper to Economic and Social Research Council seminar on Gender and Stratification, University of East Anglia, July.

GORZ, A. (1976) 'Technology, technicians and class struggle', in GORZ, A. (Ed.) *The Division of Labour*, Harvester Press.

GROSS, E. (1968) 'Plus ça change?... the sexual structure of occupations over time', *Social Problems*, 16, Fall.

HAKIM, C. (1979) *Occupational Segregation* (Report No. 9) London, Department of Employment.

HINTON, J. (1981) *The First Shop Stewards Movement*, George Allen and Unwin.

HUTCHINS, E.L. (1978) *Women in Modern Industry* (first published 1915), EP Publishing Ltd.

JEFFERYS, J.B. (1946) *The Story of Engineers 1800–1945*, Lawrence and Wishart.

Kessler-Harris, A. (1982) *Out To Work: A History of Wage-earning Women in the United States*, USA, Oxford University Press.

Lapidus, G.W. (1976) 'Occupational segregation and public policy: a comparative analysis of American and Soviet patterns', in Blaxall, M. and Reagan, B. (Eds) *Women and the Workforce: The Implications of Occupational Segregation*, University of Chicago Press.

Leacock, E.B. (1981) *Myths of Male Dominance*, Monthly Review Press.

Martin, J. and Roberts, C. (1984) *Women and Employment: A Lifetime Perspective*, London, Department of Employment and Office of Population Censuses and Surveys.

Martin, M.K. and Voorhies, B. (1975) *Female of the Species*, USA, Cambridge University Press.

Marx, K. (1954) *Capital* (Vol. I) (first published 1887), Lawrence and Wishart.

Mellaart, J. (1967) *Çatal Huyuk: A Neolithic Town in Anatolia*, USA, McGraw-Hill.

Meyer, A.N. (1972) *Women's Work in America* (first published 1891), USA, Arno Press.

Mumford, L. (1934) *Technics and Civilization*, London, Routledge and Kegan Paul.

Neff, W.F. (1966) *Victorian Working Women* (first published 1929), Frank Cass.

Noble, D. (1979) *America by Design: Science, Technology and the Rise of Corporate Capitalism*, Oxford, Oxford University Press (first published 1977, USA, Knopf).

OECD (1980) *Women and Employment: Policies for Equal Opportunities*, Paris, OECD.

Pelling, H. (1976) *A History of British Trade Unionism*, London, Macmillan.

Penny, V. (1869) *Think and Act* cited in Meyer, *Women's Work in America*, USA, Arno Press.

Pinchbeck, I. (1981) *Women Workers and the Industrial Revolution 1750–1850* (first published 1930), London, Virago Press.

Pollert, A. (1981) *Girls, Wives, Factory Lives*, London, Macmillan.

Postan, M.M. (1975) *The Medieval Economy and Society*, Harmondsworth, Penguin.

Rohrlich-Leavitt, R. (1980) 'State formation in Sumer and the subjugation of women', *Feminist Studies* 6, 1, Spring.

Rohrlich-Leavitt, R., Sykes, B. and Weatherford, E. (1975) 'Aboriginal women: male and female anthropological perspectives', in Reiter, R.R. (Ed.) *Toward an Anthropology of Women*, Monthly Review Press.

Rosenberg, N. (1982) *Inside the Black Box: Technology and Economics*, Cambridge University Press.

Rubin, G. (1975) 'The traffic in women', in Reiter, R.R. (Ed.) *Toward an Anthropology of Women*, Monthly Review Press.

Sacks, M.P. (1976) *Women's Work in Soviet Russia: Continuity in the Midst of Change*, USA, Praeger.

Slocum, S. (1975) 'Woman the gatherer', in Reiter, R.R. (Ed.) *Toward an Anthropology of Women*, Monthly Review Press.

Snell, M.W., Glucklich, Z.P. and Povall, M. (1981) *Equal Pay and Opportunities*, Research paper No. 20, Department of Employment.

SOLDEN, N.C. (1978) *Women in British Trade Unions 1874–1976*, London, Gill and Macmillan.

STANLEY, A. (1981) 'Daughters of Isis, daughters of Demeter: when women reaped and sowed', *Women's Studies International Quarterly*, 4, 3.

STANLEY, A. (1983) 'Women hold up two-thirds of the sky: notes for a revised history of technology', in ROTHSCHILD, J. (Ed.) *Machina ex Dea: Feminist Perspectives on Technology*, Oxford, Pergamon.

STRANDH, S. (1979) *A History of the Machine*, USA, A and W Publishers Inc.

TANNER, N.M. (1981) *On Becoming Human*, USA, Cambridge University Press.

TANNER, N.M. and ZIHLMAN, A. (1976) 'Women in evolution: innovation and selection in human origins', *Signs*, 1, 3, Spring.

WEMPLE, S.F. (1981) *Women in Frankish Society: Marriage and the Cloister 500–900 AD*, University of Pennsylvania Press.

WESTWOOD, S. (1984) *All Day Every Day*, London, Pluto Press.

WHITE, LYNN, JR (1962) *Medieval Technology and Social Change*, Oxford University Press.

WHITELOCK, D. (1952) *The Beginnings of English Society*, Harmondsworth, Penguin.

WILKINSON, B. (1969) *The Later Middle Ages in England 1216–1485 AD*, Longman.

ZEITLIN, J. (1979) 'Craft control, and the division of labour: engineers and compositors in Britain 1890–1930', *Cambridge Journal of Economics*, 3.

Chapter 3

The Selling of the New Technology

Frank Webster and Kevin Robins

> The promotion of the illusion of an 'electronic revolution' borders upon complicity by intellectuals in the myth-making of the electrical complex itself. The celebration of the electronic revolution is a process whereby the world of scholarship contributes to the cults of engineering, mobility, and fashion at the expense of roots, tradition, and political organization. (Carey and Quirk, 1970, p. 422)

Bookstalls in airports, railway stations, chain stores and newsagents are fascinating sociologically, since they give insight into the concerns of the mass market. Stocks are predictable: soft pornography, crime, science fiction, romance, international espionage and romance predominate. Certain titles are found almost everywhere — *The Boys from Brazil, The Valley of the Dolls, The Day of the Jackal* and *The Eagle has Landed* are obvious examples — as are authors such as Ken Follett, Len Deighton, Jackie Collins and Harold Robbins. A little non-fiction sits beside the pulp novels, and this too has easily recognizable characteristics. It will surprise no one that a current best-seller is *How to Make Love to Your Man*, a thoroughly modern manual on how to be ladylike, attractive, and liberated.

The bookstalls have become particularly interesting since late 1978 because of the unanticipated appearance of a number of paperbacks that are concerned with a 'non-sexy' topic — technology. As any publisher knows, technology does not appeal to a wide public: it is something for specialists, runs of a thousand or two, decidedly not the big time. Nonetheless, a number of titles have nudged aside stories about supermen, inter-galactic adventures, and erotic exploits. Titles such as *The Micro Millenium, The Third Wave, The Wired Society, The Micro Revolution, The Silicon Civilization* and *The Communications Revolution* have achieved sales hitherto thought impossible for this subject.

Connoisseurs of the bookstalls will be puzzled by the presence of these books only at first glance, since a look at their covers explains their location. They are about a very special technology the discovery of which is set to change our lives more thoroughly than anything previously imagined. Their blurbs announce the content: 'The Revolution that will change our lives' (Toffler, 1980); 'A tiny fragment of Silicon that will change your life beyond recognition' (Hyman, 1980); 'A revolution in technology that could bring the wholesale displacement of people from work by automation — by the robots of science fiction — or the chance of a glittering electronic future with infinite opportunities for everyone?' (Laurie, 1980).

These announce the arrival of something which will revolutionize our whole way of life — our work, leisure, education, politics, family ... and even our sexuality, if we are to credit Professor Arthur Harkins, director of the graduate program in futures at the University of Minnesota. Harkins believes that by the year 2000 people will be 'marrying' robots since, given that the 'great bulk of human relationships are formulated on a ritualistic basis' (which is to say that 'most humans, in their relationships with wives or lovers, expect a kind of metronomic precision of expected behaviour and expected responses to occur over time'), even the most intimate behaviour is programmable. Because people 'expect breakfast, lunch, and dinner to be ready at a certain time, sexual acts to be performed at certain times or in certain ways, the house to be a certain way, the vacation to be a certain way, and the children to be treated a certain way,' then these patterns can be duplicated by a sophisticated machine which also incorporates personality traits, mechanical sexual organs, and the warmth, texture and smell of humans (*Computerworld*, 17 May 1982). There will clearly be no way of escaping this new technology, and thus it is not unexpected that Information Technology has entered the best-seller listings. It is perhaps also a reasonable prediction that a future best-seller — after *How to Make Love to Your Woman* — will be *How to Make Love to Your Android*.

The bulk of these popular books on Information Technology are as escapist and unworldly as the rest of the pulp with which they displayed, despite their hard-nosed tone and assurances to the contrary. Nevertheless, they do indicate the arrival of a significant phenomenon. The development and future application of Information Technology promises to have an influence on many aspects of everyday life. For this reason, there has been a justified fascination at the human ability to create such a powerful new technology. An avalanche of futurist comment has helped divert this nascent interest into apathy and awe.

Information Technology

Information Technology (IT) is a neologism (others are télématique, communications, and informatics) coined to describe a tendency for computing and telecommunications technologies to integrate and converge. It is a generic term which encompasses word processors, office equipment, electronic mail, cable television, videotex, robotics, television games, computer networks and satellite communications. Its growth is being promoted by the rapid rise of microelectronics, which is the source of dramatically cheapened computing capacity that is the enabling technology behind recent developments.

Microelectronics is noteworthy because

- it is a heartland technology which has, in the manner of the steam engine, petrol engine and electric motor, application over an entire range of activities.

- it allows information to be handled almost everywhere it appears, since it:

    > touches every function of sensing, of control, communications and information processing — indeed, just about every kind of work now performed by people or machines except generating power or propelling vehicles. It promises to extend the impact of all that has gone before and to impinge upon virtually every organized human activity, whether institutional or personal. (Sarnoff, 1974, p. 31)

It is this availability of a cheap and reliable means of handling information that has led to the integration and convergence of computers and communications categorized by IT. This is occurring because microelectronics can now be distributed in much wider ways than was previously possible, which brings about a need to tie together disparate operations. The Howlett Committee reviewed this trend thus:

> It has been obvious for some time that the running of a moderately industrialized economy requires the collection, storing, retrieving, processing and generally moving around of a great variety of information, numerical or otherwise, often in large volumes and often very quickly. The computer makes the first four of these activities possible on a scale which was unthinkable a generation ago and every modern state is now completely dependent on computers and allied devices.... The telecommunications system makes the transporting of information possible on the scale required and there is a corresponding dependence here too. (Howlett, 1978, p. 1)

Because commentators have focused attention on microelectronics and the significance this has for computer applications, there has been a tendency to underestimate the symbiotic role of telecommunications. However, it is arguable that telecommunications is nowadays 'the most important single business in Britain' (Conservative Party, 1979, p. 41), because it is not computers in themselves which are so crucial, but the ability to network computers, to extend computer communications on a widespread scale. Telecommunications, which itself integrates many aspects of computerization for information storage, exchange functions, and network control, provides this essential means of interconnection (Baer, 1978).

The ability of telecommunications to transmit information presages a time when 'information ring mains' will link departments in offices, headquarters to divisions, central offices to individuals; when automated factory production will be capable of control from a central unit; when the home will be able to access data banks in local, national, and international locations. These prospects for an 'electronic grid', enhanced by the increased carrying capacity of cable, optical fibre, microwave and satellites, have led writers to envisage an era of a 'wired society' in which, in each home, office, shop, restaurant, school, bank, town hall, or wherever, there will be computer terminals linked to central processors which will create a situation in which the public have 'information sockets like three-pin power sockets for electricity' (Barron and Curnow, 1979, p. 31).

Another important development made possible by the 'tidal wave' (*ibid.*) of microelectronics is the emergence of industries supplying systems rather than separate products.

A number of reasons account for this:

- *integration*: one of the aspects of integration is the tendency for new products to subsume the functions of former ones.
- *convergence*: previously separate technologies are coming together with the imbrication of computers and communications.
- *product compatibility*: the trend today is towards the supply of data processing, communications equipment, and so forth, as systems that are compatible in areas such as text editing, computing, filing and reproduction.

It is for these reasons that American Telephone and Telegraph (AT&T) projects that 'More and more, the Bell System's services for business will take the form of comprehensive systems integrating virtually all aspects of information flow, encompassing voice, video, data storage, retrieval, processing and distribution, word processing and electronic mail' (*Annual Report*, 1980). Tying 'together the products of . . . various sections' (Hitachi, *Annual Report*, 1980) is most readily seen in the office, but a similar process is discernable in goods being manufactured for the home which build upon television (for example, video cassette recorders, television games, viewdata). Thus AT&T observes that 'the home communications market' is moving 'in much . . . the same direction' as business 'towards information-communications *systems*. We expect to equip the home of the future with facilities that meet a wide variety of needs: information, education, entertainment, and . . . the control of energy consumption' (*Annual Report*, 1980).

Systems will increasingly replace products in three areas (which eventually will themselves integrate):

- *production systems*: automation of manufacture, instrumentation, robotics, computer-controlled engineering, etc.
- *office systems*: integrated systems for filing, typing, data/text processing and communication, copying, etc.
- *household systems*: home entertainment/information systems incorporating video, games, computing, television, teletext, etc.

It is clear that the shift towards systems of computer-communications will neither take place overnight nor be developed at an even pace. There are good social, economic and political reasons why systems will be introduced into offices and large organizations before they fully enter the domestic sphere. And even in the office, systems will be built incrementally on a modular basis from present-day products. Nevertheless, while conceding uneven development, and that the new builds upon the old, there remain unstoppable pressures forcing the spread of IT systems.

From this it would seem that IT straightforwardly identifies a range of goods and services emerging out of the integration and convergence of computers and communications that are shifting away from disparate products towards systems. However, such a definition suggests too much neatness and fails to acknowledge both the generality and massive compass of the term. IT is in truth a vague concept, in principle encompassing any technology which handles information, though more often indicating the use of computers and communications together, that has been conjured to make sense of some deep-seated changes. In consequence, the category has a huge spread that makes it difficult to readily and comprehensively identify its constituents.

For this reason, some commentators have elided microelectronic applications in the field of product manufacture (e.g., robotics, control engineering) from the category, and have limited IT to those areas of use in more obvious information-processing spheres such as administration, education, government, and media. This does have the virtue of recognizing the major areas that are being and will be affected by the new technology. However, even this leaves IT with an enormous reach that includes 'the actual equipment used to collect, store, process, transmit and display information ... (as well as the software that controls it) ... and its interactions with human activities and the management systems necessary if the capabilities of new developments are to be fully exploited.' In these terms, the title covers

important sectors of the electronic components industry (with an emphasis on microelectronics), much electronic equipment (notably computers and their associated terminals, displays, etc.) and the whole communications industry, including the broadcasting authorities ... (telecommunications) and the users and suppliers of information — industrial, financial, commercial, administrative, professional, and individual — because their activities will be affected by new forms of information handling. (ACARD, 1980)

Therefore, though IT is an amorphous term, we can identify the following sectors as central constituents:

- data/text processing equipment (computers, peripherals)
- data/text processing (software houses)
- data/text communications carriers (chiefly telecommunications authorities outside the USA)
- data/text communications equipment manufacturers (exchanges, satellites, etc.)
- significant parts of consumer electronics (e.g., video, television)
- electronic components (TV tubes, integrated circuits, etc.)
- office equipment (copiers, typewriters, word-processors, etc.)
- information suppliers (online databases, broadcasting organizations, etc.).

Futurism wild and sober

It is this arrival of IT, unannounced and uninvited, which has been the occasion for the succession of 'mighty micro' paperbacks. But the speculation has not stopped there. There has in fact been a much more sweeping response to IT. Indeed, it is no exaggeration to say that the public has been deluged by materials such that it is hardly conceivable that anyone can be ignorant of at least some of its applications. The very scale of the response to IT compels us to take it seriously, though we cannot commend the flood of (mis)information that has burst upon society. To explain our antipathy, let us review some of the coverage of IT prior to analyzing its themes and assumptions.

IT has hardly been out of the media of late, whether as a regular source of accounts about economic restructuring caused by its take-up in the business press, features in the qualities or breathless 200-word leaders in the tabloid newspapers. Television has put out programmes — and series of programmes — that commenced in Britain with a *Horizon* special and Christopher Evans's *The Mighty Micro* in 1978, and have appeared recurrently since on the likes of *Tomorrow's World, Nova* and *The Burke Special.* Within the space of a few months, from nowhere, IT has permeated the media such that it has even entered the plots of soaps.

In these outlets futurism has been working as if there was no tomorrow to supply instant comment and projections. Wilson Dizard tells us that the

> vision of a plug-in future, of computers in the living room, of global teleconferences, of robotics factories controlled by telepresence techniques, and of a new quality of life based on access to vast information resources is ... too close to possible realization to be dismissed any longer as sci-fi fantasy. (Dizard, 1982, p. 38)

With this we are away into speculation of a cashless society, an end to letters, telecommuting, shopping from our armchairs.... The *Futurist* magazine, surely the most excitable of all the prophets, repeats in each month's issue stories on the lines that we are 'entering an era in which the science fiction of a decade ago is now technological reality', that an information-rich future heralds nothing less than a New Renaissance for the West; that IT will rescue America from its present crises as the 'new miracle brains' get into 'everything from toys to kitchen equipment to machines that will play chess and backgammon', provide 'automatic machines [that] will cut your lawn ... then rake the leaves without human hands', let 'capital ... be generous with labour without significant cost to itself', hold down inflation, leaving a contented populace with time, inclination, and money so that 'history's wheel, having rolled through despotism and oligarchy, may ... because of the miracle chip, jam forever on democracy' (all quotations from the *Futurist*, August, 1981; cf. Cornish, 1982).

There are of course more sober prognostications than these. Comment becomes markedly less star-struck the shorter its span of prediction. The immediate prospects, delineated by politicians and businessmen in the main, wonder about the likely effects on balance of payments, European strategic relations with Japan and the USA, or organizational aspects of the 'office of the future'. Scenarios here outline painful effects on traditional operations, consider the need to invest in new technology, and the requirements of education to familiarize students with IT. The talk is grim, realistic, and measured.

However, the sober and wild elements of futurism are usually wedded, in that comments imagine a dazzling future if only the difficult years of adjustment can be got through. For instance, James Callaghan, then Prime Minister, thought in late 1978 that 'we may be on the threshold of the most rapid industrial change in history' which could bring 'within reach of the budget of our people a range of goods and services they could never previously afford', but 'we must prepare for it' because 'we do not have time to lose' if we are 'to reap the maximum benefit from the new technology' (Callaghan, 1978). This oscillation between tantalizing long-term prospect and formidable problems in the near future is characteristic of much of the presentation of IT. It is, of course, the old theme of carrot and stick.

Government

The Conservative Government in Britain created a multi-million-pound campaign — Information Technology Year 1982 (*IT'82*) — offering a programme of travelling exhibitions, subsidized conferences, and demonstation projects. When it was announced 'there were assurances that [it] will not dodge the issue of social change' (*Guardian*, 29 May 1981), but what has issued forth amounts to nothing less than a massive propaganda exercise extolling IT. By late 1982, its presenters had come to define it as a means of 'informing and enthusing as many people as possible of the benefits of Information Technology' (*IT'82*, October 1982), and it was fitting that Margaret Thatcher, acknowledging the success of the campaign so far, promised that her government would 'continue to encourage people to *accept* the new technology' (Thatcher, 1982, original emphasis).

To this end, *IT'82* produced an extensive advertising campaign featuring slogans such as 'Has the revolution started without you?' 'Is your seven-year-old better equipped to run an office than you are?' and 'Is the technology in your local more advanced than the technology in your factory?!' Beneath such headings are messages, attractively illustrated, which tell us that IT is 'transforming old industries, taking away boredom, removing danger, making factories cleaner, more pleasant places to work', that IT in the office will 'take away an enormous amount of boredom from a secretary's life and provide a machine that is intrinsically interesting to use', that 'caring for prematurely born babies, continuously monitoring them, and alerting hospital doctors and nurses whenever special treatment is needed, is just one area in which IT looks after people', that 'from our earliest moments to old age, IT is involved in looking after us, and not just in terms of our health. IT is also helping to educate our children and to equip them to exploit fully the information revolution.' *IT'82* produced an irregular newsheet in similar vein: the new technology is presented as a panacea for ills found in all spheres of life — and it reaches all spheres.

The campaign also encouraged the public to hurry and accept this 'once-in-a-century chance to create new wealth, higher standards of living and a world in which routine and drudgery are alleviated and in which all of us have more time, freedom and ability to pursue our interests'. And if these words of inducement ('The important thing to remember about the IT revolution . . . is that its effects are friendly') were insufficient, if one persisted in hanging back, then *IT'82* threatened: 'one thing is certain about IT, if we don't learn its lessons now for ourselves; we'll end up having to pay someone else to teach us'; 'The one thing that is absolutely certain is that if we don't adopt IT, our competitors will. They are already doing so'; 'Without IT, Britain will decline — very fast'; 'There's no future without IT.'

Education

Education at all levels in the UK has been induced to act on IT (DES, 1978, 1979), harried by repeated calls for 'an injection of technology into the curriculum' (Gosling, 1981, pp. 16–17) because the 'task of education' is to help 'our kind to make the transition to a new lifestyle' (Gosling, 1978, p. 39). In the upper ranges, extra resources have been made available for courses on microelectronics, computing and electronic engineering, while research funds, cut almost everywhere else, have been forthcoming. 'New blood' lectureships in British universities have overwhelmingly gone to IT and cognate subjects, while other disciplines have been heavily bled. Lower down the educational ladder there is a government commitment in the UK to get a microcomputer into every secondary school by the mid-1980s; special programs have been devised to familiarize the generation which will reach adulthood in the computer age; computer camps are encouraged as worthy holiday activities; and soon all Britain's 20,000 primary schools will have a computer. Needless to say, *IT'82* has singled out the schools for special attention. To this end posters, video material, films, and literature, all appealingly packaged, have been sent gratis to teachers. The campaign also subsidized 50 per cent of a book — *Educating the Information Generation* — which was sent free to British schools early in 1983. The source of the rest of the costs, commercial sponsors, notably IBM, suggests the substance of this education. Such has been the success of these measures that the Microelectronics Education Programme, a joint venture of the Departments of Industry and Education commenced in 1980, had its budget doubled and span of life extended to 1986 the better to continue its mission in schools (Fothergill, 1983).

Government can rely upon other agencies to complement this material. For example, the press is replete with messages for the younger generation, competitions to write essays on the microelectronics revolution, personal computers to be won, badges and leaflets to be sent for. The Disney organization supports the schools with its $800 million Experimental Prototype Community of Tomorrow (Epcot) which aims 'to convince the general public that computers are as non-threatening as Mickey Mouse — and infinitely more useful'. Demonstrating the group's 'underlying principle of using entertainment as a medium of public instruction', Disneyland (one of America's more visited amusements which is supplemented by major television and film coverage) will use Epcot's robots, moving replicas of living creatures, extensive terminals, and extravagant special effects 'to portray processors as useful and approachable and to counteract the widespread perception of the machines as sinister and destructive entities' (*Computerworld*, 8 March 1982). AT&T features *Spaceship Earth* at the Epcot Center, sponsoring an exhibit which 'depicts communications from the Stone Age to the Information Age' (*Annual Report*, 1982). The spectators will doubtless appreciate how wonderfully we have evolved, and shall continue to do so, if things are left in the safe hands of the Bell System (Bass, 1983). All this and Disneyland is but the most prominent aspect of a massive industry of toys, comics and games which has hitched on to the IT juggernaut to sell its wares.

Advertising

Corporate advertisers have lately been spending fortunes, both extolling their produce and — with increased emphasis — urging public acceptance of IT and 'the future'. A whole page is bought in the *Observer* newspaper (cost in 1983 £15,750) to tell us that 'Information technology has a long and benign history. The computer, the telephone, the telegraph, the printing press, the invention of writing itself — all of them led to increased prosperity and universal improvement in the standard of living'. For all this and more to come, the paymaster adds that 'Britain will be grateful to Sinclair Research' (*Observer*, 22 May 1983), and the advertisement is repeated in other national press. In the USA, AT&T has been among the most actively committed to 'the great crusade for understanding' (Barnet and Müller, 1975, pp. 105–20), scheduling a regular series of prime-time television and newspaper advertisements which comment on an 'Information Age' in the making. The Bell organization incurs this expense because 'We believe it is in the public interest to see the benefits of that new age come to America as quickly as possible' (advertisement, *Wall Street Journal*, 14 January 1982).

United Technologies, buying space in *The Atlantic*, takes to heart the Mobil organization's maxim that 'business needs voices in the media' because 'our nation functions best when economic and other concerns of the people are subjected to rigorous debate' (Mobil advertisement, *Los Angeles Times*, 6 April 1982). To this end, United Technologies contributes to the 'rigorous debate' about technological innovation by vilifying 'Misfortune Tellers' of the past through choice quotation. Thus, 'A sampling of the now-amusing statements of old shows that naysaying is nothing new' precedes idiocies from a nineteenth-century cleric such as 'Rail travel at high speed is not possible because passengers, unable to breathe, would die of asphyxia'. Half a dozen of this sort of remark lead to the sagacious conclusion of a 'rigorous debate': 'Misfortune tellers with dark clouds in their crystal balls have always been with us. Happily, so have innovators with the vision and perseverance to reach successfully for the promise of technology' (*The Atlantic*, April 1982).

Such appeals to favour change are commonplace in discussions of IT. IBM is especially in favour of progress and vehemently against those Luddites who hinder innovation and the advantages it brings. The company presents history lessons in the pages it buys:

the action of the Luddites carries a very instructive lesson: it's not progress itself which is the threat, but the way we adapt to it. For without technology, a nation's progress would undoubtedly falter. Machines bring down the cost of production. Which in turn either creates greater profit for reinvestment, or holds down the costs of the product, so providing greater purchasing power for the pound. The result is greater wealth — the ideal climate for increased employment. And machines that relieve man of the tasks that limit his personal fulfilment. Smashing the clocks might destroy the mechanism of progress. But it will never delay tomorrow. (advertisement, *New Statesman*, 25 May 1979)

In such ways do corporate advertisers present innovation, seizing upon the idea of progress as an unqualified term of praise, tapping deeply-held beliefs of western society (Pollard, 1968; Sklair, 1970; Bury, 1932).

Many of these advertisements are aimed at particular social groups rather than the public at large. Targeting messages in the business, political and up-market press that proclaim the electronic age is evidently directed at opinion leaders (the British government's 'awareness campaign', launched by Labour in 1979, paralleled this in being aimed at '50,000 key decision makers', *Electronics Times*, 11 January 1979). Given the socio-economic situation of such readers, one can safely assume that most will be predisposed to look favourably on IT, so much of the propaganda will function to consolidate rather than change opinion. One may further speculate that, at such a time as we live in when IT is arriving amidst recession, uncertainty and apprehension, there is a special psychological need for opinion leaders to be convinced that current developments which appear unstoppable are beneficial, and that the future will indeed turn out for the best. Only with this conviction can they operate effectively as mediators between government, corporations and the wider public.

James Martin — and the entourage accompanying the James Martin Seminars — combines a boost in confidence in the future with the appealing promise of improved corporate productivity in the immediacy to those businesspeople able to attend his regular audiences in Amsterdam, London, Paris, Berlin, New York, Los Angeles, Chicago, Toronto, Atlanta or Boston. All his activities evidence the breezy confidence and evangelical fervour of one sold on progress and the future and schooled over two decades with IBM. And of even more significance is that Martin represents only the best-known face of an unceasing round of conferences, seminars, and workshops design-ed to sell IT to educationalists, academics, business, community and political representatives.

Visionaries and realists

It has been a feature of commentary on IT that much has evidenced a coexistence of fantastic futurism with grave concern for the constraints of the here and now. We mentioned this paradox earlier, and would comment further on the popularity of the 'visionary' and 'realist' approaches. A great deal unites the two by switching back and forth from a scenario for the 1990s promising wonderful achievements to the disturbing and unsettled 1980s, and it has been choice of time-scale rather than different conceptions of the significance of IT that has distinguished opinions. Thus, in spite of different emphases, it is hard to doubt that the presentation of IT, both as a herald of better, even halcyon, days and as something which must be taken up immediately to avert a further plunge into recession, has been instrumental in effecting its unopposed introduction. The probability that foreign competitors will adopt IT before us, and thereby gain markets at our expense which will worsen recession, is constantly held out as the reality which demands rapid take-up of new technology. It is such a prospect that induces the Trades Union Congress to pressure 'Britain to be in the vanguard of the technological change' (TUC, 1979), and, as this present difficulty imposes itself, the long-term futurist nirvana is drawn upon as a source of morale.

When one looks at statements from politicians about IT, one sees serious concern for immediate problems, though the electronic idylls are always on the horizon. But what is still more striking than this is the astonishing unanimity about IT in the political sphere which in fact serves to denude the issue of politics in any meaningful sense. In Britain, Labour and Tory spokespeople are in accord that IT presents the possibility of renewed glory — provided it is quickly taken up. For example, it was James Callaghan who noted that 1978 'has proved to be the year when Britain woke up to micro-electronics', urged the nation to meet head-on the challenge of IT and strive for its rewards. If we do not adopt it, he went on, 'and other major industrial countries adapt ... then the prospect for us will be of stagnation and of decline' (Callaghan, 1978). In exactly the same way, Kenneth Baker, by 1981 the Minister of Information Technology in a Conservative administration, stressed the 'enormous opportunities' IT held for the country, so long as we were not 'left behind in this technological race. We shall have to run fast to keep abreast of our European partners, and we shall have to run very fast to keep ahead of the newly emerging countries [since] we cannot resist the trend of progress' (*Hansard*, 11 July 1980, cols. 933–4). A full-scale debate on IT in Parliament held in 1980 underscored this remarkable consensus, members agreeing that 'it is difficult to decide who is a Conservative and who is a Socialist in this debate' (*ibid.*, col. 955), that in speeches 'there has been a lack of political partisanship and a genuine desire to explore the problems and possibilities of modern technology' (col. 993), that a 'feature that has characterized this debate already is the lack of party controversy' (col. 993). All this is uniformly technocratic, denying a politics of technology on the centre-stage of the polity.

We are not the first to note this consensus. Revealingly, a commercial organization, Acorn Computers, underscored it in a full-page advertisement in the *Guardian* newspaper (8 June 1983) on the eve of what was one of the most polarized and bitter political campaigns in post-war history. The text ran:

> Whatever the differences between the three major parties ... we're happy to report a certain amount of accord on, at least, one important issue. All three parties have recently affirmed their commitment to the continuing growth of information technology and to the vital role of the microcomputer in education and industry. Whoever wins tomorrow, therefore, it is certain that the microcomputer has an increasing role to play.

Acorn unabashedly staked its claim as 'one of the handful of companies that has helped Britain achieve this position' as it insisted that IT 'is basic to the future growth of this country', prior to concluding: 'Isn't it reassuring to know that, whoever is drinking the champagne on Friday, there is a shared determination to keep that industry ahead in the world?' It is fitting that a commercial outfit should in its puffery voice approval of this consensus, since it recalls an earlier example of assurances that certain things are beyond debate: as Acorn's interests in IT coalesce with those of the nation, so too did General Motors' with those of America. We may ponder the likely effects on public attitudes towards IT when political representatives — not to mention a surfeit of media, education and business opinion — present such an undifferentiated response.

So have gone — and continue to go — the instant analyses of IT. We have been swamped with projections and recommendations which acknowledge that IT will have an enormous social effect, that its adoption is unavoidable, and that in the long run it will be a fine thing for us all. These deserve closer inspection.

Technology is benign

Technology is presented as, on the whole, benign. Typically 'most of the changes are changes for the better: better education, better news media, better forms of human communication, better entertainment, better medical resources, less pollution, less human drudgery, less use of petroleum, more efficient industry, and a better informed society with a rich texture of information sources' (Martin, 1978, p. 15). To be sure, there are references to potential ill effects, generally of a transitional nature, but the overwhelming image is one of a 'benevolent technology' (*ibid.*) which may create an 'electronic renaissance' (Williams, 1982, p. 280).

In spite of the fact that reports, especially in the media, present a picture of there being a choice to be made between interpretations that are either optimistic or pessimistic, there is no balance between alternative views. The roseate picture of a post-industrial wonderland far outweighs references to the possibility of mass unemployment and authoritarian states.

Technology as spectacle

Technology is presented as a spectacle, as something which can evoke only a gee-whiz, awed response, since it entails regarding technology as a phenomenon that has arrived in society out of the blue, although it will have a devastating social effect. This conception of a desocialized technology which is set to have the most far-reaching social effects inevitably leads to Callaghan-like calls to wake up to the unexpected arrival. We are so accustomed to perceiving social change in these terms of a history of technological development ('the Railway Age', 'the world the steam engine made') somehow removed from human intent and decision that the most recent developments are readily framed in this way (Williams, 1974, pp. 9–31). History comes to be seen as a history of technological innovation, contemporary Britain the product of a 'remarkable series of inventions' (Landes, 1969), microelectronics but the latest stage of this progression. History — technological advance — comes to have its own logic and drive which shapes the society though it is devoid of social value. In this framework technology is assumed, crucially, to be separate from society at its outset (apparently having arisen from some internal process in some wierd and wonderful place such as Silicon Valley) only to be introduced at a later stage as an independent variable which is the primary cause of social change.

Because futurists, in adopting this perspective, accept as their starting-point a completed technology, they are impelled to offer the public no role other than that of consumer of the latest gadgetry. Ignoring the processes by which technology itself comes to be constituted means that one is restricted to consideration only of the likely impact the latest product will have. Such a procedure, as Young observes, necessarily excludes the public from any meaningful say in technological change, since its presentation leaves one with nothing other than the sense that 'This is beautiful, fascinating; I have been enlightened. It is serious but very palatable fare — to be consumed' (Young, 1979).

So long as consideration of technology starts from the technology as it is, then discussion can only be limited, restricted to the social implications of a constituted technology, and ignorant of the whole series of social choices that have been exercised in the production of the technology:

> What the media treat is the 'impact' of such development. Where were those media when they were being conceived and prepared for market? Today is yesterday's *Tomorrow's World*, but what debate occurred before Raymond Baxter and Co. were allowed to televise what's in store for us? (Young, 1979; *cf*. Gardner and Young, 1981)

W.A. Fallow, chairman of Eastman Kodak, in a recent speech to share-holders, unassumingly revealed the misguidedness of regarding technological innovation in the manner of futurists when he informed his audience of Kodak's criteria for development of new products as follows:

> Last year, Kodak spent more than $615 million on R&D (research and development), ranking it among the top ten US companies in total research expenditures. Right now, while we are meeting here,

there may be a Kodak scientist ... making an exciting new discovery in photographic imaging, electronic imaging, or their related fields. Such discoveries can lead to whole new technologies.

About ten years ago, for example, the continuous wave dye laser was invented during research at Kodak.... Over the last decade, it has revolutionized the field of spectroscopy. But Kodak has never produced such a laser for market, and so far we have no plans to do so. That market has never had the earnings potential to justify the cost of developing it.

I think the point is clear. Just because Kodak knows *how* to make a product doesn't mean we *should* make it.... From now on, Kodak's success will depend on our ability to apply the right mix of many technologies, in those markets characterized by solid growth potential. (Fallow, 1982)

To take Mr Fallow seriously — and, as head of one of the world's leading corporations, he merits taking seriously — is to refuse the starting-point and therefore subsequent analysis of almost all commentary on IT, and to start reexamination of the relations between technology and society from a perspective which rejects all talk of their separation.

Technology is neutral

Because technology is believed to be asocial, it is also seen as neutral, a tool to be used either appropriately or not, depending on the motives of a society. From this assumption of neutrality, most comment on IT asserts that the new technology offers choices. We shall have more to say about this rhetoric of choice, but here we offer Dizard's alternative of a 'life-enriching culture in the 21st century' or 'collapse into political latitude, economic stalemate, and social fragmentation' (Dizard, 1982, p. 1) as representative of a recurrent theme.

Across the spectrum of politics, one finds assurances that the 'technology itself is neutral: it is the way it is applied and used that determines the effects on people' (GMWU, 1980), and from a such a proposition the idea of choice is irresistible. Moreover, if IT is socially neutral and leaves policy choices to the public, then on what reasonable grounds can it be suspected?

Inevitability

It is paradoxical that these presentations of IT, so often professing 'choices' that the new technology allows, invariably carry an underlying inevitability. There is total agreement that IT must be adopted — and as quickly as possible. Thus Large's 'in a competitive world there is no alternative to using the chip as quickly and widely as possible' (1980, p. 12), and Hyman's 'the new technologies need to be introduced rapidly and creatively' (1980, p. 123), are unexceptional statements among the futurists.

As we have noted, commentators across the political divide insist that IT cannot be rejected. Tory Kenneth Baker, for example, asserts that 'The inevitable logic is that we must accept the technologies' (*Hansard*, 11 July 1980, col. 938), and he finds an echo in Labourite John Evans' words that 'The British people in all walks of life, whether they are employers, trade union members, politicians, or academics, must recognise that we have to accept the advent of the new technology' (*ibid.*, col. 1000). Moreover, though we are told in the UK that the Social Democratic Party has 'broken the mould' of orthodox allegiances, the fracture has not affected reaction towards IT, leading member Shirley Williams concurring that 'there is no alternative to adopting the new technologies' (*Guardian*, 18 November 1980).

This inevitability has been reinforced by a historical legacy of what has been called the 'ideology of industrialization', by which is meant a tradition of thought which perceives technology as a hidden hand in development apart from the social issues of power and control. David Dickson summarizes:

> The message of this ideology is that industrialization through tech-
> nological development is a practical — rather than a political —
> necessity for achieving social development. It implies an objectivity to
> the process, and seeks to remove it from debate on political issues. It
> thus gives a legitimacy to prophecies that appear to promote the
> process of industrialization, often regardless of their political, or even
> social consequences.... To stand in the way of technology is, almost
> by definition, to be labelled reactionary. Industralization is equated
> with modernization, with progress, with a better and healthier life for
> all. (Dickson, 1974, p. 42)

The past in the future

If one queries the advantages — or the need — of accepting today's techno-logical innovation, one is frequently portrayed as an unworldly romantic in sharp contrast to the this-worldliness and foresight of its advocates. This charge castigates a deep-rooted tradition in England of a rejection of 'indus-try' in favour of a retrospective ruralism (Newby, 1980). It is a remarkable feature of industrial capitalism that, .hroughout the transforming experiences of the past three centuries, the ideas of rural life have 'persisted with extra-ordinary power' (Williams, 1975, p. 10): '*Real* England has never been repres-ented by the town, but by the village, and the English countryside has been converted into a vast arcadian rural idyll in the mind of the average English-man' (Newby, 1979, pp. 11–12). This idealization of the countryside, espe-cially the agricultural past, in the most thoroughly urbanized country in the world, is evidenced in much literary and cultural output which extends from the beginnings of industrialization through writers as diverse as William Blake, Charles Dickens and D.H. Lawrence, to current vogues for Laura Ashley dresses, earthenware pots, and nostalgia for anything rural, and it can easily be shown to be misleading, ignorant of the misery, oppression, and deprivations of pre-industrialism (see, for example, George, 1962). Subscribers to a rural idyll are too often ignorant of history — the real history of the countryside in which life 'was as hard and brutal as anything later experienced' (Williams, 1975) — to be taken seriously. Because of this, opposition to new technology is readily smeared and thereby discounted by association with a tradition which can appear to desire a return to the impoverishments of an earlier time. Drawing on this imagery, Wilson P. Dizard can sneer at and condemn the 'disturbing tendency to retreat from the implications of the new machines, to deny the possibility of a viable technology-powered democratic society. These anti-technology forces, the new Luddites, seek solace in astrology, artificial Waldens, and bad poetry' (Dizard, 1982, p. 15).

Paradoxically, however, and possibly because ruralism is so deeply entrenched, perpetrators of the new technology have often tried to steal the clothes of these opponents even while ridiculing their proposals. This is achieved by projecting a return to the past in the future, the recovery of a golden age with twenty-first-century comforts, by suggesting that adoption of IT will effect a return to a lost way of life. We see this posture in the language of those who envisage the reestablishment of domestic production in the era of the electronic cottage, a period when community will be regained in a wired society, a time when pollution disappears due to 'technologies that are environmentally sound ... and nondestructive of the ecology' (Martin, 1978, p. 4).

This capacity to combine rejection of IT's critics with the argument that IT satisfies the requirements of their criticism is remarkably common. Dizard, for example, jettisons 'antitechnology forces' for their naivety and immediately proceeds to hymn the 'search for a new Eden through the melding of nature and the machine' that is a 'powerful force propelling us toward new forms of post-industrialism' which, in the 'information age', brings 'electronic salvation within our grasp' (Dizard, 1982, pp. 22–3). Alvin Toffler dismisses 'critics of industrialism' who picture the 'rural past as warm, communal, stable, organic, and with spiritual rather than purely materialistic values' because 'historical research reveals that these supposedly lovely rural communities were ... cesspools of malnutrition, disease, poverty, homelessness, and tyranny, with people helpless against hunger, cold, and the whips of their landlords and masters' (Toffler, 1980, p. 135). Toffler categorizes those who praise 'pre-technological primitivism' (Toffler, 1970, p. 284) as a 'small, vocal fringe of romantic extremists' that is 'mostly middle-class, speaking from the vantage point of a full belly, blindly indiscriminate' and guilty of desiring 'a return to a world that most of us — and most of them — would find abhorrent' (Toffler, 1980, p. 167), going so far as to label these 'future-haters' sufferers of the pathology 'technophobia' (Toffler, 1970, p. 233). Nonetheless, our best-selling futurist is no apologist for industrialism. On the contrary, 'Second Wave systems are in crisis' (Toffler, 1980, p. 139), and their institutions 'crash about our heads' (p. 367) due to crises of ecology, work satisfaction and even intimate relations. But from the ashes of this collapse, salvation rises in the form of 'third wave civilization' which is set to supercede 'second wave' (i.e., industrial) society. Here the electronic cottage will facilitate the development (and reestablishment) of the 'prosumer' who combines the role of consumer and producer while working from home. Such a trend offers a return to lifestyles that were 'common in the early days of the industrial revolution among farm populations', though now one can 'imagine this life pattern — but with twenty-first century technology for goods and food production' (p. 294).

Add this together, and what is offered is a 'practopian future' (p. 375) which looks much like — but is also much more than — the romantic visions of the past. In like manner, James Martin contends that:

> Local communities in the future may grow more of their own foods and provide their own daily needs. They will have offices for white-collar workers plugged into nationwide telecommunications networks. They will have satellite stations or other links that provide the same television facilities as in the big cities. The local bread and vegetables will be better than those that are mass-packaged for nationwide distribution. Much of the drudgery of commuting will be ended.... For many the lifestyle of rural communities with excellent telecommunications will be preferable to that in the cities. (Martin, 1978, p. 191)

The moral of all such propaganda — as if one could have missed it — is simply that

> Rather than lashing out, Luddite-fashion, against the machine, those who genuinely wish to break the prison-hold of the past and present would do well to hasten the ... arrival of tomorrow's technologies ... [because] it is precisely the super-industrial society, the most advanced technological society ever, that extends the range of freedom. (Toffler, 1970, pp. 282–3)

Neo-McLuhanism

Though this futurism which imagines 'people living in what one can recognize as the old pastoral ways ... but possessing great power because they have internalized the communication and productive capacities of the urban-scientific-industrial phase' (Williams, 1975, p. 331) has recently experienced a resurgence, it has a lengthy tradition. This was developed, especially in the United States, during the nineteenth century as a distinctive 'industrial version of the pastoral design' (Marx, 1964, p. 32), found its exemplar in Walt Whitman's celebration of the 'body electric' (Bentall, 1976), and drew together a 'powerful metaphor of contradiction', 'a strong urge to believe in the rural myth along with an awareness of industrialization as counterforce to the myth' (Marx, 1964, pp. 4, 229).

The most prominent recent member of this tradition was Marshall McLuhan. He himself had, significantly, a biographical connection with both the English school of literary criticism which held to the notion of a disappearing rural 'organic community' and the 'industrial pastoral' of his native North America (Fekete, 1978). Moreover, most of the contemporary writers on IT ought to be seen as being squarely within this tradition and its McLuhanite emphasis on the 'electronic sublime' (Carey and Quirk, 1970). Indeed, the presence of elements of McLuhan's work can be sensed in all the books, articles and television presentations to which we have referred. For example, Anthony Smith's *Goodbye Gutenberg* (1980), both a substantial book and a BBC documentary broadcast in 1980, constantly reminds us of McLuhan's *Gutenberg Galaxy* (1962), and, though he never in fact mentions his mentor, Smith's exercise should be seen as a sequel to McLuhan's. Elsewhere McLuhan is unabashedly rehashed: James Martin believing that IT's promise of satellite-age democracy will fulfil McLuhan's ideal of a global village (Martin, 1978, pp. 75–6); Sam Fedida and Rex Malik (1979) announcing their debt to McLuhan on the opening page of their report on viewdata; and Joseph Pelton, whose fantasia of the 'telecity' in an age of 'Global talk' is simply vulgar McLuhanism (Pelton, 1981).

Technological determinism

It is apposite that we recall McLuhan here, first to indicate the tradition in social thought of 'the machine in the garden' (Marx, 1964), and second — and more importantly — to point out the technological determinism which underpins the futurism now in vogue. Starting out from the technology, this comment is invariably determinist, since, acceding to the technology as it is, it then asks and only asks — what are the social implications of this technology? The technology is assumed to be a major — and isolatable — variable which causes social change, and, whether or not writers take a strong or soft line as regards the degree of causation, they all remain within a determinist frame.

In the light of recent concern with IT, we believe that it is now appropriate to revive the criticism of McLuhan's faith in the electronic millenium, since his work represents an extreme formulation of technological determinism and today retains a certain veracity as a version of the belief that technology is the motor of history. As McLuhanism resurfaces, it is salutary to indicate its two central traits. First, technology is considered a determining factor within society, for McLuhan *the* determinant factor: 'All media work us over completely. They are so pervasive in their personal, political, economic, aesthetic, psychological, moral, ethical, and social consequences that they leave no part of us untouched, unaffected, unaltered. The medium is the message' (McLuhan, 1967, p. 26). The difference between McLuhan's advocacy of 'utter human docility' in the face of technological change, and the now common statement that we must 'adapt to the world of the silicon chip' (Burkitt and Williams, 1980, p. 154), is only one of emphasis (and not much of that). Second, as detailed earlier, technology is detached from its social context and treated as an isolated phenomenon.

The conception of a determining technology is found in all popular (and not so popular) presentations of the new technology. A characteristic metaphor is that of an alien, extra-social invasion which cannot be prevented from effecting massive changes in social arrangements. The imagery of revolution created by such invaders has become the stock-in-trade of futurist offerings, and examples are legion: Burkitt and Williams commence with 'A mysterious force has come into our lives, working silently, screened from the human eye, and understood by only a tiny few. It is smaller than a fingernail, thinner than a leaf, and is covered with microscopic markings. It is powered by minute amounts of electricity ... yet it is probably one of the most significant machines ever made by man: the silicon chip' (Burkitt and Williams, 1980, p. 9). Alvin Toffler, writing of the 'great, growling engine of change — technology' (Toffler, 1970, p. 25), envisages a 'dramatically new technostructure for a Third Wave civilization' (Toffler, 1980, p. 164) which is a 'powerful tide ... surging across much of the world today, creating a new, often bizarre, environment in which to work, play, marry, raise children or retire' (pp. 17–18). Frederick Williams contends that 'our lives will never be the same again' because of the 'miracles of electronic communications' (Williams, 1982, pp. 9, 18). Joseph Pelton believes the 'process[es] of technical modernization, automation ... are seemingly irresistible forces' (Pelton, 1981, p. 203). Christopher Evans opens with 'This book is about the future.... It is a future which will involve a transformation of world society at all kinds of levels.... It's a future which is largely moulded by a single, startling development in technology whose impact is just beginning to be felt. The piece of technology I'm talking about is, of course, the computer' (Evans, 1979, p. 9). Occasionally, some of these writers aware that it is looked on with disfavour by most serious students, disclaim 'naive technological determinism' (Gosling, 1981, p. 8). At the same time, they hail a 'microelectronics revolution which is changing and shaking our whole contemporary world', bringing about an 'explosive reconstruction of human society and life' (pp. 81, 83).

Recalling these features so much in evidence, it is important to emphasize that this neo-McLuhanite perspective involves a focus on technology to the exclusion of social phenomena — the social is always adaptive and secondary to technology — and in doing so it 'abolishes history', thereby removing 'questions of human need, interest, value or goal' (Fekete, 1973, pp. 80, 78). From this perception of desocialized technologies, McLuhanites then identify an astonishing causal capability in the technology: the technology is transformed into a *deus ex machina*, influencing society yet beyond the influence of society. It is in this way that McLuhanism is a type of 'technological fetish' that is idealist in spite of its ostensible materialism. Though materialist in focusing on the things of this world (and how can one be more materialist than when concerned with technology?), the approach is idealist in so far as it excludes the world from these things to which it ascribes such social significance.

Technological socialism

There is one other feature of futurism which deserves elaboration — the aspiration towards a similar society to that offered by socialists *without* need for socialist commitment or action. This projection rests on the adage that socialism is a fine dream but is practically unattainable. Now, thanks to IT, runs the argument, the dream can be realized without the unpleasantness of political struggle. The idea that we may, following technological trends, be on a path which will produce a better society (one which will make manifest the ideals of many socialists) in a smooth, evolutionary manner is a favoured theme of futurism. It often merely suffuses prediction, making its presence felt in assurances that the information society will be a caring, communal, service-oriented one, but the appropriation of socialist language and vision can be quite explicit. Thus, for Anthony Hyman, 'the magnificent generosity of the new technology is at last beginning to make it possible for society to move in the direction of its old dream, never realisable but a splendid goal, the dream that was appropriated by Marxism and then lost in the monolithic politics of the twentieth century: from each and all according to their inclination; to each according to need' (Hyman, 1980, pp. 126–7).

On occasion, this type of comment presents IT as the means to achieve a recognizably socialistic society while also claiming it is a challenge to all orthodoxies. James Martin, for instance, impatient with the uptake of IT, appeals to 'young people especially' as he lambasts all who oppose the good life promised by the new technology, and his attack includes 'corporate Luddites' who 'attempt to prevent the spread of new technologies which they fear will harm their profits' (Martin, 1978, pp. 14–15). He announces himself a veritable firebrand, the champion of technologies that 'are in conflict with the established order' which are bound to 'encounter fierce opposition from vested interests' (p. 15). Alvin Toffler is still more of an extremist, insisting that all ideologies are conservative when contrasted with his allegiance to the 'super-struggle for tomorrow' between 'those who try to prop up and preserve industrial society and those who are ready to advance beyond it' (Toffler, 1980, p. 453). He rings the death knell on Marxism — 'The farther we move beyond industrial mass society the less tenable the Marxist assumptions' (p. 436) — and (less vigorously) on capitalism, which is 'tearing apart under the impact of an accelerating wave of change' (p. 247). Toffler, eager for battle, denounces 'Marxists and anti-Marxists alike, capitalists and anti-capitalists, Americans and Russians [who have been] bearing the same set of fundamental premises.... Both were apostles of indust-reality' (p. 115), both 'basically committed to preserving the dying industrial order' (p. 453). Our hero berates the cowardice of those who find 'frightening ... the prospect of deep political change', and contemptuously throws aside those 'pseudorevolutionaires' — 'Archaeo-Marxists, anarcho-romantics', etc. — who are 'steeped in obsolete Second Wave assumptions' (p. 456). The real revolution is coming, states Alvin Toffler, and this 'third wave' will bring down all 'second wave elites'. It is fortunate that all we need to do is catch the third wave as it rises and let it carry us safely to a shore offering material abundance, personal satisfaction, and communal bonds while it swamps all obsolete political interests.

There are other futurists who put a different inflection on the issue, though they share the domain assumptions. The promise of IT is seized upon by Christopher Evans to at once propagandize for Western capitalism and preach the immanence of 'paradise' here, where 'the emancipation of Man from the need to work for his living will have been achieved' (Evans, 1979, pp. 150–1). With Toffler and Martin, Evans believes that 'the production of fantastically cheap devices will, at long last, make the humanistic dream of universal affluence and freedom from drudgery a reality' (p. 207), which means that the world will change 'and for the better, and without the long-awaited revolution of the proletariat' (p. 205). However, this practical attainment of socialism via the microprocessor, since it is a 'creature of capitalism' (p. 209), will highlight the 'inherent advantages of the capitalist system', because IT could only have developed 'through go-for-broke capitalist exploitation' (p. 207).

Therefore, *pace* Toffler, Evans announces the 'decline of communism' because the 'most striking feature of Russia ... has been its failure to get anywhere near, let alone catch up and overtake, the living standards of its capitalist rivals' (p. 206) and, with the 'surge of affluence' the 'Computer Revolution' is bringing in the West, 'even the most ardent Marxist' will be forced 'to bow to the overwhelming testimony of the microprocessor' (p. 208), since 'the Communist world ... in the absence of capitalist incentive, is bound to lag further and further behind' (p. 207). Casting an eye over Chinese and American rapprochement, Evans considers that 'the message of the microprocessor and the fact that it is a creature of capitalism may already be getting through' (p. 209), before concluding that the 'absolute dependence of mass microprocessor technology on capitalist production and distribution methods could well be the first nail in the coffin of doctrinaire Marxist thinking' (p. 207). Professor W. Gosling has already buried Marxism. Having shifted from a university chair to the post of technical director of Plessey Electronic Systems, he brings all his scholarship to voice what Hyman, Toffler, Martin and Evans assume. The senior Plessey managers who heard his lecture must have been relieved to learn that 'Karl Marx's lack of understanding that technology is not static was one of the things, along with his psychological naivety, which made his theoretical ideas such a poor guide to policy' (Gosling, 1981, p. 67).

We scarcely need say that this promise for the future indicates no real socialist commitment on the part of these writers. It is but a consequence of IT that we will arrive at the humanization of capitalism (Hyman, Martin), perhaps with communism's collapse (Evans) or the convergence of all systems into a new civilization (Toffler). However, the hold of these commentators on a vision of the future which is socialistic is significant in one particular respect: they monopolize discussion of the future when those whose aspirations and ideals they steal appear unimaginative, reactive, and defensive. When faced with the arrival of IT, socialist responses, concerned chiefly with negative effects, have appeared pessimistic and even reactionary. It is in this way that propagandists for IT have stolen a march on the Left. It is they who have confidence, they who welcome the future, and it is they who, ironically, foresee the possibility of socialism within IT itself.

Conclusion

The speculation about IT's social import seems to us to have two effects worth special emphasis. The first is that it manages to dominate discussion in a straightforwardly quantitative manner which makes it difficult for alternative perspectives to be heard. Analyses of IT are almost totally one-sided, so that public debate and discussion is markedly impoverished. Second, the major consequence of this presentation of IT, while it may not persuade the populace to wholeheartedly welcome the new technology, is to create a general sense of acquiescence to innovation. We believe this happens because IT, without discernable origins, is something ordinary people cannot understand. The technology is a mystery and remains a mystery even when its technical functions are explained in simplified terms, because its genesis — its social history — is ignored. In this way, technology is placed in a tradition of science fiction as an arrival — fortunately benign — from another galaxy: as Margaret Thatcher appositely observes, 'Information Technology is friendly; it offers a helping hand; it should be embraced. We should think of it more like *ET* than IT' (Thatcher, 1982, p. 29). Without history, IT becomes an unstoppable force which, though incomprehensible to natives, is understood sufficiently for them to realize that it must change their whole way of life.

For good or ill, we are obliged to adjust to the things that have arrived unannounced and unexpected. Understandably in these circumstances, a common response is one of apathy. The technology has been imposed upon us irrespective of our wishes or even imaginings, and it seems that there is little we can do other than accede to its dictates. Hence we often witness a resigned acceptance of the inevitable, a sense of helplessness, and a feeling of stale familiarity and apathy after constant but uninformative media exposure.

Starting with the palpable hereness of IT, and only then moving to consider its social influence, is to accept from the outset that technology is in crucial ways out of our control. And it is because almost all comment on IT unquestioningly adopts this framework that its function is in effect to sell it to the wider public. That, in general, IT is said to be beneficient makes it that much more palatable, and that much futurism promises it will bring about a socialistic idyll makes it that much more appealing at the same time as radical critics must appear dog-inthe-manger, but these are essentially embellishments, since the starting-point — the technology in and of itself — means that alternatives are blocked from the beginning.

Finally, because futurism, wild and sober, takes on an aura of realism by commencing analysis with the technology itself, it contains a deep irony. Starting 'realistically' with IT, it can quickly and impatiently extrapolate to the wildest imaginings (or, if it so chooses, fix on the short-term prospects), all the while insisting that such dreams are but potentialities of technology which is here today. The irony is that such prospects are but castles in the air, since to start with the technology which is here in the world without looking at the world which developed and is developing the technology is to ignore realities that thwart futurist dreams ever being realized. Futurism fails to face up to the social realities that are embodied in technologies that have been created and are now being expressed in the application of IT. The procedure is something akin to starting with sight of a tiger in the bush and then imagining all manner of things it might do (attack that deer? have a sleep? run in that direction?), ignoring the whole time that the animal has been previously incapacitated by drugs, training, and perhaps extraction of teeth by someone who has carefully bred his pet and who remains constantly in control.

In spite of all the assertions of commentators on IT that they are coming to grips with existing realities and extrapolating only upon these — 'the aim of this book ... is ... to illustrate that tomorrow began yesterday and that the options sharpen and tighten every day' (Large, 1980, p. 13); 'I am under no Pollyannaish illusions' (Toffler, 1980, p. 19) — we charge that these writers are profoundly unrealistic from start to finish.

We would also note that this writing on IT, in spite of — or rather because of — its 'real-world' starting-point, exemplifies what Roland Barthes termed 'the creation of myth'. Effective mythology is not sustained by outright lies, but through what Saul Bellow has called 'concealment through candour': 'Myth does not deny things, on the contrary, its function is to talk about them; simply, it purifies them, it makes them innocent, it gives them a natural and eternal justification, it gives them a clarity which is not that of an explanation but that of a statement of fact' (Barthes, 1973, p. 143). This seems to us precisely what comment on IT achieves: it talks endlessly about the new technology, realistically, candidly, tangibly; but because it never comes to terms with the social relations of the technology and remains stuck in an account which accepts its 'naturalness', the talk amounts to a snow job. Myth 'has turned reality inside out, it has emptied it of history and has filled it with nature, it has removed from things their human meaning so as to make them signify a human insignificance' (*ibid.*, pp. 142–3).

All this is functional to those interests aiming to exploit IT for their own purposes, because it deflects attention away from the powers behind the technologies, disarms critics both with abuse and the prospect of an easily attainable electronic fairyland (provided we do not resist its application in the here and now), and above all credits IT with an independence from society, with a naturalness which renders it incomprehensible as a social, value-laden phenomenon. It is in ways such as these that comments on IT 'proclaim the future in word and ... desert the future in fact (Carey and Quirk, 1970, p. 396).

References

ACARD (1980) *Information Technology*, Cabinet Office HMSO.

BAER, W.S. (1978) 'Telecommunications technology in the 1980s', in ROBINSON G.O. (Ed.) *Communications for Tomorrow: Policy Perspectives for the 1980s*, New York, Praeger, pp. 61–125.

BARRON, I. and CURNOW, R. (1979) *The Future with Microelectronics: Forecasting the Effects of Information Technology*, Frances Pinter.

BARTHES, R. (1973), *Mythologies* (originally published 1957), Paladin.

BASS, A. (1983) 'Disney and the Corporate Con', *Technology Review*, October, pp. 18–21, 76.

BENTALL, J. (1976) *The Body Electric: Patterns in Western Industrial Culture*, London, Thames and Hudson, Ltd.

BURKITT, A. and WILLIAMS, E. (1980) *The Silicon Civilization*, W.H. Allen.

BURY, J.B. (1932) *The Idea of Progress: An Inquiry into Its Origins and Growth*, (reprinted 1960), New York, Dover Publications.

CALLAGHAN, J. (1978) *Prime Minister Announces Major Programme of Support for Microelectronics*, Press Notice, 10 Downing Street, 6 December.

CAREY, J.W. and QUIRK, J.J. (1970) 'The mythos of the electronic revolution', *The American Scholar*, 39 (Spring and Summer), pp. 219–41, 395–424.

CONSERVATIVE PARTY (1979) *Proposals for a Conservative Information Technology Policy*, Provisional Draft Report, Conservative Central Office (mimeo).

CORNISH, E. (Ed.) (1982) *Communications Tomorrow: The Coming of the Information Society*, Bethesda, World Future Society.

DES (Department of Education and Science) (1978) *Educational Implications of Microelectronic Technology*, DES, 24 October.

DES (1979) *Microelectronics in Education: A Development Programme for Schools and Colleges*, London, HMSO.

DICKSON, D. (1974) *Alternative Technology and the Politics of Technological Change*, Fontana.

DIZARD, W.P. (1982) *The Coming Information Age: An Overview of Technology, Economics, and Politics*, Longman.

EVANS, C. (1979) *The Mighty Micro: The Impact of the Computer Revolution*, London, Victor Gollancz, Ltd.

FALLOW, W.A. (1982) *Annual Meeting of Shareholders*, Rochester, New York, Kodak, May 5.

FEDIDA, S. and MALIK, R. (1979) *The Viewdata Revolution*, Associated Business Press.

FEKETE, J. (1973) 'McLuhanacy: counterrevolution in cultural theory', *Telos*, 15, pp. 75–123.

FEKETE, J. (1978) *The Critical Twilight: Explorations in the Ideology of Anglo-American Literary Theory from Eliot to McLuhan*, London, Routledge and Kegan Paul.

FOTHERGILL, R. (1983) 'The microelectronics education programme in the UK', in MEGARRY, J., *et al.* (Eds) *World Yearbook on Education 1982/3: Computers and Education*, London, Kogan Page, Ltd.

GARDNER, C. and YOUNG, R. (1981) 'Science on TV: a critique', in BENNETT, T., *et al.* (Eds) *Popular Television and Film*, British Film Institute Publishing in association with The Open University Press.

GEORGE, D. (1962) *England in Transition: Life and Work in the Eighteenth Century* (originally published 1931), Harmondsworth, Penguin.

GMWU (General and Municipal Workers' Union) (1980) *New Technology: Report to Congress*, Esher, Surrey, GMWU.

GOSLING, W. (1978) *Microelectronics, Society and Education*, Council for Educational Technology Occasional Paper No. 8.

GOSLING, W. (1981) *The Kingdom of Sand*, Council for Educational Technology Occasional Paper No. 9.

HOWLETT, J. (1978) *Report of the National Committee on Computer Networks*, presented to the Secretary of State by J. Howlett, Department of Industry, October.

HYMAN, A. (1980) *The Coming of the Chip*, New English Library.

LANDES, D. (1969) *The Unbound Prometheus: Technological Change and Industrial Development in Western Europe from 1750 to the Present*, Cambridge, Cambridge University Press.

LARGE, P. (1980) *The Micro Revolution*, Fontana.

LAURIE, P. (1980) *The Micro Revolution*, Futura.

BARNET, R.J. and MULLER, R.E. (1975) *Global Reach: The Power of the Multinational Corporations*, Jonathan Cape, Ltd.

MARTIN, J. (1978) *The Wired Society*, Englewood Cliffs, Prentice-Hall.

MARX, L. (1964) *The Machine in the Garden*, New York, Oxford University Press.

McLUHAN, M. (1962) *The Gutenberg Galaxy: The Making of Typographic Man*, London, Routledge and Kegan Paul.

McLUHAN, M. (with Q. Fiore) (1967) *The Medium is the Message: An Inventory of Effects*, Allen Lane.

NEWBY, H. (1979) *The Deferential Worker: A Study of Farm Workers in East Anglia* (originally published 1977), Harmondsworth, Penguin.

NEWBY, H. (1980) *Green and Pleasant Land? Social Change in Rural England* (originally published 1979), Harmondsworth, Penguin.

PELTON, J.N. (1981) *Global Talk*, Alphen aanden Rijn, The Netherlands, Sijthoff and Noordhoff.

POLLARD, S. (1971) *The Idea of Progress: History and Society* (originally published 1968), Harmondsworth, Penguin.

SARNOFF, R.W. (1974) 'The Electronic revolution', *Economic Impact*, 7, 3.

SKLAIR, L. (1970) *The Sociology of Progress*, London, Routledge and Kegan Paul.

SMITH, A. (1980) *Goodbye Gutenberg: The Newspaper Revolution of the 1980s*, New York, Oxford University Press.

THATCHER, M. (1982) *Speech at the Opening Ceremony of IT'82 Conference*, Press Office, 10 Downing Street, 8 December.

TOFFLER, A. (1970) *Future Shock*, Bodley Head.

TOFFLER, A. (1980) *The Third Wave*, Collins.

TUC (Trades Union Congress) (1979) *Congress*, TUC.

WILLIAMS, F. (1982) *The Communications Revolution*, Beverly Hills, Sage.

WILLIAMS, R. (1974) *Television: Technology and Cultural Form*, Fontana.

WILLIAMS, R. (1975) *The Country and the City* (originally published 1973), Paladin.

YOUNG, R. (1979) 'Science as culture', *Quarto*, December.

Chapter 4

The Information Society: Ideology or Utopia?

David Lyon

At the present moment a discussion is raging as to the future of a
civilization in the novel circumstances of rapid scientific and technological advance. (Whitehead, 1925, p. 254)

In my Eden we have a few beam-engines, saddle-tank locomotives,
overshot waterwheels and other beautiful pieces of obsolete machinery to play with: In his New Jerusalem even chefs will be cucumber-
cool machine-minders. (Auden, 1955)

The 'information society' expresses the idea of a novel phase in the historical
development of the advanced societies. Not just a 'post-industrial' society,
but the advent of new social patterns is predicted, consequent upon a 'second
industrial revolution' based above all on microelectronic technologies. A
growing proportion of people, it is claimed, is involved in an unprecedented
variety of information-related jobs. Scientific and technical workers gather
and produce information, managers and supervisors process it, teachers and
communications workers distribute it. From domestic life to international
relations, and from leisure activities to industrial relations, no sphere of social
activity is left untouched by this 'informatizing' process.

Notions such as Alvin Toffler's *Third Wave* — virtually synonymous
with 'information society' — have entered popular imagination. A television
film has been made of the *Third Wave*, and in the UK, the 'Third Wave' is the
slogan for a British Telecom advertising campaign. The 'information society'
is increasingly used as a handy catch-all for focusing discussions of 'the
future' as we approach the third millennium. Government policy also draws
upon this concept, particularly with regard to education. The British are
assured, for instance, that 'Our educational system will be a major, perhaps
the dominant, factor in ensuring the economic prosperity of the UK in a
world-wide information society' (Information Technology Advisory Panel,
1986).

However, certain questions are too frequently left unanswered or treated only to oblique or opaque responses. What are the connections between new technology and society? To what extent and under what circumstances does technological potential become social destiny? Is it warranted to see an epochal social transformation in the kinds of economic and social restructuring currently taking place? And whether or not we are witnessing the emergence of a 'new kind of society', are its advocates correct to assume, as they often tend to, that the social effects of Information Technology are generally benign?

Much of my work (Lyon, 1988) has been taken up with just such questions. Not necessarily to determine what the 'answers' might be, but to suggest some possible lines of investigation. I have tried to do this by drawing together themes otherwise treated separately, in an effort to reach balanced but yet tentative conclusions. For example, the convergence between computing and telecommunications, often treated as a separate 'technical' moment, prior to the social 'impact' of Information Technology, is shown (see Lyon, 1988) to have some important *social* dimensions itself. Again, optimistic predictions about the democratic potential of IT are brought face-to-face with darker diagnoses about the potential for IT to undermine democracy.

But at the end of the day, the question remains as to whether the information society concept should be consigned to the waste-bin of redundant ideas, or retained as a tool for social analysis. Might it have a future as an illuminating concept, as it points up one of the most significant aspects of contemporary social change, namely that associated with the diffusion of Information Technology? Or should it be abandoned precisely because it gains credibility more through the daily appearance of yet another 'microchip' gadget than because of its power to explain social realities?

There is another aspect to this question. The information society concept sounds a hopeful note in the midst of recessionary gloom. In Japan it has found ready acceptance among certain groups as a rallying cry for mobilizing research and entrepreneurial energies. While many social prognoses are pessimistic, seeing only decline (economic) or disaster (nuclear) ahead, the information society sounds positive and apparently provides some sense of purpose and social goals. Just when intellectuals bemoan the death of progress or the dearth of utopias (Levitas, 1982), an older vision is revived, of a good society growing out of the present. So not only the usefulness of the concept for social analysis, but its social role within present national and global contexts deserves examination.

In what follows I take this latter question a little further. My first concern is to comment on the long connection between politics and technology, in the light of which it would not be surprising to find that the 'information society' has ideological aspects. That is, its use may help buttress the *status quo*. Secondly, exposing the ideological uses of the information society concept leads in turn to another task, the discussion of resistance to the new technologies and to alternative proposals and strategies. Lastly, I return to the major issue, an agenda for social analysis — which in turn suggests some options for political action and public policy — which arises from the constructive critique of the 'information society'.

The politics of technology

New technologies have been infused with a potent symbolism at least since Francis Bacon's time. He proposed that science and technology be viewed as a means of overcoming the malign effects of the human 'fall' from God's grace. In fact his utopia, *New Atlantis* (1627), straddles the 'theological' and the 'natural' interpretation of human affairs. While he continues to use biblical language, the spirit of his writing underpins a dominant theme of Western culture following him, that human progress is assured through the scientific and technological exploitation of nature.

This Janus-faced character of Bacon's writings is caught in these contrasting interpretations: Arnold Pacey (1983) quotes him approvingly (and I would concur) for his emphasis on science and technology motivated by a 'love of God's creation' which issues in using the 'fruits of knowledge' not for 'profit, or fame or power ... but for the benefit and use of life' (p. 178). But in Bacon's attempt to establish a 'chaste and lawful marriage between Mind and Nature', Evelyn Fox-Keller finds a rather different spirit. Nature, almost always 'she', is brought to obedience by the (male) scientist. Though Bacon indeed admits a caring aspect to science and technology, today it is largely lost. Fox-Keller connects this loss with the move towards a more 'self-contained' science in which 'the explicit role of God has disappeared'. The modern scientist's 'kinship with Bacon survives in his simultaneous appropriation and denial of the feminine' (Fox-Keller, 1985, pp. 36, 42).

Considerable debate arises over the relative contributions of religion and politics to the origins of modern technology (e.g., White, 1978). While Max Weber is often imputed with the view that the religious — and particularly the Protestant — origins were decisive, others have challenged this. Weber stressed the contribution of Christian theology to justifications of technological activity. It is part of a God-given task of sharing his supervisory and transformative work, and is given added impetus in the context of a suffering world, cut off from immediate access to the Creator.

But for others the more decisive influence is that represented by Machiavelli. He succeeded in lowering the ultimate goals of political life while at the same time increasing the possibility of their worldly realization (Mitcham, 1983). For him, technology, when harnessed to the production of unlimited wealth, is justified by its contribution to the common good. Technological activity is thus uncoupled from religious or ethical concerns — to do with the stewardship of nature or justice in economic relations — which might otherwise serve to curb or redirect it. Attention is rather focused on appropriate techniques for attaining this-worldly ends.

By the eighteenth and particularly the nineteenth century, technology was strongly linked with belief in progress. Its close associations with burgeoning capitalism, which increasingly required new technology as a means of maintaining and boosting profit levels, assured a dominant place to the Baconian or Machiavellian doctrine. Progress, for many Victorians, was at once a political aspiration, to be achieved via the application of science and technology to all areas of life, and also a means of explaining social change. It undergirded early sociology (Kumar, 1978).

Progress, industry, science and technology were immortalized in the Great Exhibition in the Crystal Palace, London, in 1851. But although widespread British faith in technological advancement was not to wane for many decades, it could be argued that the centre of gravity of 'technological progress' shifted across the Atlantic. In the USA, as nowhere in Europe, technological progress was made by some into a panacea. Technological utopians — as Howard Segal (1985) calls them — provided detailed blueprints for the good society. Edward Bellamy, the best known, envisioned in *Looking Backward* an America criss-crossed with electrical and telegraphic communications, and in which everything from music to food was piped into homes from central sources.

The possibilities of such social and material engineering were seized upon eagerly by numerous Bellamy Clubs, for whom *Looking Backward* expressed a common belief in the inevitability of technological progress. The desired future represented no break with the present (the heyday of technological utopianism was 1883–1933), but would grow steadily out of it. Moreover, in Segal's words,

> The utopians were not oblivious to the problems technological advance might cause, such as unemployment or boredom. They simply were confident that those problems were temporary and that, furthermore, advanced technology held the solution to mankind's chronic problems, which they took to be material — scarcity, hunger, disease, war, and so forth. (1978, p. 66)

It scarcely seems necessary to bring the account up to date, given the patent connections between these earlier technological utopias, the 1960s celebrations of the 'electrical sublime' in Buckminster Fuller or Marshall McLuhan (1964)[1] and the 'wired societies' and 'silicon civilizations' of today. But the connections and continuities are significant. The technological utopia grows progressively from present conditions and will in the long term ensure the peace and prosperity of all. It is possible to rectify the less desirable consequences of technological innovation by further applications of technology. Today more stress is laid upon the effort required to bring about the new society (socialist versions emphasize the issues of justice and equality alongside technical development). And the USA is not held up unequivocally as the 'leading' society. Japan is felt to be threatening its supremacy.

Until now I have gone along with Segal's designation of these 'possible futures' as 'technological utopias'. But is this entirely appropriate? Let me sow some seeds of doubt. While 'utopia' may refer to an ideal, hoped-for and maybe even worked-for society, it often has other features as well. Thomas More's original *Utopia*, which gave its name to the genre, was a cutting critique of monarchical and clerical tyranny in sixteenth-century England. True, it traced the outlines of a good society, but this was a radical alternative to present conditions, not a continuation of them. More himself was eventually to lose his head for his temerity (in objecting to the wishes of Henry VIII).

The 'information society' shares utopian aspects with some previous technological 'good societies'. But the ways in which IT is developed and adopted frequently widens the gaps between already divided social groups and nations, extends the capacity of the state and other agencies to monitor and control people's lives and augments the power of ever-growing economic interests. In the light of this, the 'information society' also appears to have some highly charged ideological aspects.

Such 'ideological aspects' may be teased out to show how the information society concept connects politics and technology in a peculiarly modern way; it often obscures the vested interests involved in IT, it deflects attention from some embarrassing contradictions, while at the same time giving to the coming of the information society the appearance of an entirely natural and logical social progression (Giddens, 1979, pp. 193ff).

In the 1960s, a full decade before informatics entered public discussion, Jürgen Habermas argued that expanding forms of 'technocratic reason' present a serious threat to human freedom. Public communication and decision-making are distorted so that most of the population are kept in the dark about the real distribution of power and control in a given society. Habermas (1971) said that political debate is systematically reduced to a purely technical level (the language of 'controlling the economy' being a good example), and at the same time technology becomes almost a rival force to politics.

Reducing political debate to the technical means that people are denied the chance to participate freely at the level of morality and justice, and thus also to affect outcomes by means of political action. Today, IT developments illustrate this well. Slogans such as 'a computer in every school' or 'automate or liquidate' narrow any discussion to the question of means, rather than ends. 'Why do children need exposure to keyboards and screens?' and 'Who will benefit from automation?' are the unasked questions which lead logically to a consideration of valuing and purposes. Moreover political decisions are frequently presented to the public as a *fait accompli*. Few British people are privy to the reasons why a new cable infrastructure rather than an upgraded telephone network became public policy.

The further aspect of Habermas' contention, that technology becomes a rival force to politics, is also evident today. He quotes Herman Kahn's 'cybernetic dream' about the use of new techniques for surveillance and mass education, direct electronic communication with human brains and so on. The upshot would be 'planned alienation'. But IT has indeed made possible many things once dismissed as 'science fiction'. The theoretical possibility of the 1960s that political decisions could be computerized became in the 1980s sober fact. Anti-ballistic missile warning systems are a case in point.

What, then, of the 'ideological aspects' of the information society concept? First, inequalities and relations of power are very much in the background. For instance, while it is not inappropriate to hope that the diffusion of IT would have a similar positive role for democratic participation as the diffusion of print media once had, it is irresponsible to declare that this is likely to happen. The fact that more people buy ever-cheaper home computers does not add up to an 'information revolution'. Cees Hamelink concludes that

> control over and access to advances in information technology are very unevenly distributed in the world, and the fact that millions of people can fiddle with their home computers does not change this. The management structure of the information industry is not affected by the proliferation of electronic gadgets. If anything, it is considerably strengthened by the widespread use of its products. (1986, p. 11)

All manner of vested interests are involved in IT, but the concept of the information society is all too often used in ways that obscure their role. Sometimes those interests are intertwined in ways that have yet to be carefully explored. The coincidence that defence funding supports so much research in IT *and* that the world of IT frequently excludes women deserves just such exploration. Technology in general is undoubtedly associated with maleness, socially and culturally; IT no less so.

Secondly, the information society concept papers over not only the cracks but also opposing movements in society. Underlying contradictions are even less likely to be exposed than inequalities and conflicts on the surface. Opposing movements may be seen, for instance, in the IT context, along the fault-line of information as public good versus saleable commodity. The real threats of current IT development to public service broadcasting and to public libraries are manifestations of deeper dynamics of opposition.

Thirdly, the coming of the information society is viewed (by its popular proponents at least) as an entirely natural occurrence. It is the obvious way forward. The future lies with IT. The new technologies must be 'wholeheartedly embraced', declare the captains of industry. This is why educational systems have to be reoriented, the market unshackled, and high-technology research and trading deals engineered. It is also why Luddism has to be stamped out.

This particular ideological aspect — information society as a natural and logical social advance — is further buttressed by the typically Western belief in progress via unlimited economic accumulation. What Shallis calls 'silicon idolatry' resonates with this still-strong belief. As Bob Goudzwaard observes, if indeed this faith is a driving force within economic and technological expansion, then two things follow. First, the 'overdevelopment' of both spheres comes as no surprise, and second, it is 'accompanied by an expectation of happiness that relativises anything that might raise objections against them' (1975, p. 4).

Having made such comments about ideological aspects I ought to repeat and extend qualifiers. I am not arguing that a 'dominant ideology' exists to hoodwink large segments of the populations of advanced societies. Nor is there a conspiracy to deceive such publics. Rather, I am warning that the danger of using the information society concept uncritically is to disguise or gloss over the reality of domination by powerful interests.

I should also stress that the point of exposing such relations of power is not simply to replace them with others, but to open the door for a properly normative approach. Fe/male partnership in new technology will not eliminate war but, as a way of recognizing co-humanity, could begin to reorder technological priorities. Revealing contradictions of IT development is rather futile unless it leads to a questioning of economic life itself: is it about producing things, or is it fundamentally relational? (Storkey, 1986).

Resistance and alternatives

Anyone worried about the encroaching tyranny of technocratic power embodied in IT should not ignore countervailing movements also present in contemporary societies. True, the information society idea is strong and popular, but there are many for whom it is remote and unreal, and yet others who regard it with suspicion and hostility. For them, the critique of ideology may itself appear as a less than central task; more urgent is actual resistance to the adoption of new technology. Examining forms of resistance — particularly the 'Luddism' scathingly referred to above — is one thing, however; joining the quest for alternatives is another. I shall argue that both strategies are required if the information society as depicted here is not to become a self-fulfilling prophecy.

The intrusion of IT into numerous areas of life — only this week I discovered that my plastic card could buy a train ticket at the local station and that my office is soon due to be connected with a central IBM computer — has revived interest in Luddism as a mode of opposing technology. While some use it as an epithet to be directed at all 'anti-progressives' who quite irrationally wish to 'put the clock back' by refusing to adapt to new technology, others — both conservative and radical — willingly accept the label as correctly portraying their stance. 'If Luddite means the preservation of all that is good from the past and the rejection of things that destroy good', says Michael Shallis, 'then I would welcome the term' (1984, p. v).

It seems that most of those who are credited today with 'threatening our future' are members of labour unions who resist the unchecked spread of new technologies within the workplace. (In fact, plenty of anti-Luddism exists within unions. A Calderdale components factory union is on record with the following: 'You cannot hold back progress.'; 'We don't want any latter-day Luddites here,' quoted in Huws, 1982, p. 9. The first Luddites were strong in Calderdale.) The charge of Luddism is heard most frequently in celebrated cases, such as the newspaper and print workers' disputes discussed in Lyon (1988). But it occurs in other contexts as well, in mining and manufacturing (automated and robotic assembly lines, CNC machine tools) and also in offices and schools where serious doubts are expressed about installing computerized machines.

Of course the original Luddites, who attacked factories and broke new machinery in the early nineteenth century in Yorkshire, Lancashire, Cheshire and the Midlands of England, made their protest against industrialism in the days before labour unions were established. Evidence shows the hallmarks of carefully planned night-time raids, in which only specific machines thought to threaten the livelihoods and skills were destroyed (Thompson, 1968). Clearly, fear of the new was involved (Reid, 1986). But it is helpful to put Luddism in a much broader context. Those machines were symbolic of a whole new way of life which accompanied the spread of *laissez-faire* economic doctrines, the growing scale of factory enterprises, new divisions between home and work, and the loss of older patterns of mutual responsibility between employer and employee.

Among those who deliberately adopt a Luddite stance *vis-à-vis* today's technology, Frank Webster and Kevin Robins (1986), spell out the connections most clearly. They argue that contemporary Luddism demands on the one hand a refusal to submit to the dictates of *laissez-faire* political economy in which economic interests ride roughshod over customary lifestyles, jobs and skills. On the other, recalling the Luddite resistance not to machines *per se*, but to the social relationships represented by them, they insist that Luddism is a way of seeing, a '*critique* of developments which because they are presented as mere matters of technical change, appear unstopable and unobjectionable' (Reid, 1986, p. 4; See also Albury and Schwartz, 1982).

Appropriately enough, for a critique of developments within capitalist societies, those 'social relations' represented by Information Technology are seen mainly as *class* relations. Relationships of men to women, of ethnic majorities and minorities, of individuals to the state (and so on) thus tend to be interpreted in class terms also. Clearly, such analysts recognize that in modern societies labour movements have not simply been displaced by others — such as peace movements or feminism — and that, furthermore, labour movements may well act as 'carriers' for wider concerns. Added to which, it is patent that many key social issues raised by IT have to do with the world of work and employment. But there are limits to reviving Luddism as a class-based critique alone.

For a start, the labour movement is not 'inevitably the prime source of opposition in capitalist societies' (Giddens, 1985, p. 318). Opposition may originate elsewhere. (Media coverage contributed to the ending of the Vietnam war; mobilizing local opinion blocked Sunday trading in Britain.) Moreover, the labour movement may be unwilling seriously to take new technology issues on board. Cynthia Cockburn, assailing male dominance in technological change, pleads that labour unions be willing to question the direction and content of IT development. But she ruefully acknowledges that unions too often see the main challenge as ensuring that 'the benefits of change are distributed equally', and that the 'ideology of technological progress' is contested not by them, but by ecology and peace movements (1983, p. 230).

Placing too much stress on class relations and the labour movement may also deflect attention from other issues. In IT, transnational corporations predominate, but the attempt similarly to internationalize labour movements is negligible. But apart from this, if it is correct to argue that IT facilitates the massive strengthening of state powers of surveillance, then why does so little critical and adversarial activity take place in this arena? Civil liberties groups have yet to make serious dents in government complacency about the protection of citizens from unwanted and unnecessary prying and control. Questions like this (which may be extended to the cultural area in general) will not be answered satisfactorily if class is retained as a key mode of explanation and line of battle.

Lastly, Luddism as a class critique is limited by its negative and often pessimistic stance. Herbert Schiller's (1981) devastating account of global capitalism's IT interests finds its most hopeful moment in a forecast of 'social conflict in the core of the transnational corporate system'. It is unclear how this conflict will arise. But if it fails to materialize, one may be able to fall back on other 'powerful sources of potential breakdown in the overall [American] economy' (Schiller, 1981, p. 176; see also Noble, 1983). In fact, a similar negativism is found in non-Marxist Luddism. Michael Shallis concludes that IT is 'an invention of the devil ... born destructive....' which 'enchants people into false belief in a false god.... We need to be informed about the machines that "think" but we should become ashamed to use them' (1984, pp. 176–8).

Latter-day Luddism represents resistance to new technology, and is essentially negative. As such, it is an understandable reaction in the face of apparently antagonistic forces. Nevertheless, as Webster and Robins point out, the kernel of an *ethical* response is also discernible in Luddism. This again broadens the question from being merely one of class relations. It hints at the potential for positive alternative strategies.

Return for a moment to an earlier theme. Edward Bellamy's utopia *Looking Backward*, while it attracted widespread acclaim in the USA, horrified at least one English reader, William Morris. *Looking Backward* seemed more like a *dystopia* to him, and his response was to pen his own famous satirical utopia: *News from Nowhere* (1890). His utopia, though informed by Marxism, is anti-industrial as well as anti-capitalist. In his dream he looks back from a world of meaningful and artistic craft-work to a time when 'they forced themselves to stagger along under this horrible burden of unnecessary production'. In this system, little care was spent on making things, but ceaseless energy spent on turning out as much as possible, to which project 'everything was sacrificed'.

Morris offers an authentically utopian alternative to the oppressive vision of a centralized production-and-consumption-oriented world. Whether or not one agrees with the rather romantic nostalgia that appears in the details of Morris's alternative, it is undeniable that human freedom and fulfilment is a high priority. Attention to the features of the 'good society' is as significant as resistance to alienation, domination and dehumanization.

What form should be taken by 'alternative visions' to the 'information society' idea? At least two criteria should be satisfied. First, the normative basis of the alternative(s) must be made clear. Second, the different levels on which intervention might take place, and modes whereby policies may be implemented, must be indicated. This involves offering practical examples of altered practice and of the potential for choice in technological innovation.

Technocratic thought, especially that embodied in today's computer logic, tends to minimize or exclude debate about ethics. Discussion of 'alternatives' brings this into the foreground. Unfortunately, as Hans Jonas (1984) observes, an ethic suited to the global and long-term aspects of today's technology is largely lacking. The ethics of the personal is far better developed. That said, once it is recognized that the 'information society' gives the false impression that we are entering an *entirely* novel social situation, then certain long-trodden ethical paths become pertinent.

A further problem here is the relative lack of contexts within which such moral debate may take place. Professions, for instance, have always provided such opportunities (even though they have sometimes been self-interestedly abused). Medicine, involving 'technologies of the body', has traditionally been hedged by moral qualification, dating back to the Hippocratic Oath. Today's computer professionals evidence a very low level of membership or interest in any comparable organizations.

It may be that IT raises new moral problems. The ease with which data can be permanently and untraceably erased may be one, the way in which privacy is invaded by computers, another (Brown, 1985). But among the most pressing issues is that of the status of information itself. This raises old questions about the proper relation between data, information, knowledge and a fourth category, which has a low profile today, wisdom. But IT gives their ethical consideration a new urgency, and also connects them with another cluster of problems to do with property: information as a commodity. 'Information' is produced for sale in the market-place. But what should rightly be defended as 'public information', as a 'resource'? What should be the limits to commodification?

The second criterion is that of realism about strategies. It is all very well for 'processed' (read 'alienated') San Francisco office-workers to parade the streets wearing cardboard visual display terminals over their heads, but such demonstrations do not exhaust the possibilities of strategic action relating to IT. The kind of realism required is that which connects possibilities for alternative action with actual conditions in a given social context. Despite the apparent cohesiveness of the 'information society' vision, it is unlikely that alternatives to it will be similarly homogeneous.

Although it may be possible theoretically to show how modern societies are increasingly divided between classes of people with and without control over and access to information,[2] in real life their struggles are on numerous and often unconnected fronts. The labour process and industrial relations offer some obvious examples of appropriate strategies. New Technology Agreements, for whatever reason they are introduced, may be used to monitor and control the process of adapting to new technologies. Demonstrations of automation and robotics whose introduction does not deskill or displace labour are vital here (Council for Science and Society, 1981).

Other strategies run through a spectrum including formal political activity within existing parties, involvement in the political process by social movements, attempts to influence communications or educational policy, and local grass-roots action. Legislative change, such as data protection, clearly requires activity of the former sort. But concern for IT alternatives may also be expressed in conjunction with other movements. In Britain, the 'Microsyster' organization attempts to redress the gender imbalance within IT, while 'Microelectronics for Peace' encourages the fostering of alternatives to military developments, mainly within the big IT transnationals. Similar organizations, such as the American 'Computer Professionals for Social Responsibility', exist elsewhere.

As information and communication become increasingly important categories both at a global and a local level, so groups and movements emerge whose aims are to rechannel such developments or to broaden participation within them. Some such strategies have an egalitarian impulse, in which access and control are key issues, whereas others go beyond this to inquire as to whether in certain contexts proposed or established new technologies are appropriate at all. On the international level, the debate over the New World Information and Communication Order laudably considers both sorts of question, although legitimate doubts have been expressed both about the viability and efficacy of the UNESCO forum and about the intentions of some participants.

On the more local level the twin concerns of justice and appropriateness may be confronted again. On the one hand are the attempts to found a decentralized communications system to which public access is guaranteed. Examples range from the Homa Bay radio experiment in Kenya (Ansah, 1979) to community television pilot schemes in Western Europe or North America (McCron, 1984). On the other are projects which explicitly aim to reverse the common pattern of technological development, starting with research on social and personal 'needs'. These relate in particular to disadvantaged groups, such as the disabled, single-parent families, isolated elderly people, and so on. The German study *Sozialpolitische Chancen der Informationstechnik* (Lang *et al.*, 1982, cited in *Communication Research Trends*, 1984, p. 9) is one example, Elisabeth Gerver's *Humanizing Technology* (1986) is another.

The information society problem

The 'information society', paradoxically, has both ideological and utopian aspects. It should not be abandoned on either count. By way of conclusion let me offer four important reasons for saying this, with accompanying qualifications.

Firstly, the 'information society' raises questions about new social circumstances, but not always for the reasons its better-known protagonists think. As I have shown (Lyon, 1988), expectations for this 'new society' are frequently based on highly dubious economic arguments about the predominance of a new 'information sector'. Its adjuncts, the widening dependence on microelectronics, computing and telecommunications, and the growing cadre of 'information workers', provide the supposed social dimension which justifies talk of an 'information revolution' and an 'information society'.

It is not at all clear that the information society is emerging in any of its dimensions. The centralism, monopolies and inequalities of capitalism are not disappearing, and services continue to expand (as ever) *alongside* industrial production (though some of the latter is displaced into the southern hemisphere). Participatory democracy, with immediate access of all to information sources, does not appear to be just around the corner either. And what is absent in the political realm is also missing in the cultural. Where exactly are these promised new choices in diverse and individualized cultural experience and activity to fill the widely augmented leisure time offered by automation?

That said, it does appear that the process of 'informatizing' social, economic and cultural life raises significant sociological questions. While it is perfectly true that, for instance, surveillance by state agencies and by employers has a long history prior to the introduction of informatics, the impact of the new technologies at a time of general economic restructuring may turn out to have long-term (and unforeseen) consequences.

At economic, political and cultural levels the effects of informatics appear to be profound. Its influence within industrial relations, both direct and indirect, is far from negligible. The rising awareness of the (often unwelcome) monitoring of personal lives by computerized agencies may stimulate new kinds of social movement in response. And, judging by past history, the media through which information passes and the kinds of human image enshrined within 'smart machines' may be expected to contribute to alterations in our cultural experience.

Secondly, the technological convergence expressed in the term 'Information Technology' is socially as well as technically significant. The once-clear categories now blurred by the diffusion of IT have important social ramifications. Concepts like 'journalism' or 'middle management' acquire new connotations with the arrival of direct-entry text and the computerized marshalling of data. More widely, I have indicated that surveillance, though made more efficient by mere computerization, is massively strengthened by computerization *with* telecommunications. Furthermore, it is in precisely this area that rapid changes are now taking place (Smith, 1985). Again, in the global context, the debate about communication and cultural dominance of North over South takes on a quite different complexion as IT makes those same communications the conduits of economic power.

The 'convergence factor' also has policy implications, as William Melody explains with this example. In a situation where industrial policy promotes rapid expansion of telecommunications networks, including cable television, direct broadcast satellite and integrated services digital networks, imports of equipment could expand drastically. The new networks could open the country to further imports of data-processing and information-related services, 'displacing domestic production and services ranging from databases to television production. This in turn could bring about a serious balance of payments problem and result in more jobs lost than created, and undercut domestic cultural policy' (Melody, 1985).

As indicated above, the same issue bristles with ethical problems, above all those associated with the plethora of uses of 'information'. Questions of social, personal, public, private, commercial and cultural information are all pertinent here. Each requires appropriate ethical analysis in the context of their revised technical and social usage.

Thirdly, in all 'information society' discourse it must be remembered that technological potential is not social destiny. The easy slide from discussing the technical breakthrough to proclaiming its social benefits is simply unwarranted. (Even the technical breakthrough is a social construction. Research, experiment and planning take place for a long time before an innovation is launched as an *economically* viable product.) This is not to say, however, that IT has inevitable socially malign or sinister aspects.

Without doubt, there are many innovations based on microelectronics for which we have cause to be grateful. Writers like myself are not the only ones to be glad of the increased efficiency gained through word-processing. Robotics and other forms of automation within factories and offices often reduce the level of soul-destroying drudgery. Computerized irrigation and crop-production systems, and satellite sensing of natural and animal resources, make possible huge strides in conservation. Computerized medical diagnosis increases the likelihood of correct and speedy detection of disease.

But in so far as the information society idea depends upon versions of technological determinism it should be resisted. Such determinism is demonstrably false. Technological development does not have pre-set social effects which are predictable, universal or, for that matter, just or beneficial. It can be shown to be the outcome of social shaping itself, including certain deliberate political, economic and cultural choices. Although the pattern of technical advance does sometimes appear to be 'self-augmenting' (in Jacques Ellul's terms), even that process could not continue without the recursive involvement of human agents.

Equally, the spectre of social determinism should be exorcized. This may take more than one form. Theorists such as Harry Braverman and Michel Foucault, though writing from within different traditions, are guilty of underplaying the role of human agency in their accounts of technology-and-society. But there is another aspect to this, namely that new technologies and systems should be seen as overdetermined by social forces. Information Technology may itself be a semi-independent factor within social change. When British Rail computerized their freight yards, for instance, the new system had quite unpredictable consequences for management structures.

Rejecting the determinism latent in 'information society' thinking means that the concept may be opened up into a forum for the consideration of alternative futures. If social and personal choice are involved, then their role should be highlighted. At the same time, those choices, and their motivations, will not always be unambiguous. The impulse behind the timing of data protection law in the UK, for instance, was not concern over privacy as such, but fear of losing important information markets on the continent because British law was out of step with the European Convention.

Fourthly, and following from the previous point, the problem of the information society is a political as well as an analytical one. Social analysis has a role within IT policy. I am thinking of such 'policy' at different levels, from international forums, through national government planning, to the level of the firm and the school, and even the neighbourhood organization. What currently passes as policy frequently lacks an ethical dimension and social awareness.

Within today's political climate, overshadowed as it is by technology policy (whether to remain economically competitive or militarily secure), strenuous attempts are made to co-opt social science for technological ends. Research money is available for those willing to investigate the conditions under which new technology may be adopted, and people adapted to it, successfully. To question social goals, to explore the possibilities for emancipatory, appropriate technology, to examine the ethics or cultural dimensions of new technology, these are not perceived to be priorities.

The task ahead involves a reassertion of the classic role of social inquiry, which is to act as a form of 'public philosophy'.[3] Social analysis has unavoidable moral dimensions, and is concerned in profound ways with the 'human condition'. This is why issues of the magnitude of the social shaping and social consequences of Information Technology may not be siphoned off into mere social engineering. Social scientists dare not sell their moral and analytical birthright for a mess of technological pottage. Social analysis must remain in, but not of, the 'information society'.

Notes

1 The original edition began by asserting that we are in 'the electronic age whose media substitute all-at-onceness for one-thing-at-a-timeness' (see James Carey and John Quirk, 1970).
2 This is an extension of the views expressed in, e.g., Abercrombie and Urry (1983), and Touraine (1974, 1981).
3 The term comes from Bellah *et al.* (1984); see also Sullivan *et al.* (1983).

References

ABERCROMBIE, N. and URRY, J. (1983) *Capital, Labour and the Middle Classes*, London, Allen and Unwin.

ALBURY, D. and SCHWARTZ, J. (1982) *Partial Progress: The Politics of Science and Technology*, London, Pluto Press.

ANSAH, P. (1979) 'Problems of localising radio', *Ghana Gazette*, 25, 4, pp. 1–16.

AUDEN, W.H. (1955) 'Vespers' from *Collected Shorter Poems 1927–1957*, London, Faber.

BELLAH, R. *et al.* (1984) *Habits of the Heart*, Berkeley, University of California Press.

BROWN, G. (1985) 'Privacy and information: a new moral problem?', *Education, Culture and Society/Universities Quarterly*, 39, 2, pp. 114–26.

CAREY, J. and QUIRK, J. (1970) 'The myths of the electronic revolution', *The American Scholar*, 39, 3.

COCKBURN, C. (1983) *Brothers: Male Dominance and Technological Change*, London, Pluto Press.

Communication Research Trends (1984), 5, 2.

COUNCIL FOR SCIENCE AND SOCIETY (1981) *New Technology: Work, Employment and Skill*, London, CSI.

FOX-KELLER, E. (1985) *Reflections on Gender and Science*, New Haven and London, Yale University Press.

GERVER, E. (1986) *Humanizing Technology*, New York, Plenum.

GIDDENS, A. (1979) *Central Problems in Social Theory*, London, Macmillan.

GIDDENS, A. (1985) *The Nation-state and Violence*, Cambridge, Polity Press.

GOUDZWAARD, B. (1975) *Aid for the Overdeveloped West*, Toronto, Wedge.

HABERMAS, J. (1971) *Towards the Rational Society*, London, Heinemann.

HAMELINK, C. (1986), in TRABER, M. (Ed.) *The Myth of the Information Revolution*, London and Beverly Hills, Sage.

HUWS, U. (1982) *Your Job in the Eighties*, London, Pluto Press.

INFORMATION TECHNOLOGY ADVISORY PANEL (1986) *Learning To Live With IT*, London, Her Majesty's Stationery Office.

JONAS, H. (1984) *The Imperative of Responsibility*, London and Chicago, University of Chicago Press.

KUMAR, K. (1978) *Prophecy and Progress*, Harmondsworth, Penguin.

LANG, B.-P. *et al.* (1982) *Sozialpolitische Chancen der Informationstechnik*, Frankfurt and New York, Campus Verlag.

LEVITAS, R. (1982) 'Dystopian times? The impact of the death of progress on utopian thinking', *Theory, Culture and Society*, 1, 1, pp. 53–61.

LYON, D. (1988) *The Information Society: Issues and Illusions*, Cambridge, Polity Press.

MCLUHAN, M. (1964) *Understanding Media*, London, Routledge and Kegan Paul.

MCCRON, R. (1984) 'New technologies: new opportunities?', *Journal of Educational Television*, 10, 1, pp. 7–18.

MELODY, W. (1985) 'Implications of the information and communications technologies: the role of policy research', *Policy Studies*, 6, 2.

MITCHAM, C. (1983) 'The religious and political origins of modern technology', in DURBIN, P. and RAPP, F. (Eds) *Philosophy and Technology*, New York and Frankfurt, Reidel Publishing Company.

MORRIS, W. (1890) *News From Nowhere*, in BRIGGS, A. (Ed.) (1962) *William Morris: Selected Writings and Designs*, Harmondsworth, Penguin.

NOBLE, D. (1983) Present tense technology', in *Democracy*, Spring, Summer and Fall.

PACEY, A. (1983) *The Culture of Technology*, Oxford, Basil Blackwell.

REID, R. (1986) *Land of Lost Content*, London, Heinemann.

SCHILLER, H. (1981) *Who Knows? Information in the Age of the Fortune 500*, Norwood, New Jersey, Ablex.

SEGAL, H. (1978) 'American visions of technological utopia 1883–1933', *The Markham Review*, 7 (Summer).

SEGAL, H. (1985) *Technological Utopianism in American Culture*, Chicago and London, University of Chicago Press.

SHALLIS, M. (1984) *The Silicon Idol*, Oxford, Oxford University Press.

SMITH, M.F. (1985) 'UK information technology: 1990s', *Information Technology Training*, 3, 3, pp. 69–71.

SULLIVAN, W. *et al.* (Eds) (1983) *Social Science as Moral Inquiry*, New York, Columbia University Press.

STORKEY, A. (1986) *Transforming Economics*, London, SPCK.

THOMPSON, E.P. (1968) *The Making of the English Working Class*, Harmondsworth, Penguin.

TOURAINE, A. (1974) *The Post-industrial Society*, London, Wildwood House.

TOURAINE, A. (1981) *The Voice and the Eye*, Cambridge, Cambridge University Press.

WEBSTER, F. and ROBINS, K. (1986) *Information Technology: A Luddite Analysis*, Norwood, New Jersey, Ablex.

WHITE, L. (1978) *Medieval Religion and Technology*, Berkeley, University of California Press.

WHITEHEAD, A.N. (1925) *Science and the Modern World* (reprinted 1985), London, Free Association Books.

Chapter 5

Mass Production, the Fordist System and its Crisis

John Mathews

Modern factory work, despite its universality and the battery of technical arguments supporting its supposed necessity, is in fact a very recent invention. The familiar components of factory work — mechanization, hierarchical supervision, time discipline — were all added piecemeal to previous forms of work organization only in the nineteenth, and in some cases, the twentieth century. Modern scholarship traces the evolution of the industrial system backwards through at least three distinct phases:

- mass production — origins of the corporation, scientific management and assembly line;
- factory production — centralization and mechanization;
- proto-industrialization — cottage industry, putting-out system.

The days are gone when the industrial past was nothing but a dim memory of 'dark Satanic mills'. Our first task is to shed light on the rise of the factory, looking in particular at the social negotiations and struggles that accompanied it. Our aim is to trace the evolution of the labour process to its modern form.[1]

Pre-factory modes

In pre-industrial times, the majority of people lived in rural villages, and agricultural labour, on their own or others' land, occupied most of their time. Work was regulated by the natural rhythms of the seasons, sunrise and sunset. Frequent saints' days provided opportunities for rest and recreation. Work was organized largely in family units.[2] Extra work, producing handicrafts, was taken in as fluctuating conditions allowed, to increase households' meagre incomes. In time, households came to specialize in such activities as weaving, basketmaking or pottery. Such *cottage industries* became a feature of eighteenth-century Europe.

The pinnacle of this system was the proud and highly skilled master craftsman, who owned his own tools, hired his assistants, bought his own materials and sold his product direct to the market. Technologies and production processes were relatively stable, and were known in minute detail by the independent artisan, through his apprenticeship and membership of a guild.

The skills and general scientific and technical culture of the craft workers should not be underestimated. As Braverman put it in a famous passage from *Labor and Monopoly Capital*:

> The working craftsman was tied to the technical and scientific knowledge of his time in the daily practice of his craft. Apprenticeship commonly included training in mathematics, including algebra, geometry, and trigonometry, in the properties and provenance of the materials common to the craft, in the physical sciences, and in mechanical drawing. Well-administered apprenticeships provided subscriptions to the trade and technical journals affecting the craft so that apprentices could follow developments. But more important than formal or informal training was the fact that the craft provided a daily link between science and work, since the craftsman was constantly called upon to use rudimentary scientific knowledge, mathematics, drawing, etc., in his practice. Such craftsmen were an important part of the scientific public of their time, and as a rule exhibited an interest in science and culture beyond that connected directly to their work. (1974, p. 133)

Shortage of capital meant that few cottage producers could establish themselves as completely independent businesses, buying raw materials from the proceeds of sales of finished articles. Such independence was reserved for the master craftsmen, such as shoemakers. The majority of cottage producers depended on merchants to supply them with raw materials, and to pay standard prices for finished work. This system, called *proto-industrialization*, is a primitive form of industrialization that prefigured the later factory mode.[3]

Proto-industrialization

Modern scholarship locates the beginnings of the capitalist system proper (i.e., a system of production for profit using wage labour) in the putting-out and contracting systems. Early merchant capitalists advanced capital (funds accumulated, for example, through trade) to buy raw materials, and provided these to, say, weavers in their cottages, and collected the finished cloth from them. In this way, they 'put-out' work in the form of raw materials, advanced wages to the workers and collected the finished product, for sale in the market.

The 'putting-out' system was practised on a very large scale; some operations involved thousands of workers in a district coordinated by a large merchant. It was, in other words, a selfregulating industrial system. (It survives today, in a new guise, in the 'outwork' systems that operate in the clothing industry and in the fabrication at home of a host of other consumer items. Indeed, computerization is adding a further chapter to this story, by encouraging home work at a computer terminal.)

The putting-out system was a transformation of work imposed on workers by merchant capitalists who found a way to place themselves between the producers and the market. But it was also a transformation of the merchants, who came to amass fortunes, and began to 'integrate vertically', as we would put it today. They bought looms and other means of production, and let them out to workers as the workers became financially ruined and were forced to surrender their independence.

The putting-out system, or proto-industrialization, provided the conditions out of which the present industrial system developed. It created a stratum of skilled workers; it allowed capital to accumulate in the hands of merchants who had an incentive to reinvest it in manufacturing; and it encouraged the growth of markets and a division of labour.

On the other hand, the putting-out merchant was at perpetual war with his workers, and was plagued by problems of irregularity of production, loss of materials in transit, embezzlement, uncertainty and lack of uniformity in the finished product — and, above all, by an inability to modify the process of production, which was totally under the control of the worker in his home. Hence it was but a short step for the capitalist — but a big step for humankind! — to set up a centralized manufactory where the craft workers could all be brought under one roof, and be subject to the employer's discipline.

Factory system

Between the middle of the eighteenth century and the end of the nineteenth century, the putting-out system and what remained of independent craft work gave way to the modern system of factory production. The conventional technological determinist account explains the rise of factories as 'caused' by the need of new power-driven machinery for centralized power sources.[4] The logic of central power sources like water wheels and, later, steam engines, required an end to production being scattered throughout workers' homes — so we are told.

However, modern scholarship in labour process studies has now shown that this view stands the real situation on its head. In fact, the real impetus for the setting up of early factories (i.e., manufactories, meaning places where manual work was done) was to overcome the perceived deficiencies of the putting-out system, by imposing a discipline of work under one roof. Once work was aggregated in this way, it became possible to harness external power sources, such as water wheels and, later, steam engines. But the aggregation of work, as a conscious *political* act, *preceded* the application of new sources of power.[5]

The factory was created in a climate of great social violence. Independent workers would starve rather than submit to its discipline. Riots and arson frequently accompanied a new factory's appearance. So hated were the factories, that early owners were largely dependent on pauper children for their workforce, or on the inmates of workhouses. Starving agricultural labourers, turned off the land as a result of the enclosure movement, were also early factory fodder.

Who then were the early factory masters? Andrew Ure, writing in 1835, at a time when spinning was still the only industry unequivocally dominated by factory production, wrote admiringly of Arkwright who was credited with being the founder of the factory system:

> The main difficulty lay above all in training human beings to renounce their desultory habits of work, and to identify themselves with the unvarying regularity of the complex automation. To devise and administer a successful code of factory discipline, suited to the necessities of factory diligence, was the Herculean enterprise, the noble achievement of Arkwright. Even at the present day, when the system is perfectly organized and its labour lightened to the utmost, it is found nearly impossible to convert persons past the age of puberty, into useful factory hands.

Arkwright could be seen as the Taylor of the eighteenth century, the man who got his hands dirty and imposed the first major transformation of the labour process on some extremely unwilling workers. Another pioneer factory owner-operator was Josiah Wedgwood, of pottery fame. He established a pottery manufactory, and sought to control the irregular habits of his employees by imposing a clocking-in procedure, the chiming of bells for starting and finishing and even an embryonic assembly-line system (McKendrick, 1961).

In spite of the opposition to them, factories became entrenched, and eventually skilled workers had to submit to their discipline. But the point is that this was not through technical superiority, but through an organization of labour imposed as a social choice by the employers and reinforced by economic benefits. The important economic stimulus for employers to establish manufactories was the possibility of extending the division of labour. This would break a single craft production process into a number of 'detailed' jobs, many of which could be performed by unskilled workers, and hence more cheaply. This factor was studiously avoided by Adam Smith in his famous discussion of the division of labour in his *Wealth of Nations* in 1776 — but it was stated forthrightly by Charles Babbage in his book, *On the Economy of Machinery and Manufactures,* in 1832, as a principle:

> That the master manufacturer, by dividing the work to be executed into different processes, each requiring different degrees of skill or of force, can purchase exactly that precise quantity of both which is necessary for each process; whereas, if the whole work were executed by one workman, that person must possess sufficient skill to perform the most difficult, and sufficient strength to execute the most laborious, of the operations into which the art is divided.

Braverman, who is chiefly responsible for rehabilitating Babbage, identified this as the key motive behind the drive to fragment work into smaller and smaller details, each requiring less skill to perform. He called it the 'Babbage principle'.

The other major economic benefit that factory production brought to employers was the more obvious one of allowing them to dictate longer hours of work. This did not increase productivity in itself (indeed, it probably lowered it, as the workers' fatigue became overwhelming) but it allowed fixed plant to be worked more intensively, and thereby lowered unit costs. Economically there was no limit to the optimal working time, and employers would have had workers at the mill for twenty-four hours a shift if it were humanly possible. The only remedy to prevent a total collapse of civilized values was legal regulation of the length of the working day — and this was of course the source of the great agitation for factory regulation during the first half of the nineteenth century.

Mechanization

The factory, to modern eyes, is pre-eminently the place where workers no longer operate tools, as in 'manufacture' (i.e., hand or manual production) but where machines operate workers. Once the factory system had been imposed, it offered undreamt-of possibilities for applying centralized power sources and harnessing them with large-scale machinery. Machinery was not only very productive, and therefore profitable, but it was also a powerful instrument to discipline workers as 'dead labour'. No one has surpassed Marx in his description of the effects of mechanized factory work on their inmates. In 'Machinery and Modern Labour' he writes:

> The life-long speciality of handling one and the same tool, now becomes the life-long speciality of serving one and the same machine.... In handicrafts and manufacture, the workman makes

use of a tool; in the factory, the machine makes use of him. There the movements of the instrument of labour proceed from him; here it is the movements of the machine that he must follow. In manufacture the workmen are parts of a living mechanism. In the factory we have a lifeless mechanism independent of the workman, who becomes its mere living appendage.... By means of its conversion into an auto-mation, the instrument of labour confronts the labourer, during the labour-process, in the shape of capital, of dead labour, that domin-ates, and pumps dry, living labour-power. The separation of the intellectual powers of production from the manual labour is, as we have already shown, finally completed by modern industry erected on the foundation of machinery.... The technical subordination of the workman to the uniform motion of the instruments of labour, and the peculiar composition of the body of workpeople, consisting as it does of individuals of both sexes and of all ages, give rise to a barrage of discipline, which is elaborated into a complete system in the factory, and which fully develops the before-mentioned labour of overlooking, thereby dividing the workpeople into operatives and overlookers, into private soldiers and sergeants of an industrial army. (Marx, 1970, chapter 15)[6]

It is easy to be overwhelmed by machinery and see it as the ultimate force for disciplining labour — as Marx apparently did in the passage quoted above. Mechanization has been the principal source of technological change in the workplace over the past century, taking over former 'craft' areas one by one. In the way it has been introduced, its effect has certainly been to deskill formerly personalized skilled work and to offer factory owners greater con-trol over their employees, or 'hands' as they were called. But this is not a *technical* effect, inherent in the machinery — it is the *social* outcome of the way technology was designed and installed. And this social outcome was not predetermined. Workers managed to counter the effects of mechanization, imposing constraints on the way it was used, and in some cases determined the outcome themselves, through their union demands.

Research is now starting to be done on the complex series of negotiations and social interactions which have shaped the organization and mechanization of work in factories. Let us look at two case studies of the technical and social transformations that occurred in the nineteenth century — in the cotton trade in the first half of the century, and in the boot trade in the latter half. The case of 'automation' of spinning, through the use of the 'self-acting mule', shows not only how workers were able to shape the manner in which machinery was used, but it was also a case where Marx was beguiled by capitalist propaganda and believed that exactly the *opposite* had occurred. These studies provide us with fundamental insights when we look at the wave of computerization that is currently sweeping through industry.

Case study: automation of cotton spinning

We now have a reasonably complete picture of the forces which shaped technological change in the cotton industry in the UK and US — the industry that was the pace-setter of the industrial revolution.[7] Spinning of thread had been done since time immemorial by hand, and then later, in cottages, using a hand-operated spinning jenny. A technical advance led to the development of the (common) mule used for spinning in factories. This was a machine operated by a spinner working on a subcontract basis, hiring his own 'piecers' to join the threads, a 'creel-filler', and cleaners. The spinner was an adult male and his hired help would be children, often his own. In the 1780s mule-spinning was performed on a putting-out basis; in the late 1780s mule-shed manufactures arose; and by the 1790s factory mule-spinning predominated. Already by the 1790s, mule-spinners had organized themselves into strong unions. By 1810, for example, the mule-spinners were well organized in Manchester, where they staged a massive four-month strike which only failed when they ran out of funds; in 1811 several spinners were imprisoned for the offence of 'combining'. In the early years of the nineteenth century several more strikes were staged, mainly to control the level of piece-rates and impose uniformity on wages, but also to stop capitalists putting women onto the mules and paying them less.

The employers were desperate to find a means to curb the power of the spinners, and for forty years there was constant experimentation to find an automatic, or 'self-acting', mule that would put the spinners out of work. Mule-spinning was a delicate craft, and to automate it was in those times a technical feat. Lazonick describes how between 1818 and 1830 at least six types of self-acting mules were put into experimental operation. Finally Richard Roberts patented a successful self-actor in 1832. By June 1833, about 100,000 spindles had been put into operation, on 250 to 300 machines (some of which were common mules converted to self-actors) and a further 120,000 were on order. Clearly employers wasted no time in taking up the innovation. The spinners and their union looked like being wiped out.

At this point the capitalist apologist Andrew Ure, writing in 1835 in his book *The Philosophy of Manufactures*, noted that 'the effect of substituting the self-acting mule for the common mule, is to discharge the greater part of the men spinners, and to retain adolescents and children'. He suggested that the self-actor, among other things, would 'put an end ... to the folly of trades' unions'. He went on to assert, in a phrase picked up by Marx, that 'This invention confirms the great doctrine ... that when capital enlists science into her service, the refractory hand of labour will be taught docility'. Ure was simply expanding on the claims made by Roberts' company, Sharp, Roberts and Co., Manchester, who promoted their self-acting mule as having the prime advantage of 'saving of a spinner's wages to each pair of mules, piecers only being required, one overlooker being sufficient to manage 6 or 8 pairs of mules or upwards'. So Ure swallowed the manufacturer's claims, and Marx swallowed Ure's claims. But what actually happened?

In fact, the same subcontracting system was perpetuated, this time with a self-actor 'minder', and 'ciphers' and 'little piecers' as assistants. Lazonick argues that it was simply beyond the resources of capitalists to switch to a completely automatic mechanism because, paradoxically, this would have required constant and close supervision over the minder to ensure that snarled thread was not hidden inside the 'cop' where it could become a nuisance in subsequent operations. It was therefore easier to partly mechanize the process and subcontract it to the minder, to avoid the necessity for close supervision. In time the minders developed their own strong unions, and merged with the decaying mule-spinners' union. This system of work organization persisted until the twentieth century. As Lazonick concludes:

> The case of the self-acting mule in Lancashire, therefore, does not demonstrate the unfettered triumph of capital over labour through the use of division of labour and machinery ... there was continual process of conflict, compromise and even cooperation between capitalists and workers, over the form and content of the components of technical change — mechanization, division of labour and intensification of labour. The resistance of workers to changes in these aspects of the technical structure of production often took the active forms of organized work stoppages and slow-downs, as well as the passive form of individual workers holding back in their exertion of their labour-power unless closely supervised. (Lazonick, 1979)[8]

Case study: mechanization of bootmaking

Bootmaking was a flourishing trade in Melbourne, supplying the local colonial Victorian market and, by the 1870s, exporting as well.[9] Power-driven machinery was unusual, and it was still possible for an enterprising bootmaker with a few hundred pounds to set up as a manufacturer. Virtually all finishing work on boots was 'put-out' to home workers. As Raelene Frances describes it:

> These outworkers were supplied by an army of lads who swarmed over Melbourne and [the inner suburbs] Fitzroy and Collingwood, pushing barrow loads of boots in various stages of construction. Nor were the manufacturers anxious to bring the finishers inside the factories, as they took up valuable space and were considered a 'nuisance, trouble and expense as they must have gas burning' (i.e., to keep their pots of pitch warm). (Frances, 1986)

By the mid-1890s, the industry was completely transformed, with large, highly mechanized factories dominating the trade. Small producers had been eliminated, as had outwork, and the previously strong bootmakers' union was close to collapse. This would appear to be yet another case of machinery being used to teach 'docility to the refractory hand of labour', as Ure had put it. But the situation was more complex. In fact, the changes were sparked by the union itself campaigning to end the putting-out system used in finishing boots. In 1884 all of Melbourne's major boot factories were involved in a strike and lockout over this issue:

> The unionists could see that it was impossible to prevent reductions in piece rates so long as men were scattered throughout the inner-city suburbs, doing the work in their own homes. By bringing the finishers inside the factories, they hoped to organize more effective resistance. The employers did not want this to happen for several reasons. They could see that more effective unionisation would be the result, and they were also unwilling to spend money on buildings to provide the additional accommodation. After a bitter struggle lasting thirteen weeks the manufacturers agreed to provide this accommodation and bring all the finishers inside. It seemed that the union had won — but their victory had unexpected long-term effects. No longer able to cut costs by simply cutting wages, employers began to look more closely at other ways of reducing their production costs. Many began to experiment with new machinery and subdivision of labour, hoping simultaneously to reduce their labour costs and weaken the union by replacing hand-labour with machinery. As unemployment rose in the boot trade in the late 1880s, these strategies began to pay off. By the time the depression deepened in 1891, the employers were ready for a full-scale re-organisation of the industry. (Frances, 1986, pp. 7–8)

This story is pregnant with lessons. The 'victory' the unions had won in 1884, sacrificing the independence of the outworker to maintain piece-rates, had ramifications that the workers failed to foresee. By advocating an extension of the factory system, the union was powerless to oppose the concomitant extensions of factory discipline and further subdivision of tasks. While opposing the move from piece-rates to weekly wages in general, the union conceded that subdivisions and weekly wages could be used in conjunction with the new machines (thereby preserving the *status quo* for hand-workers). But this only accelerated the installation of new machines.

Raelene Frances argues that had the union not succeeded in eliminating outwork in the 1880s, then the employers would have been more likely to respond to the depression of the 1890s by cutting piece-rates, rather than mechanizing and subdividing labour. Thus the industry might have taken a different course. It is not that the bootmakers' union was 'wrong', any more so than the employers: the point is that neither side in this story had any real understanding of the social complexity and ramifications of changes in technology and work organization. These mistakes need not be repeated during the current wave of change associated with computerization.

Internal organization of the factory

How was work organized in nineteenth-century factories, before the ranks of managers that came into existence in the twentieth century? Modern labour process scholarship identifies a transitional form of work organization which allowed the early capitalists to get around a dilemma: they had little technical knowledge of production, and could not attract or supervise workers to run or 'manage' the process for them. One solution was 'inside contracting'. Skilled workers were attracted into the factory by being allowed to hire their own assistants. They contracted to perform work for a price, and the difference between that price and their costs could be kept as profit. The alternative, namely direct control by a technically competent entrepreneur, was not nearly as common as popularly believed.

The internal contractor became the basis for the notion of an 'aristocracy of labour', which was posited by such writers as Hobsbawm as constituting a stratum 'bought off' by the employers and holding back the development of a class-consciousness on the part of the workers. The more recent labour process literature shows this to be a rather crude notion, and not helpful in understanding the dynamics of the transformation of the labour process.

Inside contracting therefore constituted a self-consistent system of organization of work. It was used extensively in both the US and the UK, even in technically advanced sectors of industry (notably by the highly profitable Singer Sewing Machine Company in the 1870s).[10] Why then did it disappear (apart from its continued survival in the construction industry, which is a rather special case)?

Clawson (1980) argues that the system did not decline by virtue of any technical inferiority. It was a series of social choices on the part of employers, towards the end of the nineteenth century, that led to its demise. Some contractors were able to make a lot of money, and were able to earn far more than a salaried foreman could hope to achieve. But even more importantly, the contractors were seen as rising 'above their stations'. Towards the end of the century they were dressing in silk hats and frock coats, and were rivalling the firm's managers in social prestige. Therefore they 'had to go'.

In the case of the UK, Littler (1982) argues that the system lost working-class support as the contractors started to 'sweat' their employees more and more during the depression years of the 1870s and 1880s. There were several celebrated internal trade union clashes, for many contractors formed a union themselves, and either admitted less-skilled colleagues only to inferior positions in the union, or refused admission and forced them to form separate organizations.

How was the inside-contracting system destroyed? There were a number of factors. One was the use of piecework payments systems. Piecework offered employers direct control over the conditions in which workers laboured and a means of compiling data on the times taken to complete different tasks. It also set worker in competition against worker, thus undermining solidarity; it was therefore opposed by unions. But we saw above that the bootmakers' union was at the same time *opposing* the introduction of weekly wage rates in favour of piece-rates. The situation was far from simple.

In Britain the spread of piecework in the engineering industry was rapid. In 1886 it covered 5 per cent of workers; in 1906 it covered 27.5 per cent; and by 1927, only forty years later, it reached nearly 50 per cent (by then including premium bonus schemes as well as simple piecework).[11] Thus wage systems based on Payment By Results (PBR) became extensive. The essence of piecework was that it replaced a system of payment where the employer handed over a lump sum to the contractor, not knowing how and in what proportions he dispensed it to his 'gang', to one where all employees were paid directly by 'the office'. This was an important bureaucratic innovation, and one with far-reaching consequences, although these may not have been seen at the time. The employer required the worker to make a weekly return of his or her output (or else this was done by the supervisor) in order that the wage and premium could be calculated. Hence the employer was able to accumulate records of production. At the time, these were used simply in the endless skirmishes between employer and workers over fixing the rate per piece — with the employers trying to lower the rate and workers trying to maintain it. In order to do so, workers learnt to restrict output so that they would not earn inflated wages, and at the same time they had to close ranks to prevent over-keen 'rate busters' from producing too great an output and thereby give the employer justification for lowering the rate. Later, these records were to serve as the foundation for further, more detailed 'time and motion' studies of workers; they represented the first, hesitant steps towards the bureaucratic forms of control characteristic of the twentieth century.

Mass production

Throughout the nineteenth century, the impetus towards mass production gained ground over its craft-production technological rival. Its basic rationale was reduction of cost by standardizing the production of parts, and the use of repetitive mechanical methods to substitute for skilled labour. Following the principles outlined by Charles Babbage in 1832, the mass-producing firm strove to break the process of production into smaller and smaller fragments, each requiring less skilled (and so cheaper) labour to perform, and substituting mechanical dexterity for human dexterity wherever possible.[12]

The victory of mass production was complete. As Michael Piore and Charles Sabel put it in their seminal book, *The Second Industrial Divide:*

> Manchester cotton goods, Waltham clocks, Lynn shoes, Colt revolvers, Yale locks, McCormick reapers, Singer sewing machines, Remington typewriters, American Tobacco cigarettes, US steel and Standard oil, — industry after industry came under the domination of giant firms using specialized equipment to turn out previously unimagined numbers of standard goods, at prices that local producers could not meet. When, in 1913, Ford's Model T rolled out of his Highland Park, Michigan, plant, it was the culmination of a century's experience with mass production: the machinery for making the parts was so precise that no hand-finishing was necessary, yet it was so easy to operate that workers just off the farm could operate it; and the final assembly of the product — paced by the endless circulating chain that moved the work in progress from one station to another — required no more traditional craft skill than the operation of the automatic equipment that the engineers privately called farm tools. The indisputable contribution of these techniques to the American success in World War I made mass production a matter not just of commercial prudence, but of national survival. (Piore and Sabel, 1984, p. 20)

The technology of mass production was dependent on standardization and interchangeability of parts. It was perfected in the US in the years after 1850 in the small-arms (Colt revolvers) and locks industries. It then spread to new areas, such as in the production of sewing machines, typewriters and bicycles.

Mass production, involving low-skill workers driven by piece-rate incentives, was the antithesis of skilled artisan craft production. The contest between these two modes was unequal from the start. There were economic, ideological and technical factors involved. Each bears some consideration, if we are to fully understand the pressures that shaped the modern industrial system.

Economic consolidation: rise of the corporation

Standardized production of hundreds of interchangeable parts, in aggregated workshops making large purchases of raw materials, required a level of coordination far more sophisticated than that given by inside contracting.

Mass production required large investments to be made in highly specialized equipment and in narrowly trained workers. In the terminology of manufacturing, these resources were 'dedicated' or suited to the manufacture of one particular product. Once the market for that particular product declined, then the resources would have no place to go. Mass production was therefore profitable only with markets that were large enough and standard enough to absorb an enormous output of a single, standardized commodity. Markets of this kind, like markets in general, did not occur naturally, but had to be created. Piore and Sabel argue that in the United States, the modern corporation was organized for this purpose.

The corporation arose as the agglomeration of smaller firms, each producing parts that were required to be assembled into a final product. In place of the market being allowed to coordinate their activity, through the price system, firms found it more efficient to internalize their parts production, thus distributing costs across more and more branches, and reducing uncertainty. (This was a case study in capitalist departure from neo-classical economic theory that preaches the superiority of the market as a means of organizing production.) There were real, material reasons for the shift: as equipment became dedicated to long runs of standardized products, it could not be used for alternatives, as required by efficient, price-sensitive markets; similarly, semi-skilled workers specializing in a particular branch of standardized production could not easily transfer to other work, as envisaged by an 'efficient' labour market. The corporation was the legal form in which an economic solution to these problems was found.

Ideological consolidation: scientific management

Mass production, even when organized in the new corporation that emerged at the end of the nineteenth century, lacked an ideology. It was not enough that it should conquer craft production in the market-place: the skill and knowledge of production retained by craftsmen were still seen as a threat to the dominance of the new mode of production.

Along came Frederick Winslow Taylor, as the apostle of a new creed of 'scientific management' that was to justify the expropriation of skill from the trained worker by an emergent management bureaucracy.[13]

The essence of Taylor's thought lay in his concept of control. Employers have tried to control workers in different ways since the Industrial Revolution. These had largely consisted of systems of rules, discipline and other external features of the labour process. What Taylor achieved was to raise the concept of control to an entirely new plane. He maintained that it was an absolute necessity for adequate management to dictate to the worker the precise manner in which work was to be performed. Management, Taylor insisted, could only be a limited and frustrating undertaking while it left to the worker any power to take decisions about work.

As Taylor himself put it, in his classic text 'The Principles of Scientific Management':

> What the workmen want from their employers beyond anything else is
> high wages and what employers want from their workmen most of all
> is low labour cost of manufacture . . . the existence or absence of these
> two elements forms the best index to either good or bad management.
> (Taylor, 1972, p. 93)

Taylor's system could be distilled into three fundamental principles. These are:

1 *Dissociation* of the labour process from the skills of the workers, i.e.,
  management appropriation of all traditional knowledge and skills
  which workers have used, and their reduction to systematic formulae
  and rules.
2 *Separation* of conception from execution, i.e., removing all possible
  brainwork from the shop floor and relocating it in a planning or layout
  department.
3 Use of this monopoly over knowledge to *control* each step of the
  labour process and its mode of execution, i.e., dictating how each job is
  to be done through complete written instruction, describing in detail
  the task that is to be done, how it is to be done and the time it is to take.

These then were the principles of 'scientific management'. It can be
argued that they have been adopted, in one form or another and without
necessarily being called 'Taylorist', in all subsequent schemes of production
engineering, time and motion study and work study in general.[14]

Taylor's system, and its successors in the form of time and motion study,
made a big impact on industry in the period 1880 to 1930 — a half century of
reorganization and rationalization of management methods that have had a
lasting effect on the labour process and on the worker.[15]

In the UK, scientific management was not taken up with any degree of
enthusiasm before the First World War, being seen as faddishly American.
But as UK industry faced the threat of competition in the 1920s and firms
started going to the wall, UK firms looked to new management systems for
salvation.

The most popular in Britain was the Bedaux system, marketed interna-
tionally by the Bedaux organization in the 1920s and 1930s. This system was
based on the B, a 'universal' unit of work that also incorporated a rest factor
(one of the weaknesses of Taylor's system being that he never acknowledged
the physiological need for rest and recovery). Any worker taking a normal
time for recovery was rated as being able to produce 60B per hour, no matter
what particular work he or she was doing. Anything in excess of 60B (as
measured by the time and motion engineers) would attract a bonus. By 1939,
most of the leading companies in Britain, like ICI, Lucas, Lyons and Wolsey,
had adopted the Bedaux system — but not without provoking major strikes at
such places as the Wolsey Hosiery Company in 1930–34, organized by the

Hosiery Union, with a largely female membership, and not previously noted for its militancy (Littler, 1982).

In other countries, such as Australia, the impact of scientific management was felt more gradually. It only became a central part of the ethos of manufacturing capital after the Second World War. The excesses of time and motion study, and the use of the stopwatch, were resisted successfully by metalworkers in many engineering plants in Australia in the 1950s and 1960s, and in munitions and defence establishments. This resulted in a variant called MTM ('Methods Time Management') being adopted, a procedure which worked out 'time-allowances' in advance, and eliminated the provocation of direct timing. Rationalization was eventually achieved through some major success stories, such as at the Standard Motor Company in Melbourne, where the Works Study Department introduced changes which led to substantial gains for the company (Cochrane, 1985).

Scientific management can be seen as a breathtaking shift of power in favour of the employers, dispossessing workers of their skills and instituting a dictatorship in the workplace.

On the other hand, the rationalization of work methods did in practice lead to productivity gains and so to greater security of employment for workers. Hence continued blanket opposition on the part of unions was neither feasible nor productive. Exactly the same dilemma confronts unions today as they face up to the challenges of computerization.

Technical consolidation: the assembly line

The modern assembly line dates essentially from the system installed by Henry Ford at his vehicle plant in Highland Park, Detroit, in 1913. This introduced an endless-chain conveyer to vehicle production for the first time (although the idea arose in the meat industry in the 1880s). Despite conventional claims that it was the technical superiority of the assembly line that led to its introduction, in fact the engineering of the line was quite primitive. The reality was that its essence lay in control — and in particular, control over the pace of production. For instead of a situation where the worker goes to the job, as in batch production, with the assembly line the job comes to the worker, at a pace dictated by the employer.[16]

The assembly line has become the symbol of mass production, as immortalized in Chaplin's film *Modern Times*, made in 1936. It was the clearest instance where the technical requirements of a shift from batch to flow production were combined with a new drive for management control.[17]

Like other innovations in the organization of work, the assembly line was introduced under conditions of social violence and worker resistance. Workers reacted to the assembly line by leaving in droves, and Ford found recruitment to be a big problem. In 1913 labour turnover was 380 per cent. In

1914 the International Workers of the World ('Wobblies') began an intensive unionization drive in Ford plants. Ford's response to the double threat of a flight of workers and unionization was the announcement of a new wage level of $5 per day in 1914 — nearly double the standard rate at the time. This was a brilliant move which solved both problems at a stroke, and gave Ford a quiescent workforce on which to impose further job intensification. As Henry Ford himself wrote in his autobiography: 'The payment of five dollars a day for an eight-hour day was one of the finest cost-cutting moves we ever made'. The assembly line was then consolidated as the centrepiece of Ford's work organization, forcing competitors to follow suit or face extinction.

Outside the motor industry, the assembly-line principle was consolidated more slowly — but in sector after sector it surely came to oust the older 'batch' methods of production. Like previous reorganizations of work, its introduction was fought bitterly. It represented a new degree of degradation of labour that was already smarting from the discipline of the factory and from time and motion study.

The assembly line became the dominant paradigm even outside manufacturing. For example, in the meat trade the 'solo' practices of slaughtering and butchering were displaced around the turn of the century by the 'chain' method of continuous 'dis-assembly' of carcasses. (Ironically, it was early examples of chain conveyors used in Chicago meat works in the 1890s that are said to have inspired Henry Ford.) In some cases, the struggle to oppose the 'chain' method brought unions to the point of destruction.[18]

Diffusion of mass production

Mass production drove out its competitors, and rose to dominance in the years immediately following the First World War. Along with Taylorist and post-Taylorist principles of 'scientific management', it spread to Europe and Japan, becoming the worldwide, dominant industrial paradigm.

In *The Second Industrial Divide*, Michael Piore and Charles Sabel characterize the rise of the mass-production system as a first 'industrial divide' that split it off from craft and batch production methods. They are at pains to point out that this was anything but a predetermined outcome. As they put it: 'The triumph of a technological breakthrough over competing adaptations depends on its timing and the resources available to its champions — rather than on its intrinsic superiority' (1984, p. 15).

This is the point I have stressed throughout. The evolution of production technology and work organization cannot be understood as a *technically determined* process — despite the dominant ideology which reads developments since the Industrial Revolution in this light. It can only be understood as the outcome of a complex social process: technologies bear the scars of the social conflicts which have shaped them.

For better or worse, then, the mass-production system came to dominate industry in the twentieth century. But just as its development was contingent on numerous social and economic factors, so is its survival. And that is just what is now in doubt. It is to this issue that we turn in the next section.

The concept of Fordism

As we have seen, a revolutionary mode of organizing production had become established in the US by the 1920s, and from there it spread to Europe, Japan and elsewhere. This new mode encompassed mass production, assembly-line techniques and scientific management in one or other of its guises. It was so successful that it led to rapid increases in productivity and increases in employment and wage levels — with, of course, regional variations. Lack of overall regulation plunged the world economy into an overproduction crisis in the 1930s. This highlighted the absolute necessity, if mass production were to become established, for measures to ensure that consumption be encouraged to keep pace with production.

Henry Ford himself was quick to realize that the economies of scale inherent in mass production could only be reaped if mass markets could be created for mass-produced goods. For this to be achieved, purchasing power had to be raised and maintained — which was one of the factors influencing Ford to introduce his $5-a-day wage. Ford's ability to affect the whole system was of course limited — but the need for markets to be created for mass-produced goods from the 1920s onwards, underlies many of the social and economic developments that are conventionally seen as arising independently. These include: Keynesian macroeconomic policies and the New Deal with their acknowledgment of the role of government in holding up levels of domestic demand for mass-produced goods; various forms of the welfare state; and acceptance of mass trade unions and collective bargaining as legitimate elements of the economic order. This was the 'consumption' side of a comprehensive system of regulation that complemented the 'production' side. In deference to Gramsci and to Henry Ford himself, this system has come to be called *Fordism*.[19]

Fordism is now seen as the dominant political-economic framework of the twentieth century.[20] There is nothing magic in the name: it merely serves as a means of identifying the major features of the dominant industrial system, and what distinguishes it from the pre-war regime of accumulation.

The diffusion of Fordism followed different paths in the US, Europe and Japan; indeed one can distinguish quite distinct *national paths* of Fordism. The US was pre-eminently the Fordist heartland, and it was US corporations that fashioned the elements of the model. Prior to the rise of mass unionism in the US, the industrial relations of Fordism were paternalistic: this was the period of 'welfare capitalism', when firms attempted to soften the brutality of job fragmentation, skill destruction and punitive supervision by company welfare schemes and 'human relations' innovations.[21] The Depression put paid to all that, and the Fordist system in the US was henceforth shaped by the liberal compromise of the New Deal and accommodation with mass industrial unions (recognized in the Wagner Act of 1935).

Expansion of Fordism — and its limits

The post-war period, with reconstruction in Europe and the boom triggered by the Korean War, set in train a period of growth unprecedented in the history of capitalism. All the elements of the Fordist system worked together: markets for consumer goods expanded as purchasing power grew, and mass-producing corporations supplied these markets with standardized goods, maintaining their competitive edge through technological supremacy and productivity growth. World trade proceeded on a relatively ordered basis through the Bretton Woods system of fixed exchange rates, premissed on the supremacy of the US dollar. Keynesian demand management techniques allowed consumer markets to maintain their buoyancy, diminishing the effects of the traditional business cycle of boom and slump, while new social security measures coped with the marginal elements in each society, preventing them from becoming too disruptive. The Western labour movement shared in this prosperity, and its leadership subscribed to Fordist principles of labour management as the price to be paid for general affluence.

Of course the picture was not all rosy. The Second World War sparked a series of national liberation movements in the Third World that led to colonial wars of intense bitterness and brutality — e.g., in Algeria, in Vietnam and in the Portuguese colonies in Africa. There were upheavals in the East, notably the victory of Chinese Communists in 1949 and the Hungarian revolt in 1956. There was the Cold War and then nuclear standoff as the Soviet Union, and then China, developed their own nuclear weapons.

But these events, momentous as they were, were not central to the confident expansion of mass production and mass consumption or to the dominant modes of economic life in the post-war era. It seemed that this system would go on forever — but of course it didn't. From the late 1960s on it suffered a series of shocks that have shaken the system to its foundations.[22]

The first of these was the social upheaval of the late 1960s, when country after country was shaken by worker and student revolts — May 1968 in France, the hot autumn in Italy and the emergence of militant mass movements against the Vietnam War in the US, UK, Australia, and many other places. These upheavals, even if they did not lead to 'revolution', showed that the post-war consensus and the much-trumpeted 'end of ideology' was in fact a facade; social tensions would henceforth be an integral part of the business environment.

Secondly, the dominance of European and American firms was challenged from the East, firstly from Japan, and then from mass production imitators like South Korea, Hong Kong, Taiwan and Singapore. Trade wars came to be a dominant feature of the world economy in the 1970s, with whole industries in the 'core' countries being threatened with extinction — and becoming extinct — under the impact of cheaper imports. This process moved through phases: firstly it affected the cheaper consumer items like toys, clothing and footwear; then it touched electronic goods such as radios and TV sets; and later its effect moved into major products like cars, computers and steel.

Thirdly, the system of fixed exchange rates that had created financial security and had underwritten much of the post-war boom was exploded in the early 1970s by the introduction of floating exchange rates, which in effect meant the end of dollar supremacy. The world financial system was given further severe shocks by the first OPEC oil price rise in 1974, and then again by the second in 1978. These created a wash of billions of dollars that had to be accommodated within an inflexible system, and had irreversible effects on the pattern of world industrial development and trade.[23]

Fourthly, the 1970s were characterized by runaway inflation accompanied, paradoxically, by stagnation in economic output, making the domestic economies of the core OECD countries increasingly difficult to manage. This meant that mass markets for mass-produced goods could no longer be guaranteed in the metropolitan countries.

We could go on enumerating the difficulties encountered by world business in the 1970s — the environmental concerns that led to the imposition of statutory controls on emissions, pollution and mining practices; the worker health concerns that forced companies to comply with stricter standards; the quickening pace of technological change that made it increasingly risky to invest in long production runs with long payback periods — and so on. The point is clear that the 1970s saw the end of the heyday of the Fordist elements: stable growing markets for mass-produced, standardized goods were a thing of the past.

Now, the point of introducing a theoretical category such as 'Fordism' lies in our being able to use it to identify the essential characteristics of our industrial system and to be able to diagnose its crisis. It is the prelude to being able to formulate the outlines of a viable successor to this system. We seek to know, in other words, whether the current industrial crisis affecting the whole of the Western world (stagnation of markets, difficulties in innovating, stagflation, etc.) is caused by external shocks that in time will pass — or is it caused by internal developments that mean it will never be the same again?

The Fordist paradigm allows us to account for the general pattern of experiences in the 1970s, as the outgrowths of the success of the mass-production/mass-consumption system. This is therefore an *internal* explanation of the series of events that were experienced by the system as 'external' shocks. The paradigm gives us, in other words, a conceptual handle on reality.

It allows us to account for the basic successes of the Fordist system as the saturation of domestic markets for consumer goods, and the successful imitation of the practices of the core countries by the peripheral countries. Each interacted with the other. Let us trace how this occurred.

The saturation of domestic markets radically undermined the Fordist logic. Despite the frantic efforts of mass producers of consumer goods, who have resorted to such methods as aggressive marketing, advertising, building-in 'obsolescence', and creating or stimulating new desires, there are only so many cars, TV sets, washing machines or radios that people can absorb. By 1979, for example, in the US, there was one car for every two residents — and the road system had reached its absolute capacity. There just wasn't room in cities for more cars. As Piore and Sabel comment:

> Because of this saturation, it became more and more difficult to increase economies of mass production through the expansion of domestic markets alone. Further development along the trajectory of mass production thus brought the major industrial economies into direct competition for one another's markets and for those of the developing world. (1984, p. 184)

Market saturation was exacerbated by the rise of competing industrial powers in the periphery, who learned the mass-production game and imitated it most effectively. This was not a haphazard development, but one that was dictated by the very success of the mass-production model. Once a country exploits mass production to its own advantage — as was done by the US and then by Europe — it forces other nations to do the same or lose their independence. This is the basic contradiction at the heart of the system: *the more a production process or product is standardized, the more susceptible it becomes to emulation.* Its standardization contains the seeds of its own competitive destruction. This is why Eastern European and Far Eastern producers have been able to compete in Western markets for consumer goods, while holding market share in their own domestic countries, and gradually driving the previously dominant suppliers out of the US and European markets. The core countries could not prevent this from happening; indeed, part of their output was mass-produced factories and assembly lines for simple products, that engineering firms in the US, Germany, France and the UK were only too willing to supply to potential Third World mass-production competitors.

The spread of mass-production techniques and strategies only added to the glut of goods all seeking an outlet in increasingly saturated markets. This radically undermined the inner workings of the Fordist regime.

The various crises we referred to above can now be ascribed to a cause: they are manifestations of the *limits of Fordism*. What then have been the counter-strategies invoked by firms caught in this crisis — and can they overcome what appear to be insoluble contradictions?

Responses to the crisis in Fordism

The major responses of firms, and their political allies, to the manifestations of crises in the system, have taken the form either of an *intensification* of the strategy that seemed to work before, or of a modification of Fordism towards innovation and specialization. We shall refer to these strategies, following Charles Sabel, as variants of *neo-Fordism*.

Intensification

One significant variant of neo-Fordism involves the intensified application of mass-production principles by firms — expanding outwards, on a world scale; contracting inwards, behind heavy protectionist measures; or rationalizing and reorganizing production, utilizing computers, along Taylorist lines, in broader and broader sectors of the economy. All these strategies are evident in business trends today.

There has firstly been an intensified internationalization of production, with major producers in the core countries locating off-shore in the low-wage competing countries of South-East Asia and South America. Typical examples include the strategy to produce a 'world car' with interchangeable components manufactured in plants around the world; and the location of electronics firms' assembly plants in South-East Asian 'export zones' to utilize low-wage female labour without restrictions. While these 'out-sourcing' strategies have staved off collapse, they have not provided long-term relief, and are now being reversed. They have run into systemic obstacles, such as: rising costs and coordination difficulties in out-sourcing so many components; rising domestic opposition to the 'export' of jobs; rising inflexibility in missing national nuances in taste; bureaucratic inflexibilities in coordinating global production, assembly and marketing operations.

Further, the basic insight of Henry Ford and of the New Deal, that a mass production system needs to pay high wages to support mass consumption, is completely missing in this out-sourcing strategy. The *failure* of the Fordist system to be extended in this way underlines the significance of the panoply of social and economic support structures that underwrote expansion in the early post-war years.

As a complement to out-sourcing, some firms have pursued intensified protection of domestic markets, through erection of trade barriers (tariffs, quotas, etc.), through intensified efforts at stimulating domestic demand (large tax cuts), and through manipulation of currency values (e.g., maintenance of high interest rates in the US, despite huge trade deficits). This too has run into systemic limits in a situation where there are too many players in the world financial markets and where deregulation has ensured that they have access to all major markets. National protectionist strategies under these circumstances are doomed.

A third neo-Fordist strategy pursued has been one of rationalization and computerization, seeking through automation to further reduce wage costs and expand productivity. Intensified technological innovation has also been pursued, in a bid to open up new markets for mass production. There has been partial success with this strategy. The development of the micro-processor has opened up a whole series of new outlets and new markets — but again subject to the basic Fordist contradiction that success is quickly imitated, and the successful imitators soon become innovators in their own right. Japan is now unquestionably the dominant electronics innovator, while imitators like South Korea are set to challenge it in the 1990s. Computeriza-tion of production is certainly leading to productivity gains — but while it is applied along Taylorist lines, it quickly comes up against structural limits in the form of poor-quality goods or inflexibility of supply. The divorce of conception from execution — the basic Taylorist principle — has led to productivity gains in a simple mechanically-based mass-production system, but firms are finding that it represents an absolute *limit* to productivity growth in complex computer-integrated manufacturing systems, where worker flexibility and power of innovation are at a premium.

Innovation and specialization

An alternative neo-Fordist response has been for firms to pursue a strategy of *innovation* and *specialization*, within a continuing Taylorist framework. In other words, some firms have abandoned mass production in favour of specialty production, but have attempted to keep intact the Fordist apparatus of work organization, industrial relations and skills restriction.

Typical examples of this strategy are evident in the steel and chemicals industries. In the steel industry, over-capacity in the core countries and the rise of new raw steel suppliers in Japan and now the peripheral countries as well, has plunged former dominant suppliers like US Steel or Australian Iron and Steel into crisis. While some firms have opted for intensification (e.g., US Steel led the fight for protection against imports in the US in the 1970s), others have gone a different route, to mini steel mills with more flexible output, and to specialty steels. Specialty steels are aimed at small market niches and carry high 'value added'. They need to respond flexibly to changes in demand, and are produced in smaller electric arc furnaces rather than in huge blast furnaces.

In the chemical industry it is the same story. Basic staples like artificial fibres, pesticides and industrial chemicals (e.g., sulphuric acid, ammonia) were running into problems of overcapacity and oversupply as mass producers appeared around the world in the 1970s. While some firms have sought to cope with this by intensification, others have abandoned existing mass-product markets and are seeking to move into production of specialty items like rare earths, engineering plastics and ceramics, pharmaceutical intermediaries, and new yarns. The chemicals giants, like Dow, DuPont, ICI and Rhone-Poulenc, are 'tumbling over one another in the rush to get into specialties', commented the international trade journal, *Chemical Week*, in 1981.

Again, these strategies come up against the limits of the Fordist base on which they are erected. Specialization and innovation strategies place a premium on a highly skilled and motivated workforce — but this is incompatible with the Taylorist assumptions built into virtually all existing work organization, which is reinforced with computerization.

Limits to neo-Fordism

The twin responses of intensification and of innovation/specialization are thus running into the systemic limits of Fordism itself. Firms have tried to get round this problem with all sorts of 'work humanization' programmes developed in the 1970s, involving 'job enrichment', job enlargement and group work, as well as imported models like Quality Circles. We discuss all these in detail below — here it suffices to say that such schemes, for as long as they leave intact the fundamentals of Taylorist organization and do not allow for modifications in industrial relations, can result only in superficial relaxation of the 'rigidities' that are built into Fordist structures.

There is a limit to how far a firm can go in asking for loyalty and motivation and skilled innovation from a workforce that is consulted only in a superficial way. In the car industry, for example, some of the major producers have sought greater flexibility while maintaining intact their assembly lines; 'work humanization' programmes that bypassed the unions, or which stayed clear of industrial relations and basic job design issues, are now being abandoned. Even giants such as General Motors are having to look at alternatives — and they are now actively experimenting with totally new approaches (Streeck, 1987).

So, the twin responses of intensification and of innovation/specialization cannot be expected to recreate the golden years of the Fordist system. Nothing is predetermined however. No doubt there will be examples of successful neo-Fordist strategies, particularly in the emerging industrial powers of South-East Asia and South America. But the failures are likely to outnumber the successes.

The point of this discussion is not, to adapt Marx, to predict the future, but to change it. What I am attempting to show is that the dominant industrial system we have inherited, involving mass production of goods as its key competitive feature, is in crisis, and cannot easily be rescued. This means that the apparatus of work organization and industrial relations erected under Fordism, with its Taylorist fragmentation of jobs, deskilling and divorce of conception from execution, is becoming less and less relevant. *It was 'productive' and 'efficient' only under the very special conditions prevailing within mass production*. If these conditions cease to apply, then the rationale for such a system of alienating and dehumanizing work organization also ceases to have any foundation. Conversely, if the new economic conditions of specialist market niches and rapid innovation require a highly skilled and motivated workforce, to enable firms to be able to respond to the conditions, then it follows that treating workers seriously as responsible and adult humans, who are capable of making sensible contributions, is an *optimal strategy* for firms to follow. The participative and democratic workplace then becomes, under this reasoning, the most efficient and productive workplace.

These are truly momentous conclusions. They mean that the long-cherished aims of the labour movement, to dignify labour and the working man and woman, are no longer seen as swimming against the tide of economic efficiency and rationality. Social goals are no longer seen as being incompatible with economic performance. This is the significance of the crisis in Fordism, and of the current desperate search for a way out of this crisis. It means that the labour movement has a positive contribution to make, and in fact can play a decisive role in determining what sort of exit strategy is to be pursued out of the Fordist crisis.

This is the final step in our argument. What are the possible post-Fordist futures that can guide the labour movement's intervention at this strategic juncture?

Alternative routes to a post-Fordist future

From around the world, indications are starting to emerge of a willingness, on the part of forward-thinking firms, to depart decisively from the assumptions of Fordism.

New production concepts

The German industrial sociologists Horst Kern and Michael Schumann, advance the thesis that we are witnessing the appearance in core industries of 'new production concepts' — by which they mean post-Fordist concepts, that are no longer based on fragmentation of tasks, divorce of conception from execution, and subject to supervision and surveillance.

They argue that such a strategy is evident in core areas of West German industry — in the motor, chemical and machine tools sectors. They detect a strategy that is placing greater reliance on the contribution of skilled labour to productivity, reversing the previous dominant trend towards elimination of labour as a 'disruptive' and 'uncontrollable' factor of production. In their most recent text, entitled *End of the Division of Labour?*, they cite memoranda written by motor industry executives that spell out in detail the disadvantages to firms of staying with a labour strategy that divides tasks and divorces responsibility from job execution.[24] They argue that this trend amounts to a 'reprofessionalization' of production work, and they link it with an explicit market strategy on the part of firms to enhance the quality and diversity of products (i.e., an innovation and specialization strategy that departs from Fordist assumptions). They observe:

> There are today — one can confidently say, for the first time in the history of the motor industry — relevant restructuring projects, some of them already completed, that do not as a matter of course draw on Taylorist recipes and on the method of polarisation of tasks so dear to production planners in the 1960s. (Kern and Schumann 1984, cited in Streeck, 1987)

Kern and Schumann are realists. They recognize 'reprofessionalization' and the development of 'new production concepts' as employer strategies, induced by new market opportunities and the productive potential of new, computerized technologies. They do not see these strategies as evidence of a new form of 'humanism' or as a sign of 'weakness' on the part of employers. But they argue that the labour movement stands to gain by accommodating these strategies, and seeking to influence them. Their texts have attracted much debate on both sides of industry in Germany.

Human-centred manufacturing

The arguments of Kern and Schumann are complemented in the Anglo-Saxon world by a new emphasis on 'human-centred' advanced manufacturing systems, by such authors as Dr Mike Cooley and Professor Rosenbrock in the UK.[25]

Arising out of the experience of the Lucas Aerospace Alternative Plan, this notion has been pursued as an explictly post-Fordist industrial category. It is conceived as a general design criterion that will complement, and to some extent counteract, the usual implicit design criteria of efficiency and cost-minimization taught in engineering schools. It has now been taken up as a criterion in ergonomics and the design of advanced manufacturing technology.[26] More to the point, projects are now running in industry which are designed to demonstrate that 'human-centredness' is a productive and competitively successful notion to employ in advanced manufacturing.[27]

Flexible specialization

Piore and Sabel in *The Second Industrial Divide* locate the seeds of a post-Fordist future in the elements of craft production that have always coexisted alongside mass-production industries. They argue that the key to a crafts-man's skill lay not merely in the possession of a sequence of specialized procedures, but in the ability to take on a novel job and respond with an appropriate set of tools and techniques; it is the *flexibility* of response that is the secret of superiority of specialized craft production. For Piore and Sabel, it is this aspect of work which will be called on in future by operators of computerized equipment — leading to a radical break with Fordist methods of work organization. They state:

> Flexible specialization is a strategy of permanent innovation; ac-comodation to ceaseless change, rather than an effort to control it. This strategy is based on flexible — multi-use — equipment; skilled workers; and the creation, through politics, of an industrial commun-ity that restricts the forms of competition to those favouring innova-tion. For these reasons, the spread of flexible specialization amounts to a revival of craft forms of production that were emarginated at the first industrial divide. (1984, p. 7)

They give, as an instance of a flexible specialization strategy at work, the networks of technologically sophisticated, flexible small manufacturing firms in central and north-western Italy.[28] The claims of Piore and Sabel, while controversial, have been extremely influential in the 1980s.[29]

Diversified quality production

As an extension or elaboration of the notion of flexible specialization, the German sociologists Arndt Sorge and Wolfgang Streeck have introduced a further category of 'diversified quality production'. They argue that 'micro electronic circuitry has progressively eroded, in the course of the past decade, the traditional distinctions between mass and specialist productions.... The result is a restructuring of mass production in the world of customised production' (1988). Sorge and Streeck identify four distinct 'production strategies', organized around the distinction between high- and low-volume production, and between standardized price-competitive production and customized quality-competitive production. They argue that the term 'flexible specialization' is now too closely identified with the idea of small, indepen-dent craft production to be applied usefully to high-volume production.

Functional flexibility

All these post-Fordist production concepts can be described from the pers-pective of 'flexibility', as giving firms 'functional' or 'technical-organizational' flexibility.[30] This is seen as enabling them to respond at the micro level to external market pressures. The category of 'functional flexibility' provides a link between the mainstream debates on 'flexibility' and the literature that utilizes categories of Fordism and post-Fordist strategies.

There is by now strong evidence that all these categories are much more than 'rhetorical' or 'hypothetical' devices, but do in fact describe trends that construct a genuine alternative to mass production systems of organization — particularly in West Germany, Scandinavia and Japan.[31]

At this stage, all that can be said is that they are straws in the wind. They indicate a tendency, a potential — but they could be blown away by a major recession, by adverse political developments, or by adamant obstruction on the part of backward-looking trade unions. On the other hand, they represent tendencies that could be *reinforced* by appropriate strategic intervention on the part of the unions, governments and professional organizations.

For this is the point: the exit from Fordism will not be selected at random, but as the outcome of a series of political negotiations.

It would be a naive soul indeed who thought, because efficiency of computerized operations could be enhanced by a democratic work organization, that employers would rush to embrace industrial democracy. They will not. There are other routes towards efficiency, and they all figure prominently on the current political agenda.

The 'flexible firm' alternative

One strategy that is being pursued as an alternative to that observed by Kern and Schumann is for firms to adopt an innovative and flexible system of production involving an elite of highly trained and competent workers who are virtually manager-engineers in their own right. This is what may be called a 'skills polarization' strategy. In this case, Taylorism and its associated work organization is openly abandoned — but only for the few, and only then at the price of the total allegiance of this elite to the firm and its aims. Many of the firms operating in the new-technology sectors — computer systems, software production — are openly pursuing this sort of strategy. It either bypasses the unions, or engages with an elite minority, in order to ward off the majority. Under this strategy, there are still plenty of unskilled jobs to be done — but they will be done under Taylorist conditions or worse. Piore and Sabel have likened this approach to one resembling 'the old Bourbon Kingdom of Naples, where an island of craftsmen, producing for the court, was surrounded by a sub proletarian sea of misery' (1984, p. 279). Hence this strategy of 'polarization' may be dubbed the 'Naples' route.

Such a strategy will come increasingly to be identified politically with the New Right. It will depend on there being a weakened union movement unable to make claims for workers as a whole, or to advance a strategy for comprehensive national industrial development. It will be encouraged by incentives, such as tax concessions and training subsidies, that are paid for by the declining parts of industry and the general public. It will offer high job security for the few and casual employment for the many — and so it will seek to roll back social and unemployment benefits and keep social wage expenditure to a minimum. The role of government will be restricted to supporting technological innovation in a hard-nosed business manner, eschewing all social overtones to this process.

This is the strategy which the labour movement must defeat if it is to survive and prosper in the next century.

A labour movement strategy

In the face of the post-Fordist challenge, a labour movement strategy must draw on all the concepts identified in their various ways by Kern and Schumann, Piore and Sabel, Cooley and Rosenbrock. It will rest on a notion of *strategic accommodation* between capital and labour. Employers and unions may pursue their own interests, but with a *common interest* defined by the need to develop a flexible, innovative and efficient industrial system. We shall call this a post-Fordist strategy. The key question then arises: what is the appropriate set of policies that should guide industry, and specifically the labour movement, in its pursuit of such a strategy?

Nothing is predetermined; nothing can be taken for granted. No labour movement anywhere in the world has found a complete answer to this question. But much valuable experience is available to be drawn on.

Our task is to formulate specific policies around the issues of new technology, work organization, skills formation and industrial relations that will *favour* a post-Fordist strategy of flexible specialization, to replace the Fordist structures and processes currently existing.

The theoretical underpinning of such a stance is that technology and work organization is ultimately a social construct, the summation of innumerable choices made in the past, and susceptible to social influence, within certain limits, in the future.[32] This is to explicitly deny the validity of any notion of 'technological determinism' that binds industry to some predetermined trajectory.

We are at an exciting historical juncture. The chance to eliminate Tayloristic practices, and thereby release the creativity and imagination that has been dammed up in workers forced to submit to the discipline of mass production, has never been more real. But it will not happen automatically. Strategically informed intervention is necessary, organized around a politics of democratization. It is to contribute to the formation of such a politics that this chapter has been written.

Notes

1 An extensive literature on the labour process has been generated, much of it sparked by Harry Braverman, *Labor and Monopoly Capital* (1974). Braverman was an editor of Monthly Review Press in New York, and colleague of the leading US Marxist Paul Sweezy. He was a self-taught worker, and publication of *Labor and Monopoly Capital* (*LMC*) in 1974 was his crowning achievement. He died two years later, in 1976, having received the C. Wright Mills Award for his book from the Society for the Study of Social Problems.

For general surveys of the labour process literature, see: Zimbalist (1979) (a collection of studies of particular industries in the US, inspired by Braverman's *LMC*; the introduction by Zimbalist provides a useful overview of the debate on the labour process over its first five years); Thompson (1982); and Campbell (1983) (a 450-page survey of the labour process debates, which Campbell describes as a new and distinct 'field' of Marxist studies: his survey is oriented towards conceptual clarification and a critique of the notion of 'capitalist control' set against a simple notion of 'worker control').

In general, it is fair to say that much of the labour process literature of the 1970s and early 1980s has 'dated' quickly. The emphasis on 'capitalist control' has provided little leverage for the formation of a labour movement strategy of intervention. Nevertheless a number of fundamental studies of the evolution of forms of work organization have been generated: these are referred to in the course of the chapter.

2 For a useful overview of the literature on this topic, see Watkins (1987).

3 For key texts on this issue, see Mendels (1972) and Medick (1976). For a response to criticisms of the concept of proto-industrialization, see Kriedte *et al.* (1986).

4 For example, Mantoux, the standard historian of the Industrial Revolution, contended that 'the factory system was the necessary outcome of the rise of machinery. A plant with interdependent parts and which was worked from a central power source could only be set up in one main building where it could be supervised by a disciplined staff' (Mantoux, 1961, p. 252).

5 For an early statement of this point of view, see Marglin (1974). For a more recent assessment of the whole debate over the origins of factories, see Cohen (1981).

6 For an illuminating discussion of Marx's attitudes towards mechanization, see MacKenzie (1984).

7 The studies of William Lazonick and of Tine Bruland are fundamental in this matter. See Bruland (1982) and Lazonick (1981). Lazonick's account of the social relations surrounding the automatic ('self-acting') mule is in Lazonick (1979).

8 Lazonick goes on to comment:

> The craft control which mule spinners had developed on the common mule from the late 18th century was maintained well into the 20th century, despite the fact that any possible technical basis for such control had been undermined. In the transition to the self-actor in the 1830s and 1840s, minders were able to retain a dual role as

both operative and supervisor, not because they collectively forced this hierarchical division of labour on capitalists, but because capitalists had no leeway to experiment with new divisions of labour, particularly given the need for close supervision of younger workers. By the time capitalists realised that the special role of the minder as supervisor and recruiter of labour was forming the basis for re-emergence of an occuptation which, through its well-organised unions, could demand a 'craft' wage, they did not have the ability, even if they had the incentive, to significantly alter the minder-piecer system.

Lazonick's study shows the importance of attention to detail, and how much we still have to learn about the great transformations of the labour process that have occurred during the modern era. In particular, it shows that mechanization was not the simple cure-all that capitalists desired.

9 This case study is based on the post-graduate work of Raelene Frances at Monash University, Melbourne. See Frances (1986).

10 See Clawson (1980) and Littler (1982). Clawson examined the transformation of US industry over the sixty years from 1860–1920. Using such primary sources as the hearings of a special committee of the US House of Representatives to investigate Taylorization of work, particularly at the US government arsenal at Watertown, Massachusetts, held in 1912, Clawson has painted a plausible picture of the workplace subject to a whole series of successive transformations, all originating from the attempts by employers to gain access to the skill and knowledge held by workers and, through this, to gain control over the labour process. Littler followed a similar course, but widened his focus to make it a comparative study of the transformations of the labour process in Britain, Japan and the USA.

11 See Littler (1982). Workers fought the piecework system with bitterness. In 1912 there was a famous '*grève du chronometrage*' (time-study strike) staged against piecework, while in Germany a popular union slogan was '*Akkord ist Mord*' — Piecework is Murder. In the US around the turn of the century, the Machinists' Union was waging a campaign against piecework. Clawson notes that it was so widespread that 50 per cent of the strikes and 60 per cent of the strike benefits paid out were associated with the issue. But the figures on the spread of the system show that these struggles were not successful.

Another means through which inside contracting was eliminated was via internal union disputes. In Britain, for example, there was a celebrated clash at the Hawarden Bridge steelworks between the Ironworkers' Union (formed by the contractors) and the Steel Smelters' Association (formed in 1886 to represent the underhands). This particular dispute went to the Trades Union Congress for resolution, and the TUC sided with the contractors. Despite this setback, and a period that it spent outside the TUC in disgust, the Steel Smelters grew rapidly. As Littler notes, 'Wherever they secured recognition they soon succeeded in negotiating an end to internal contracting. . . . It was the collective pressure of the unskilled which was the vehicle of the decline of internal contract in numerous firms'.

This again shows that workers' unions are themselves major factors in the evolution of the organization of work.

12   For the definitive accounts of the rise of mass production in the USA, see Hounshell (1984) and Piore and Sabel (1984). These texts, particularly that by Piore and Sabel, have exercised a dominant influence on subsequent discussion of industry politics.

13   Taylor's life spans the transition from the nineteenth to the twentieth century. He was born in 1856 into a wealthy Philadelphia family. He was to go to Harvard but dropped out because of poor eyesight, and in 1874 began an apprenticeship as a pattern maker and machinist. In 1878 he took a job at the Midvale Steel Company and quickly rose to be foreman. It was here that he enforced a greater pace of work, but in the end had to leave because of his unpopularity. At the Bethlehem Steel Company he reorganized the handling of pig iron, using the unfortunate Schmidt as his celebrated subject. It was this experience that allowed him to formulate the principles of management, which he began to discuss in papers in the 1890s. By the early 1900s he was the dominant figure in the new 'scientific management' movement, and he and a small group of disciples were busy as consultants to companies through the period to the First World War.

14   In *Labour and Monopoly Capital*, Braverman's major contribution was to show what a fundamental role Taylor and his system played in reshaping the labour process this century. As Braverman put it:

> It is impossible to overestimate the importance of the scientific management movement in the shaping of the modern corporation and indeed all institutions of capitalist society which carry on labour processes. The popular notion that Taylorism has been 'superseded' by later schools of industrial psychology or 'human relations', that it 'failed' because of Taylor's amateurish and naive views of human motivation or because it brought about a storm of labour opposition or because Taylor and various successors antagonised workers and sometimes management as well — or that it is 'outmoded' because certain Taylorian specifics like functional foremanship or his incentive-pay schemes have been discarded for more sophisticated methods: all these represent a woeful misreading of the actual dynamics of the development of management.

15   Clawson (1980) discusses the impact in detail in the US, particularly on the auto industry (the Packard plant, for example, was largely 'Taylorized' in 1912–13) and on the US government arsenal at Watertown, Massachusetts, which was the subject of a special investigation by a US House of Representatives Committee in 1912. Referring to the testimony given to this hearing, Clawson makes the point that:

> The Taylor system went beyond simply making the workers' skill unnecessary: it was designed to make the production process *incomprehensible* to workers, to structure the situation so that workers not only did not need to understand the production process, *they could not understand it*.

As an example, Clawson cites the new system of naming tools at the Watertown arsenal. In place of the previous common names, tools were given code names and only referred to by these names in instructions. The intention was that in the end, workers would not even have a language to use to describe their work.

16 For an account of the establishment of the Ford assembly line, and the social struggle that surrounded it, see Gartman (1979).

17 As David Hounshell notes: 'Henry Ford and the Ford Motor Company were largely responsible for bringing mass production into the American's vocabularly and consciousness. Ford's ghost written article by that title, commissioned for the 1926 edition of *Encyclopedia Britannica* and published as a Sunday feature in the *New York Times*, defined and focused attentions on the expression' (1984, p. 303).

18 For an account of the battles fought in Australia in the 1930s, see Willis (1985).

19 The Italian theorist Antonio Gramsci discussed Fordism in his *Prison Notebooks* (1971).

20 The literature on Fordism as a global system encompassing a mode of production ('mass production') and a mode of regulation ('mass consumption') is now immense.

   Decisive contributions have been made in France by Michel Aglietta and by Benjamin Coriot (1979). These have given rise to a body of work now called the 'French regulation school'.

   For a general and penetrating treatment in the context of Third World development debates, see Alain Lipietz (1987). Very useful reviews of the concept are contained in the articles by Annemieke Roobeek (1987) and Rianne Mahon (1987).

   In the US, it has been discussed extensively by Sabel (1982) and Piore and Sabel (1984), in texts which have come to be as influential in the 1980s as that by Braverman in the 1970s.

21 For Marxian critiques of these innovations, utilizing the categories of 'labour process' studies, see Friedman (1977) (this work revises some of Braverman's theses, particularly regarding worker resistance and types of managerial stategies; Friedman coined the term 'responsible autonomy' to describe a management strategy alternative to outright Taylorization), and Edwards (1979) (a major 'revision' of Braverman by a leading US radical economist: Edwards takes the view that Taylorization was just one in a series of failed management strategies; however, he goes on to posit a subsequent form of 'bureaucratic control' which is not far from Braverman's notion of modern Taylorism).

22 For comprehensive accounts of the decline of the 'post-war boom', see Boyer (1988) (written from a French regulation school perspective, and employing the category of Fordism); and OECD (1987).

23 For an illuminating account of the post-war international financial order, and its present problems, see Wachtel (1986).

24 Kern and Schumann (1984). This remains untranslated into English. For a statement of their views in English, see Kern and Schumann (1987). For an extended review of their text see Sorge (1985).

25 Mike Cooley, one of the architects of the Lucas Aerospace Alternative Plan has made major contributions to the definition of a 'post-Fordist' 'human-

centred' manufacturing system. See his brief text *Architect or Bee?* (1980) and Cooley and Crampton (1986).

Howard Rosenbrock, professor of control engineering at the University of Manchester Institute of Science and Technology, has long been a proponent of 'human-centred' industrial design. His description of a number of years of work is contained in Rosenbrock (1987).

26 See, for example, the special issue of the journal *Applied Ergonomics* on 'Ergonomics matters in AMT', March 1988. In particular, see Corbett (1988).

For a specific application within computer-aided design, see Majchrzack *et al.* (1987).

27 Firms mounting such projects in the UK include Rolls-Royce and BICC.

On BICC's approach to 'human-centred' computer-integrated manufacturing, see Ainger (1988). A number of demonstration projects are being mounted in BICC Technologies Group factories in the UK.

These projects, and others like them, are supported financially by the European Economic Community through its *Esprit* project 1217 (1199), 'Human-Centred Manufacturing'.

28 For descriptions of the Renaissance of small-scale manufacture using advanced computerization techniques in Italy, see Sabel (1982), Piore and Sabel (1984) and the special issue of *The Entrepreneurial Economy*, July/August 1987, on 'Flexible Manufacturing Networks'.

29 A weakness of their position from our perspective is that they offer no explicit role for trade unions in their post-Fordist exit strategy, concentrating more on small high-tech firms that are the modern equivalent to previous craft shops. On the whole, they tend to regard unions as part of the Fordist problem, rather than as contributors to a solution.

The literature commenting on their thesis is growing. For a sympathetic review, see Lane (1988). On the other hand, there is much literature seeking to 'refute' Piore and Sabel, by demonstrating how much of industry is still determined to introduce advanced manufacturing technology along Taylorist lines. See, for example, Shaiken *et al.* (1986) and Bramble (1988). This literature misses the point that Piore and Sabel are not *describing* a dominant trend, but pointing to a *tendency* that could become manifest in the 1990s given appropriate conditions.

30 See the special issue of *Labour and Society* on 'Labour market flexibility'. In particular, see Meulders and Wilkin (1987).

31 On Scandinavia, see, for example, the report on the 'Development Program' (Swedish Work Environment Fund, 1988). On Japan, see, for example, W.G. Ford (1986) and Koike (1988).

32 In addition to the general literature on Fordism, there is a further literature devoted specifically to the links between the crisis in Fordism and long-term changes in 'technological regime'. Representative accounts of this point of view are to be found in Perez (1983, 1985). In the latter article, Perez makes the succinct but pregnant statement:

> The present period is seen as one such transition [from one technological regime to another]. The mode of growth that led to the boom of the 1950s and 1960s has run its course. The world must

now make the transition from a set of social and institutional arrangements, shaped by the characteristics — and fostering the full deployment — of a constellation of mass production technologies based on low-cost oil, to another capable of fruitful and appropriate interaction with a new system of flexible technologies, based on low-cost electronics (1985, p. 441).

References

AGLIETTA, M. *A Theory of Capitalist Regulation: The US Experience*, London, Verso.

AINGER, A.W.S. (1988) 'CIM — the human centred approach', *Technology in Action*, January, pp. 28–31.

BABBAGE, C. (1963) *On the Economy of Machinery and Manufactures*, London (reprint New York).

BOYER, R. (Ed.) (1988) *The Search For Labour Market Flexibility: The European Economies in Transition*, Oxford, Clarendon Press.

BRAMBLE, T. (1988) 'The flexibility debate: industrial relations and new management practices', *Labour and Industry*, 1, 2, pp. 187–209.

BRAVERMAN, H. (1974) *Labor and Monopoly Capital: The Degradation of Work in the Twentieth Century*, New York, Monthly Review Press.

BRULAND, T. (1982) 'Industrial conflict as a source of innovation: three cases', *Economy and Society*, 11, May, pp. 91–121.

CAMPBELL, I.G. (1983) Recent Marxist Studies of the Capitalist Labour Process — The Limitations of the Theme of Capitalist Control, MA thesis, Dept of Sociology, La Trobe University, Victoria.

CLAWSON, D. (1980) *Bureaucracy and the Labor Process — The Transformation of US Industry 1860–1920*, New York, Monthly Review Press.

COCHRANE, P. (1985) 'Company time: management, ideology and the labour process, 1940–60', *Labour History*, 48, May, pp. 54–68.

COHEN, J.S. (1981) 'Manager and machinery: an analysis of the rise of factory production', *Australian Economic Papers*, June, pp. 24–41.

COOLEY, M. (1980) *Architect or Bee?*, Slough, Langley Technical Services.

COOLEY, M. and CRAMPTON, S. (1986) 'Criteria for human-centred systems', *Proceedings*, CIM Working Conference on Production Systems, Bremen, May.

CORBETT, M. (1988) 'Ergonomics in the development of human-centred AMT', *Applied Ergonomics*, 19, 1, pp. 35–9.

CORIOT, B. (1979) *'L'Atelier et le Chronometre: Essai sur la Production de Masse* [The Workshop and the Clock: Discourse on Mass Production], Paris, Editions Bourgeois.

EDWARDS, R. (1979) *Contested Terrain; The Transformation of the Workplace in the Twentieth Century*, New York, Basic Books.

FORD, W.G. (1986) 'Learning from Japan: the concept of skill formation', *Australian Bulletin of Labour*, 12, 2, pp. 119–27.

FRANCES, R. (1986) 'Technology, skill and the sexual division of work', paper delivered to the seminar 'Work in society/Work in history', University of Melbourne, July.

FRIEDMAN, A. (1977) *Industry and Labour — Class Struggle at Work and Monopoly Capitalism*, London, Macmillan.

GARTMAN, D. (1979) 'Origins of the assembly line and the Capitalist control of work at Ford', in ZIMBALIST, A. (Ed.) (1979) *Case Studies on the Labor Process*, New York, Monthly Review Press.

GRAMSCI, A. (1971) *Prison Notebooks*, London, Lawrence and Wishart.

HOUNSHELL, D. (1984) *From the American System to Mass Production, 1800–1932: The Development of Manufacturing Technology in the United States*, Baltimore, The John Hopkins University Press.

KERN, H. and SCHUMANN, M. (1984) *Das Ende der Arbeitsteilung? Rationalisierung in der Industriellen Produktion*, Muenchen, Verlag CH Beck.

KERN, H. and SCHUMANN, M. (1987) 'Limits of the division of labour, new production and employment concepts in West German industry', *Economic and Industrial Democracy*, 8, pp. 151–70.

KOIKE, K. (1988) *Understanding Industrial Relations in Modern Japan* (translated by Mary Saso), London, Macmillan.

KRIEDTE, P., MEDICK, H. and SCHLUMBOHM, J. (1986) 'Proto-industrialization on test with the guild of historians: response to some critics', *Economy & Society*, 15, 2, pp. 254–72.

LANE, C. (1988) 'Industrial change in Europe: the pursuit of flexible specialization in Britain and West Germany', *Work, Employment and Society*, 2, 2, pp. 141–68.

LAZONICK, W. (1979) 'Industrial relations and technical change: the case of the self-acting mule', *Cambridge Journal of Economics*, 3, pp. 231–62.

LAZONICK, W. (1981) 'Production relations, labour productivity, and choice of technique: British and US cotton spinning', *The Journal of Economic History*, XLI, 3, pp. 491–516.

LIPIETZ, A. (1987) *Mirages and Miracles: The Crises of Global Fordism*, London, Verso.

LITTLER, C. (1982) *The Development of the Labour Process in Capitalist Societies — A Comparative Study of the Transformation of Work Organization in Britain, Japan and the USA*, London, Heinemann Educational Books.

MCKENDRICK, N. (1961) 'Josiah Wedgwood and factory discipline', *Historical Journal*, 4, 1, pp. 30–55.

MACKENZIE, D. (1984) 'Marx and the machine', *Technology and Culture*, 25, 3, pp. 473–502.

MAHON, R. (1987) 'From Fordism to ?: new technology, labour markets and unions', *Economic and Industrial Democracy* 8, 1, pp. 5–60.

MAJCHRZACK, A. *et al.* (1987) *Human Aspects of CAD*, Philadelphia and London, Taylor and Francis.

MANTOUX, P. (1961) *The Industrial Revolution in the Eighteenth Century*, London, Jonathan Cape, Ltd.

MARGLIN, S. (1974) 'What do bosses do? The origins and functions of hierarchy in capitalist production', in GORZ, A. (Ed.) (1978) *The Division of Labour: The Labour Process and Class Struggle in Modern Capitalism*, Humanities Press (also in NICHOLS, T. (Ed.) (1980) *Capital and Labour: Studies in the Capitalist Labour Process*, London, Fontana).

MARX, K. (1970) *Capital, Vol. 1*, London, Lawrence and Wishart.

MEDICK, H. (1976) 'The proto-industrial family economy: the structural function of household and family during the transition from peasant society to industrial capitalism', *Social History*, 1, 3, pp. 291–315.

MENDELS, F. (1972) 'Proto-industrialization: the first phase of the industrialization process', *Journal of Economic History*, xxxii, pp. 241–61.

MEULDERS, D. and WILKIN, L. (1987) 'Labour market flexibility: critical introduction to the analysis of a concept', *Labour and Society*, 12, 1, pp. 2–17.

OECD (1987) *Structural Adjustment and Economic Performance*, Paris, OECD.

PEREZ, C. (1983) 'Structural change and assimilation of new technologies in the economic and social systems', *Futures*, October, pp. 357–75.

PEREZ, C. (1985) 'Micro-electronics, long waves and work structural change: new perspectives for developing countries', *World Development*, 13, 3, pp. 441–63.

PIORE, M. and SABEL, C. (1984) *The Second Industrial Divide: Possibilities For Prosperity*, New York, Basic Books.

ROOBEEK, A. (1987) 'The crises of Fordism and the rise of a new technological paradigm', *Futures*, April, pp. 129–54.

ROSENBROCK, H. (1987) 'The combined social and technical design of production systems', paper presented to International Seminar on Advanced Information technology, Milan, October.

SABEL, C. (1982) *Work and Politics: The Division of Labor in Industry*, Cambridge, Cambridge University Press.

SHAIKEN, H. *et al.* (1986) 'The work process under more flexible production' *Industrial Relations*, 25, 2, pp. 167–83.

SORGE, A. (1985) Review of Kern and Schumann (1987), *Economic and Industrial Democracy*, 6, pp. 501–3.

SORGE, A. and STREECK, W. (1988) 'Industrial relation and technical change: the case for an extended perspective', in HYMAN, R. and STREECK, W. (Eds) *New Technology and Industrial Relations*, Oxford, Basil Blackwell.

STREECK, W. (1987) 'Industrial relations and industrial change: the restructuring of the world automobile industry in the 1970s and 1980s', *Economic and Industrial Democracy*, 8, 4, pp. 437–62.

SWEDISH WORK ENVIRONMENT FUND (1988) *A New World of Work*, Stockholm, Swedish Work Environment Fund.

TAYLOR, F.W. (1972) 'The principles of scientific management', in TAYLOR, F.W. *Scientific Management*, Westport, Conn., Greenwood Press.

THOMPSON, P. (1982) *The Nature of Work — An Introduction to Debates on the Labour Process*, London, Macmillan.

URE, A. (1835) *The Philosophy of Manufactures*, London, (reprinted, New York, A.M. Kelly, 1967).

WACHTEL, H. (1986) *The Money Mandarins: The Making of a Supranational Economic Order*, New York, Pantheon Books.

WATKINS, P. (1987) *An Analysis of the History of Work*, Canberra, The Curriculum Development Centre.

WILLIS, E. (1985) 'Trade union reaction to technological change: the introduction of the chain system of slaughtering in the meat export industry', *Promotheus*, 3, 1, pp. 51–70.

ZIMBALIST, A. (Ed.) (1979) *Case Studies on the Labor Process*, New York, Monthly Review Press.

Chapter 6

Life After Henry (Ford)

Robin Murray

During the first two centuries of the industrial revolution the focus of employment shifted from the farm to the factory. It is now shifting once more, from the factory to the office and the shop. A third of Britain's paid labour force now work in offices. A third of the value of national output is in the distribution sector. Meanwhile 2,500,000 jobs have been lost in British manufacturing since 1960. If the Ford plants at Halewood and Dagenham represented late industrialism, Centrepoint and Habitat are the symbols of a new age.

The Right portrayed the growth of services as a portent of a post-industrial society with growing individualism, a weakened state and a multiplicity of markets. I want to argue that it reflects a deeper change in the production process. It is one that affects manufacturing and agriculture as well as services, and has implications for the way in which we think about socialist alternatives. I see this as a shift from the dominant form of twentieth-century production, known as Fordism, to a new form, post-Fordism.

Fordism is an industrial era whose secret is to be found in the mass-production systems pioneered by Henry Ford. These systems were based on four principles from which all else followed:

a) products were standardized; this meant that each part and each task could also be standardized. Unlike craft production — where each part had to be specially designed, made and fitted — for a run of mass-produced cars, the same headlight could be fitted to the same model in the same way.

b) if tasks are the same, then some can be mechanized; thus mass-production plants developed special-purpose machinery for each model, much of which could not be switched from product to product.

c) those tasks which remained were subject to scientific management or Taylorism, whereby any task was broken down into its component parts, redesigned by work study specialists on time and motion principles, who then instructed manual workers on how the job should be done.

d) flowline replaced nodal assembly, so that instead of workers moving to and from the product (the node), the product flowed past the workers.

Ford did not invent these principles. What he did was to combine them in the production of a complex commodity, which undercut craft-made cars as decisively as the hand-loom weavers had been undercut in the 1830s. Ford's Model T sold for less than a tenth of the price of a craft-built car in the US in 1916, and he took 50 per cent of the market.

This revolutionary production system was to transform sector after sector during the twentieth century, from processed food to furniture, clothes, cookers, and even ships after the Second World War. The economies came from the scale of production, for although mass production might be more costly to set up because of the purpose-built machinery, once in place the cost of an extra unit was discontinuously cheap.

Many of the structures of Fordism followed from this tension between high fixed costs and low variable ones, and the consequent drive for volume. First, as Ford himself emphasized, mass production presupposes mass consumption. Consumers must be willing to buy standardized products. Mass advertising played a central part in establishing a mass consumption norm. So did the provision of the infrastructure of consumption — housing and roads. To ensure that the road system dominated over rail, General Motors, Standard Oil and Firestone Tyres bought up and then dismantled the electric trolley and transit systems in forty-four urban areas.

Second, Fordism was linked to a system of protected national markets, which allowed the mass producers to recoup their fixed costs at home, and compete on the basis of marginal costs on the world market, or through the replication of existing models via foreign investment.

Third, mass producers were particularly vulnerable to sudden falls in demand. Ford unsuccessfully tried to offset the effect of the 1930s depression by raising wages. Instalment credit, Keynesian demand and monetary management, and new wage and welfare systems, were all more effective in stabilizing the markets for mass producers in the post-war period. HP and the dole cheque became as much the symbols of the Fordist age as the tower block and the motorway.

The mass producers not only faced the hazard of changes in consumption. With production concentrated in large factories, they were also vulnerable to the new 'mass worker' they had created. Like Taylorism, mass production had taken the skill out of work, it fragmented tasks into a set of repetitive movements, and erected a rigid division between mental and manual labour. It treated human beings as interchangeable parts of a machine, paid according to the job they did rather than who they were.

The result was high labour turnover, shop-floor resistance and strikes.

The mass producers in turn sought constant new reservoirs of labour, particularly from groups facing discrimination, from rural areas and from less developed regions abroad. The contractual core of Taylorism — higher wages in return for managerial control of production — still applied, and a system of industrial unions grew up to bargain over these wage levels. In the US, and to an extent in the UK, national systems of wage-bargaining developed in the post-war period, centred on high-profile car industry negotiations, that linked wage rises to productivity growth and then set wage standards for other large-scale producers and the state. It was a system of collective bargaining that has been described as implementing a Keynesian incomes policy without a Keynesian state. As long as the new labour reservoirs could be tapped, it was a system that held together the distinct wage relation of Fordism.

Taylorism was also characteristic of the structure of management and supplier relations. Fordist bureaucracies are fiercely hierarchical, with links between the divisions and departments being made through the centre rather than at the base. Planning is done by specialists, rule-books and guidelines are issued for lower management to carry out. If you enter a Ford factory in any part of the world, you will find its layout, material, even the position of its Coca Cola machines, all similar, set up as they are on the basis of a massive construction manual drawn up in Detroit. Managers themselves complain of deskilling and the lack of room for initiative, as do suppliers who are confined to producing blueprints at a low margin price.

These threads — of production and consumption, of the semi-skilled worker and collective bargaining, of a managed national market and centralized organization — together make up the fabric of Fordism. They have given rise to an economic culture which extends beyond the complex assembly industries, to agriculture, the service industries and parts of the state. It is marked by its commitment to scale and the standard product (whether it is a Mars bar or an episode of *Dallas*); by a competitive strategy based on cost-reduction; by authoritarian relations, centralized planning and a rigid organization built round exclusive job descriptions.

These structures and their culture are often equated with industrialism, and regarded as an inevitable part of the modern age. I am suggesting that they are linked to a particular form of industrialism, one that developed in the late nineteenth century and reached its most dynamic expression in the post-war boom. Its impact can be felt not just in the economy, but in politics (in the mass party) and in much broader cultural fields — whether American football or classical ballet (Diaghilev was a Taylorist in dance), industrial design or modern architecture. The technological hubris of this outlook, its Faustian bargain of dictatorship in production in exchange for mass consumption, and above all its destructiveness in the name of progress and the economy of time — all this places Fordism at the centre of modernism.

Why we need to understand these deep structures of Fordism is that they are also embedded in traditional socialist economics. Soviet-type planning is the apogee of Fordism. Lenin embraced Taylor and the stopwatch. Soviet industrialization was centred on the construction of giant plants, the majority of them based on Western mass-production technology. So deep is the idea of scale burnt into Soviet economics that there is a hairdresser's in Moscow with 120 barbers' chairs. The focus of Soviet production is on volume and because of its lack of consumer discipline, it has caricatured certain features of Western mass production, notably a hoarding of stocks and inadequate quality control.

In social-democratic thinking, state planning has a more modest place. But in the writings of Fabian economists in the 1930s, as in the Morrisonian model of the public corporation and Labour's post-war policies, we see the same emphasis on centralist planning, scale, Taylorist technology, and hierarchical organization. The image of planning was the railway timetable, the goal of planning was stable demand and cost-reduction. In the welfare state, the idea of the standard product was given a democratic interpretation as the universal service to meet basic needs, and although in Thatcher's Britain this formulation is still important, it effectively forecloses the issue of varied public services and user choice. The shadow of Fordism haunts us even in the terms in which we oppose it.

Fordism as a vision — both left and right — had always been challenged — on the shop floor, as in the political party, the seminar room and the studio. In 1968 this challenge exploded in Europe and the US. It was a cultural as much as an industrial revolt, attacking the central principles of Fordism, its definitions of work and consumption, its shaping of towns and its overriding of nature.

From that time we can see a fracturing of the foundations of predictability on which Fordism was based. Demand became more volatile and fragmented. Productivity growth fell as the result of workplace resistance. The decline in profit drove down investment. Exchange rates were fluctuating, oil prices rose, and in 1974 came the greatest slump the West had had since the 1930s.

The consensus response was a Keynesian one, to restore profitability through a managed increase in demand and an incomes policy. For monetarism the route to profitability went through the weakening of labour, a cut in state spending and a reclaiming of the public sector for private accumulation. Economists and politicians were refighting the battles of the last slump. Private capital on the other hand was dealing with the present one. It was using new technology and new production principles to make Fordism flexible, and in doing so stood much of the old culture on its head.

In Britain, the groundwork for the new system was laid not in manufacturing but in retailing. Since the 1950s, retailers had been using computers to transform the distribution system. All mass producers have the problem of forecasting demand. If they produce too little they lose market share. If they produce too much, they are left with stocks, which are costly to hold, or have to be sold at a discount. Retailers face this problem not just for a few products, but for thousands. Their answer has been to develop information and supply systems which allow them to order supplies to coincide with demand. Every evening Sainsbury's receives details of the sales of all 12,000 lines from each of its shops; these are turned into orders for warehouse deliveries for the coming night, and replacement production for the following day. With computerized control of stocks in the shop, transport networks, automatic loading and unloading, Sainsbury's flowline 'make to order' system has conquered the Fordist problem of stocks.

They have also overcome the limits of the mass products. For, in contrast to the discount stores which are confined to a few fast-selling items, Sainsbury's, like the new wave of high street shops, can handle ranges of products geared to segments of the market. Market niching has become the slogan of the high street. Market researchers break down market by age (youth, young adults, 'grey power'), by household types (dinkies, single-gender couples, one-parent families), by income, occupation, housing and, increasingly, by locality. They analyze lifestyles', correlating consumption patterns across commodities, from food to clothing, and health to holidays.

The point of this new anthropology of consumption is to target both product and shops to particular segments. Burton's — once a mass producer with generalized retail outlets — has changed in the 1980s to being a niche-market retailer with a team of anthropologists, a group of segmented stores — Top Shop, Top Man, Dorothy Perkins, Principles and Burtons's itself — and now has no manufacturing plants of its own. Conran's Storehouse group — Habitat, Heals, Mothercare, Richards and BHS — all geared to different groups, offered not only clothes, but furniture and furnishings, in other words entire lifestyles. At the heart of his organization in London was what amounted to a factory of 150 designers, with collages of different lifestyles on the wall, Bold Primary, Orchid, mid-Atlantic and the Cottage Garden.

In all these shops the emphasis has shifted from the manufacturer's economies of scale to the retailer's economies of scope. The economies come from offering an integrated range from which customers choose their own basket or products. There is also an economy of innovation, for the modern retail systems allow new product ideas to be tested in practice, through shop sales, and the successful ones then to be ordered for wider distribution. Innovation has become a leading edge of the new competition. Product life has become shorter for fashion goods and consumer durables.

A centrepiece of this new retailing is design. Designers produce the innovations. They shape the lifestyles. They design the shops, which are described as 'stages' for the act of shopping. There are now 29,000 people working in design consultancies in the UK, which have sales of £1,600 million per annum. They are the engineers of designer capitalism. With market researchers they have steered the high street from being retailers of goods to retailers of style.

These changes are a response to, and a means of shaping, the shift from mass consumption. Instead of keeping up with the Jones, there has been a move to be different from the Joneses. Many of these differences are vertical, intended to confirm status and class. But some are horizontal, centred round group identities, linked to age, region or ethnicity. In spite of the fact that basic needs are still unmet, the high street does offer a new variety and creativity in consumption which the Left's puritan tradition should also address. Whatever our responses, the revolution in retailing reflects new principles of production, a new pluralism of products, and a new importance for innovation. As such it marks a shift to a post-Fordist age.

There have been parallel shifts in manufacturing, not least in response to the retailers' just-in-time system of ordering. In some sectors where the manufacturers are little more than subcontractors to the retailers, their flexibility has been achieved at the expense of labour. In others, capital itself has suffered, as furniture retailers like MFI squeeze their suppliers, driving down prices, limiting design, and thereby destroying much of the mass-production furniture industry during the down-turns.

But the most successful manufacturing regions have been ones which have linked flexible manufacturing systems, with innovative organization and an emphasis on 'customization', design and quality. Part of the flexibility has been achieved through new technology, and the introduction of programmable machines which can switch from product to product with little manual resetting and down time. Benetton's automatic dyeing plant, for example, allows it to change its colours in time with demand. In the car industry, whereas General Motors took nine hours to change the dyes on its presses in the early 1980s, Toyota have lowered the time to two minutes, and have cut the average lot size of body parts from 5,000 to 500 in the process. The line, in short, has become flexible. Instead of using purpose-built machines to make standard products, flexible automation uses general-purpose machines to produce a variety of products.

Manufacturers have also been adopting the retailers' answer to stocks. The pioneer is Toyota, which stands to the new era as Ford did to the old. Toyoda, the founder of Toyota, inspired by a visit to an American supermarket, applied the just-in-time system to his component suppliers, ordering on the basis of his daily production plans, and getting the components delivered right beside the line. Most of Toyota's components are still produced on the same day as they are assembled.

Toyota's prime principle of the 'elimination of wasteful practices' meant going beyond the problem of stocks. His firm has used design and materials technology to simplify complex elements, cutting down the number of parts, and operations. It adopted a zero defect policy, developing machines which stopped automatically when a fault occurred, as well as statistical quality control techniques. As in retailing, the complex web of processes, inside and outside the plant, were coordinated through computers, a process that economists have called systemation (in contrast to automation). The result of these practices is a discontinuous speed-up in what Marx called the circulation of capital. Toyota turns over its materials and products ten times more quickly than Western car producers, saving materials and energy in the process.

The key point about the Toyota system, however, is not so much that it speeds up the making of a car. It is that in order to make these changes it has adopted quite different methods of labour control and organization. Toyota saw that traditional Taylorism did not work. Central management had no access to all the information needed for continuous innovation. Quality could not be achieved with deskilled manual workers. Taylorism wasted what they called 'the gold in workers' heads'.

Toyota, and the Japanese more generally, having broken the industrial unions in the 1950s, have developed a core of multi-skilled workers, whose tasks include not only manufacture and maintenance, but the improvement of the products and processes under their control. Each breakdown is seen as a chance for improvement. Even hourly-paid workers are trained in statistical techniques and monitoring, and register and interpret statistics to identify deviations from a norm — tasks customarily reserved for management in Fordism. Quality circles are a further way of tapping the ideas of the workforce. In post-Fordism, the worker is designed to act as a computer as well as a machine.

As a consequence, the Taylorist contract changes. Workers are no longer interchangeable. They gather experience. The Japanese job-for-life and corporate welfare system provides security. For the firm it secures an asset. Continuous training, payment by seniority, a breakdown of job demarcations, are all part of the Japanese core wage relation. The EETPU's lead in embracing private pension schemes, BUPA, internal flexibility, union-organized training and single-company unions are all consistent with this path of post-Fordist industrial relations.

Not least of the dangers of this path is that it further hardens the divisions between the core and the peripheral workforce. The cost of employing lifetime workers means an incentive to subcontract all jobs not essential to the core. The other side of the Japanese jobs-for-life is a majority of low-paid, fragmented peripheral workers, facing an underfunded and inadequate welfare state. The duality in the labour market, and in the welfare economy, could be taken as a description of Thatcherism. The point is that neither the EETPU's policy nor that of Mrs Thatcher should be read as purely political. There is a material basis to both, rooted in changes in production.

There are parallel changes in corporate organization. With the revision of Taylorism, a layer of management has been stripped away. Greater central control has allowed the decentralization of work. Day-to-day autonomy has been given to work groups and plant managers. Teams linking departments horizontally have replaced the rigid verticality of Fordist bureaucracies.

It is only a short step from here to subcontracting and franchising. This is often simply a means of labour control. But in engineering and light consumer industries, networks of semi-independent firms have often proved more innovative than vertically integrated producers. A mark of post-Fordism is close two-way relations between customer and supplier, and between specialized producers in the same industry. Cooperative competition replaces the competition of the jungle.

These new relationships within and between enterprises and on the shop floor have made least headway in the countries in which Fordism took fullest root, the USA and the UK. Here firms have tried to match continental and Japanese flexibility through automation, while retaining Fordist shop-floor, managerial and competitive relations.

Yet in spite of this we can see in this country a culture of post-Fordist capitalism emerging. Consumption has a new place. As for production, the keyword is flexibility — of plant and machinery, as of products and labour. Emphasis shifts from scale to scope, and from cost to quality. Organizations are geared to respond to rather than regulate markets. They are seen as frameworks for learning as much as instruments of control. Their hierarchies are flatter and their structures more open. The guerrilla force takes over from the standing army. All this has liberated the centre from the tyranny of the immediate. Its task shifts from planning to strategy, and to the promotion of the instruments of post-Fordist control — systems, software, corporate culture and cash.

On the bookshelf, Peters and Waterman replace F. W. Taylor. In the theatre, the audience is served lentils by the actors. At home, Channel 4 takes its place beside ITV. Majorities are transformed into minorities, as we enter the age of proportional representation. And under the shadow of Chernobyl even Fordism's scientific modernism is being brought to book, as we realize there is more than one way up the technological mountain.

Not all these can be read off from the new production systems. Some are rooted in the popular opposition to Fordism. They represent an alternative version of post-Fordism, which flowered after 1968 in the community movements and the new craft trade unionism of alternative plans. Their organizational forms — networks, workplace democracy, cooperatives, the dissolving of the platform speaker in favour of meetings in the round — have echoes in the new textbooks of management, indeed capital has been quick to take up progressive innovations for its own purposes. There are then many sources and contested versions of post-Fordist culture. What they share is a break with the era of Ford.

Post-Fordism is being introduced under the sway of the market and in accordance with the requirements of capital accumulation. It validates only what can command a place in the market; it cuts the labour force in two, and leaves large numbers without any work at all. Its prodigious productivity gains are ploughed back into yet further accumulation and the quickening consumption of symbols in the post-modern market place. In the UK, Thatcherism has strengthened the prevailing wind of the commodity economy, liberating the power of private purses and so fragmenting the social sphere.

To judge from Kamata's celebrated account, working for Toyota is hardly a step forward from working for Ford. As one British worker in a Japanese factory in the north-east of England put it, 'they want us to live for work, whereas we want to work to live'. Japanization has no place in any modern *News From Nowhere*.

Yet post-Fordism has shaken the kaleidoscope of the economy, and exposed an old politics. We have to respond to its challenges and draw lessons from its systems.

First there is the question of consumption. How reluctant the Left has been to take this on, in spite of the fact that it is a sphere of unpaid production and, as Gorz insists, one of creative activity. Which local council pays as much attention to its users as does the market research industry on behalf of commodities? Which bus or railway service cuts queues and speeds the traveller with as much care as retailers show to their just-in-time stocks? The perspective of consumption — so central to the early socialist movement — is emerging from under the tarpaulin of production; the effects of food additives and low-level radiation, of the air we breathe and surroundings we live in, the availability of childcare and community centres, or access to privatized city centres and transport geared to particular needs. These are issues of consumption, where the social and the human have been threatened by the market. In each case the market solutions have been contested by popular movements. Yet their causes and the relations of consumption have been given only walk-on parts in party programmes. They should now come to the centre of the stage.

Secondly, there is labour. Post-Fordism sees labour as the key asset of modern production. Rank Xerox is trying to change its accounting system so that machinery becomes a cost, and labour its fixed asset. The Japanese emphasize labour and learning. The Left should widen this reversal of Taylorism, and promote a discontinuous expansion of adult education inside and outside the workplace.

They should also provide an alternative to the new management of time. The conservative sociologist Daniel Bell sees the management of time as the key issue of post-industrial society. Post-Fordist capital is restructuring working time for its own convenience: with new shifts, split shifts, rostering, weekend working, and the regulation of labour, through part-time and casual contracts, to the daily and weekly cycles of work. Computer systems allow Tesco to manage more than 130 different types of labour contract in its large stores. These systems, and employment and welfare legislation, should be moulded for the benefit, not the detriment, of labour. The length of the working day, of the working week, and year, and lifetime, should be shaped to accommodate the many responsibilities and needs away from work.

The most pressing danger from post-Fordism, however, is the way it is widening the split between core and periphery in the labour market and the welfare system. The EETPU's building of a fortress round the core is as divisive as Thatcherism itself. We need bridges across the divide, with trade unions representing core workers using their power to extend benefits to all, as IG Metall have been doing in Germany. A priority for any Labour government would be to put a floor under the labour market, and remove the discriminations faced by the low-paid. The Liberals pursued such as policy in late nineteenth-century London. Labour should reintroduce it in late twentieth-century Britain.

Underlying this split is the post-Fordist bargain which offers security in return for flexibility. Because of its cost, Japanese capital restricts this bargain to the core; in the peripheral workforce flexibility is achieved through insecurity. Sweden has tried to widen the core bargain to the whole population with a policy of full employment, minimum incomes, extensive retraining programmes and egalitarian income distribution. These are the two options, and Thatcherism favours the first.

Could Labour deliver the second? How real is a policy of full employment when the speed of technical change destroys jobs as rapidly as growth creates them? The question — as Sweden has shown — is one of distribution. There is the distribution of working time: the campaign for the thirty-five-hour week and the redistribution of overtime should be at the centre of Labour policy in the 1990s. There is also the distribution of income and the incidence of tax. Lafontaine's idea of shifting tax from labour to energy is an interesting one. Equally important is the need to tax heavily the speculative gains from property, the rent from oil, and unearned and inherited income. Finally taxes will need to be raised on higher incomes, and should be argued for not only in terms of full employment, but in terms of the improvements to the caring services, the environment and the social economy which the market of the 1980s has done so much to destroy. Full employment is possible. It should be based on detailed local plans, decentralized public services and full employment centres. It cannot be delivered from Westminster alone.

Thirdly, we need to learn from post-Fordism's organizational innovations, and apply them within our own public and political structures. Representative democracy within Fordist bureaucracies is not enough. What matters is the structure of the bureaucracy and its external relations. In the state this means redefining its role as strategist, as innovator, coordinator and supporter of producers. In some cases the span of coordination needs to be extended (notably in integrating public transport and the movement of freight): in others production should be decentralized and the drive for scale reversed (the electricity industry, education and health have all suffered from overcentralized operations). Public services should move beyond the universal to the differentiated service. Nothing has been more outrageous than the attack on local government as loony leftist, when councils have sought to shape policies to the needs of groups facing discrimination. Capitalist retailers and market researchers make these distinctions in the pursuit of sales, and socialists should match them in pursuit of service. If greater user control and internal democracy were added to this, then we would be some way towards the dismantling of mass-produced administration, and the creation of a progressive and flexible state.

Lastly, there is private industry. In many sectors both industry and public policy are frozen in Fordism, even as the leading edge of competition has shifted from scale to product, and from costs to strategy. In spite of the restructuring that has taken place in the 1980s, largely at the expense of labour, manufacturing competitiveness continues to decline. By 1984 only five out of thirty-four major manufacturing sectors did not have a negative trade balance.

The Left's response to this decline has been couched largely in terms of macro policy: devaluing the pound, controlling wage levels and expanding investment. Industrial policy has taken second place, and centred on amalgamations and scale and the encouragement of new technology. This has been Labour's version of modernization.

The fact remains that size has not secured competitiveness. Neither has a declining exchange rate with the yen, nor wage levels which have made UK one of the cheap labour havens of Europe. The changes are much deeper than this.

An alternative needs to start not from plans but from strategies. Strategic capacity within British industry is thin, and even thinner in the state and the labour movement. Sector and enterprise strategies need to take on board the nature of the new competition, the centrality of skilled labour, the need for specialization and quality, and for continuous innovation.

What public policy should do is to find ways of ensuring that the resultant restructuring takes account of social priorities: labour and educational reform is one part of this; industrial democracy another; environmental and energy saving a third; user concerns about quality and variety a fourth. Some of these will require new laws; others incentive schemes; others collective bargaining. They all need to be a part of strategic restructuring.

In each sector there will be giants barring the path towards such a programme. One will be the stock market. A priority for a Labour government will be to reduce the stock market's power to undermine long-term strategic investment (in this we need to follow the example of the Japanese). Another will be multinationals, who dominate so many industrial and service sectors in the economy. The urgent task here is to form coalitions of states, unions and municipalities across the European Community to press for common strategic alternatives at the European level. A third will be the retailers. In some cases retailers will be important allies in restructuring industry progressively (the co-op has a role here); in others the conduct of retailers is destructive, and a Labour government should take direct measures against them.

At the same time, Labour needs to develop a network of social industrial institutions, decentralized, innovative and entrepreneurial. For each sector and area there should be established one or more enterprise boards. They would be channels for long-term funds, for new technology, for strategic support across a sector, for common services, and for initiatives and advice on the social priorities.

Public purchasing should be coordinated and used not just to provide protection in the old manner, but as supporters of the sectoral programme, as contributors to the improvement of quality, and as a source of ideas. New technology networks should also be set up, linking universities and polytechnics with the sectors and unions (this is an effective part of Dukakis' Massachusetts programme).

In short we need a new model of the public economy made up of a honeycomb of decentralized yet synthetic institutions, integrated by a common strategy, and intervening in the economy at the level of production rather than trying vainly to plan all from on high. The success of the Italian consortia and that of the German industrial regions have been centrally dependent on such a network of municipal and regional government support.

A key role in taking forward this industrial programme should be played by the unions. Restructuring has put them on the defensive. They have found their power weakened and their position isolated. Few have had the resources to develop alternative strategies and build coalitions of communities and users around them. Yet this is now a priority if unions are to reclaim their position as spokespeople of an alternative economy rather than defenders of a sectional interest. Research departments should be expanded, and commissions given to external researchers. There should be joint commissions of members, users and other related groups, as well as supportive local authorities. The production of the policy would itself be a form of democratic politics.

Mrs Thatcher has led an attack on the key institutions of Fordism: on manufacturing, on the centralized state, on industrial unions and on the national economy. She has opened up Britain to one version of post-Fordism, one that has strengthened the control of finance and international capital, has increased inequality and destroyed whole areas of collective life.

There is an alternative. It has grown up in the new movements, in the trade unions and in local government over the past twenty years. It has broken through the bounds of the Left's Fordist inheritance, in culture, structure and economics. From it can develop — as is already happening in Europe — an alternative socialism adequate to the post-Fordist age.

Chapter 7

The Cultural Production and Consumption of IT

Leslie Haddon

Cultural Studies and technological products

Cultural Studies can add to our social perspectives on technology. This chapter begins by indicating the nature of the 'discipline' and the fields which Cultural Studies embraces. This leads us into a discussion of how our understanding may be improved through considering technology as a text. Emerging themes are then illustrated in relation to the British home computer market in general, and to the BBC micro in particular: we see how the microcomputer technology which appeared was the result of a cultural process shaped by various producer interests and visions. We then turn to examine Cultural Studies approaches to the consumption of the micro, charting in more detail the examples of the significance of computer games and the role of the hacker. The last section notes the broader applicability of Cultural Studies to the study of technology, taking us beyond analyses of specific technological products.

What is Cultural Studies and what does it mean for technology?

There has been only a limited amount of writing within Cultural Studies which has focused explicitly on technology. Even so, the strategy of this chapter is in no sense to review comprehensively the insights of particular authors who have tackled this topic. Instead, the main aim is explore some of the general approaches adopted within Cultural Studies as a basis for drawing out the key forms of analysis which the 'discipline' might bring to the study of technology.

The first problem is that defining a particular 'Cultural Studies' approach to technology is difficult because Cultural Studies is itself an umbrella term for a variety of approaches. These different strands originate from, and merge

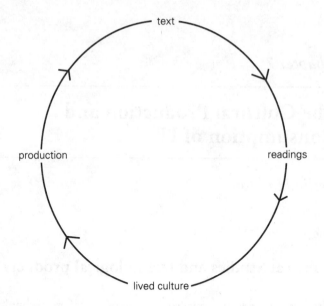

Figure 7.1

with, disciplines such as sociology, social anthropology, history, English and media studies. Alternatively, Cultural Studies can be defined in terms of the many theoretical traditions on which it draws, such as semiotics, structuralism, discourse analysis and psychoanalytic theory, together with Marxist and feminist traditions. In addition, Cultural Studies courses include borrowings from writers who may not necessarily conceptualize their own work as belonging to this field of study. In sum, the boundaries of the subject are blurred.

In these circumstances, a useful starting point for our purpose is Richard Johnson's attempt to define Cultural Studies and to locate different types of research within a wider schema (Johnson, 1983, 1986). Clearly, any one writer cannot capture all the nuances and subtleties within so heterogeneous a discipline. And his key themes are, of necessity, simplified in this chapter. Yet the strength of his writing is precisely that it does try to impose some coherent overview of Cultural Studies, and so provides a relatively easy introduction to those unfamiliar with the area.

Johnson suggests that we can view the various forms of analysis within Cultural Studies as addressing different stages (or 'moments') in the circuit of cultural production, as depicted in Figure 7.1. The cultural products (or 'cultural forms', or 'cultural objects') which move around this circuit constitute the focus of study. Past examples of cultural products which have been researched include TV soap operas (e.g., Hobson, 1982), public discourses about law and order (e.g., Hall *et al.*, 1978) and youth (sub)cultures (e.g., Hall and Jefferson, 1976; Hebdige, 1979).

Textual studies can trace their origins back to literary and linguistic analyses of written texts. Johnson refers to their important role in providing formal descriptions of patterns in textual cultural products terms of the analysis of narratives, of genre, or, in the work of semiologists, of signs. Cultural Studies analysts focusing on this moment in the circuit may be showing the processes at work in films, in music, in visual art or in the form and content of a TV programme, as they pull out the elements within the text and discern the various layers of meaning which are operating. But textual analysis extends beyond these written, audio and visual texts. Political arguments and imagery, public rituals and clothing fashions have all been treated as texts to be interpreted. The argument of this chapter is that technological artefacts can also be viewed as texts and that such a perspective extends our understanding of the social nature of technology.

Looking back to the previous moment in the circuit (production), we have the studies which focus on how and why cultural objects are constructed. Such research might include analysis of the political economy of production. An example would be an analysis of the institutional and economic considerations which shape the production of mass media (e.g., Murdock and Golding, 1974). While this is an important level of influence to consider, Cultural Studies analyses are more likely to focus specifically on 'cultural' production. That is to say, they would examine the way in which existing cultural elements such as ideas of national heritage, past discourses about the nature of education, or images of gender roles, are drawn upon by producers and embodied in new cultural products. It is possible to see such elements in the production of advertising, for example, but we should look at how they shape the very design of products — as will be seen presently.

The stage following the textual moment in the circuit shows the studies which highlight the 'readings' of texts — which examine how people from different social backgrounds interpret these cultural forms. One central theme of writing within Cultural Studies has been that although the text may have been devised (or 'encoded') to contain certain ('preferred') meanings, those interpreting the texts do so against a background of their own previous experiences. An example would be the different ways in which people interpret TV programmes (Morley, 1980). Hence, an audience can derive meanings which were not necessarily intended by scriptwriters. Equally, where the cultural objects are physical artefacts, people may use them in ways unanticipated by the manufacturers. A number of studies have called this process the 'appropriation' of cultural products (see Hebdige, 1979).

The fourth stage in the diagram shows the studies of 'lived culture'. These analyses examine the daily experience of particular social groups which forms the backdrop to reading texts. Here, we might be talking about the educational, work and 'leisure' experiences of young working-class boys or girls (Willis, 1980; Griffin, 1985), or about particular social movements or subcultures (Hebdige, 1979). Of interest in this chapter are the ways in which people encounter and use technologies or relate to discourses about technology, and how both artefacts and ideas are fitted into, or perhaps change, their daily experience.[1] Clearly, it may still be possible to talk about 'impacts' of technology to the extent that new commodities and services alter practices in everyday life; but it is important to remember that 'consumers' have an active role to play in this process.

To complete the circuit, various types of producer — from manufacturer to publisher to Government representative — themselves 'read' these everyday cultural practices. Producer interpretations might be derived from sources such as market research, media reportage or forms of personal observation.[2] The important point is that these interpretations feed back into further cultural production as new 'raw material'.

Technology as a text

Johnson actually uses a 'technological product' to illustrate several moments in his circuit of cultural product. In his description of the Metro car as a text, we can see how Cultural Studies emphasizes the symbolic dimensions of artefacts.

> The Metro was the car that was going to save the British car industry, by beating rivals from the market and solving Leyland's acute problems of industrial relations. It came to signify solutions to internal and external national threats. The advertising campaigns around its launching were remarkable. In one television advert, a band of Mini-Metros pursued a gang of foreign imports up to (and apparently over) the White Cliffs of Dover, whence they fled in what looked remarkably like a landing craft. This was Dunkirk in reverse with the Metro as nationalist hero. Certainly there are some forms — nationalist epic, popular memory of World War II, internal/external threat — that I would want to abstract for further, formal analysis (1983, p. 18).

Johnson then proceeds to the question of how these texts are read by various social groups, as opposed to charting the range of possible interpretations of these texts which professional analysts could derive.

> Supposing that we answered these questions affirmatively ... there would still be some unposed questions. What was *made* of the Metro phenomenon, more privately, by particular groups of consumers and readers? It would be unwise to infer this from public representations. For one thing, we would expect great diversity of response. Leyland workers, for example, were likely to view the car differently from those who only bought it. Beyond this, the Metro (and its transformed meanings) found some kind of lodgement in the ways of life

and subjectivities of those groups for which it had salience. It became a way of getting to work or picking the kids up from school. But it may also have helped produce, for example, orientations towards working life, connecting industrial 'peace' with national prosperity (1983, p. 18).

This second paragraph underlines the argument that 'consumers' or 'audiences' are not passive in their interpretation of texts or in their use of artefacts. Their readings are likely to structured by such social relations as gender, class, age, race, etc., but also by other influences within their milieux. In the example above, working for BL would be one factor which might well shape the way in which employees read these texts. Johnson's second theme in this passage then illustrates how cultural objects can subsequently enter into and become part of lived culture, reinforcing or changing orientations.

Clearly, this outline highlights the fact that the Metro as a cultural object consists of far more than just a physical artefact. Johnson notes:

> This raises interesting questions too about what constitutes the 'text' (or raw material for such abstractions) in these cases. Would it be enough to analyse the design of the Metro itself as Barthes once analysed the lines of the Citroen? How could we exclude the adverts and garage showroom displays? Shouldn't we include, indeed, the Metro's place in discourses upon national economic recovery and moral renaissance? (1983, p. 18)

In one sense, we can consider the Metro cultural object as being constituted by an ensemble of interrelated texts. Johnson has referred to the appearance of the car itself, the representations of the Metro in adverts and through the displays in the showroom, and possibly politicians' statements and the media portrayal of the product. These all add layers of meaning to the Metro.

Another approach to the same theme is to view technologies like the Metro as being open to numerous levels of analysis. One level that Johnson does not mention, but which has been the concern of many writers examining the social shaping of technology, is the functional design of the artefact — i.e., its structure and specifications. In the case of the Metro, we might be talking abour such parameters as size, speed and power, but also the tolerances of certain components which would have ramifications for reliability. Design of the capacities of cars can reflect an underlying view of what the image of the product should be — e.g., an 'economical' car, or a vehicle which is convenient for operating in the city. In the case of computer, the equivalent dimensions might be memory, speed, input-output facilities and the functions on offer. Cultural Studies analyses are hardly likely to say that the technological form fully determines the way people read these texts; nevertheless, what the machine is actually capable of doing is one element which enters in the way we interpret the role and identity of artefacts.

Next we have the industrial design to which Johnson refers — the shaping of the artefact in terms of appearance (see Forty, 1986; Fry, 1982; Goodall, 1983). This in itself can be considered as being one of the various dimensions which falls under the rubric of 'marketing'. Beyond the advertising mentioned above, which could be extended to PR in general, marketing encompasses elements such as the pricing, the support and servicing arrangements, and the channels of distribution, as well as promoting particular images of the company itself.

Finally, all these marketing considerations are not simply tacked onto the 'black box' after the functional design has been achieved. Marketing textbooks would certainly have us believe that these process are all integrated and flow from the 'product concept'. The actual integration may not be so neat, with re orientations of the product occurring during development, and with perhaps competing product ideas at work in the same commodity so that a technological product eventually emerges as a mixture of conflicting elements. The point is that we should not place too great an emphasis on the shaping of the technical dimensions of the product as the core concern. Rather, it is the underlying conceptions of the artefact which may make sense both of design and of marketing decisions.

Production

Johnson's outline was never intended to provide specific guidelines for analyzing technology as a cultural object. His analysis constitutes an attempt to provide a broad schema for conceptualizing the scope and methods of cultural studies. Hence, Johnson's rather generalized overview needs to be made far more complex and multi-layered when applied to particular technologies, such as microcomputers. The following section adds a few more issues to this picture, illustrating some of the elements which might be considered through examining the development of the BBC microcomputer.

Underlying conceptions

One first extra consideration is the interplay between a focus on any brand of product and a product family in general. For instance, to appreciate the significance of decisions about the BBC machine, this product has to be located within broader trends. Therefore, it is important to be aware of how other micros were developing.

Since the late 1970s, American manufacturers in particular had been considering developing a home machine which would be very different from that which was geared to the hobbyist market. They envisaged a multi-purpose product capable of providing information, entertainment, processing power, and perhaps later telecommunications and home control functions.

The computer would be regularly used by different members of the family and provide 'useful' applications. We can label this underlying conception the 'infrastructural machine' since the micro was supposed to become deeply embedded in the practices of everyday life (Haddon, 1988a, 1988b). Many of the later criticisms which claimed that the home micro failed to achieve its full potential (and became 'just a games machine') drew implicitly upon this ideal.

In contrast to this policy, which involved distancing the micro from its purely hobbyist connotations, the early products in Britain emphasized the key element of hobbyist interest — most significantly though the strategies of Sinclair Research. Sinclair, and to some extent Acorn, managed to initiate a mass market by selling machines whose main goal was to allow users to find out about computers. The underlying conception might be termed the 'self-referential' machine, in that the micro's central purpose was to enable examination of the workings of a computer rather than to deliver further benefits. While later machines offered actual applications, this goal of exploring the capabilities of the computer remained a significant undercurrent — even when games-playing came to predominate.

Many commentators saw the BBC machine as being the micro which most represented notions of an infrastructural computer in the British market. Yet Acorn's policy reveals an ambiguity between the two different conceptions of the nature of micros, which was made manifest in the ensemble of elements making up their product.

The company's self-perception and outside reputation was based around technical innovation and high quality. This 'quality' dimension was reflected in the fact that both the BBC machine and its predecessor the 'Atom' computer were designed with keys which resembled those of a typewriter (in contrast to Sinclair's cheaper membrane keyboards). The dimensions of the keyboard and hence spaces between the keys were also determined by reference to the standard size of typewriters. Such decisions were in keeping with a machine intended for regular and convenient use.

Meanwhile, the general visual design of the machine drew upon the 'wedge of cheese' shape associated with the American Apple computer. One requirement was that the micro had to fit neatly under a monitor. This partly anticipated a role in schools, but also reflected the fact that the home-based machine was supposed to achieve a constant location in relation to TV sets or monitors. The BBC micro was not intended to be be brought out occasionally and reassembled like most of its competing machines or video games devices.

Initially there were few advertisements for the BBC machine. The product was so successful in the first years following its launch that Acorn were already struggling to keep up with demand. But once adverts eventually appeared, the company went to greater lengths than many competitors to stress the multiple uses of their machine, and portrayed a variety of family members using the machine in the home (Haddon, 1988a).

On the other hand, the origins of Acorn in catering for a hobbyist market had left its mark. The fact that the company shared with Sinclair a certain emphasis on the micro as a self-referential machine was made manifest in several design decisions.

For example, the machine was supposed to help people learn computer programming. Hence, BBC Basic was specifically structured to encourage a good programming style. Acorn staff appreciated the fact that people did not only learn about computers through programming, but also through exploring applications — through exploring what could be achieved with the technology. Thus, it was seen as important that the micro was very open-ended in terms not only of having more functions than existing machines, but also of being expandable through the purchase of further equipment such as peripherals. This influenced Acorn's decision to provide so many input/output sockets.[3]

Lastly, using the micro to control other hardware was an area which potentially fitted in with both conceptions of the micro's role. The earliest application area which came to mind for one of Acorn's co-founders was that the machine might be used for controlling switches and devices in the home.[4] This was another motive for developing interfaces on the machine. Acorn had an advantage in this respect in that the company had previously been involved in a project to create a microprocessor-controlled fruit machine. The product needed to be controlled in 'real-time', which meant that Acorn had developed a form of the Basic computer language which operated very quickly. This expertise later meant that the BBC's Basic was faster than its rivals, but also that it was more practical for the BBC to control appliances. Apart from the fact that control of home appliances constituted yet another role for the multi-purpose BBC, this facility could also be seen as being yet another avenue through which users could explore the micro's potential.

The range of producers

Producers of meaning

Johnson's discussion of the Metro car example indicated the variety of agencies who 'produce' meanings around technology apart from manufacturers. In the case of the micro, discourses about IT in general and about its role in the future in the UK clearly set the scene for this product. In relation to the micro, of particular relevance here would be *IT'82* — the consciousness-raising 'Year of Information Technology', with its advertising campaigns, open days and exhibitions — the speeches of Government ministers, the British Broadcasting Corporation's Computer Literacy Campaign and the DTI initiative to finance microcomputers in schools (Linn, in this volume; Skinner).

Apart from supporting the appearance of micros in general, some of these initiatives were of central relevance specifically for the BBC machine. While BBC Enterprises often provides supporting material for its TV programmes, the BBC went to unprecedented lengths in the case of its computer literacy campaign by commissioning and lending its name to a particular brand of hardware.

In certain ways, the BBC interest in developing a micro shared some of the same ambiguities as Acorn with regard to the two different conceptions of the machine. On the one hand, the micro was seen as having a central place in the home, and as having really useful applications. The BBC did not want a micro which would end up being stored or thrown away. And the BBC negotiators certainly wanted a micro which was more accessible to the everyday user than many previous hobbyist-orientated computers had been. It was as important for the Corporation as for Acorn that later adverts portrayed multiple use and multiple users.

On the other hand, the broadcast programmes were ultimately part of a 'literacy' campaign and emphasized learning about the nature and applications of computers. For this reason, the programming features of Acorn's machine were welcomed, as were its range of options and expandability. In addition, the BBC commissioned a range of software to act as 'tasters' for their viewers and provide familiarity with potential application areas.

Apart from these contributions and role in drawing up specifications and negotiating the machine's design, the Corporation's involvement had one other vital influence on the meaning of this micro-text. By virtue of lending its name to the product, the BBC made this particular brand of micro respectable. The BBC computer was an 'official' machine whose capabilities and future were to an extent guaranteed by the Corporation's involvement. Further sanctioning of this micro took place when the DTI initially cited the BBC micro as the only 'home' computer which it was supporting in schools.

Interrelated products

Magazine, software and peripherals producers also contributed products which were symbiotic with the micro and which could be seen as interrelated texts. Amongst microcomputer producers, Acorn was one of the few to set up its own software arm 'Acornsoft' to support hardware sales. In addition to this, a veritable cottage industry arose around the BBC micro, encouraged by the computer's 'official' status, the clearly rising demand and the options offered by the machine's design. This support not only made the machine a safer purchase in terms of guaranteeing that the BBC machine would have applications, but enhanced the image of the micro as a versatile computer both as an infrastructural machine and, especially, as one to explore applications.

The major development which was to engulf the home computer market generally was the rise of games-playing and the narrowing of the micro's role to one of a games machine. Clearly, user interest in this application (as expressed by consumers' purchasing patterns and by the time spent playing games) was a key influence on the changing conception of the micro's role. This was an instance where there was a degree of user appropriation of technology — challenging the role, and therefore the identity, of the product as these had been intended by its producers.

However, the picture is more complex. On the one hand, all hardware producers were ultimately concerned by this development, since it threatened to lessen the perceived status and long-term value of their products. Consequently, there have been on-going attempts to promote other applications — such as telecoms or music synthesis — to break with the predominance of games. Yet, these manufacturers were always ambivalent on this issue. Commodore had, right from the start, hoped to take sales from the increasingly popular video games market. Nor were other firms averse to capitalizing on the demand stemming from the popularity of games. Hence as time went on, the various hardware manufacturers increasingly supplied programming manuals showing how to create games effects, while many adverts were designed to demonstrate the micro's games potential.

But perhaps the more dramatic producer influence on the course of the micro's developments was the support which games received from the software and magazine industries. The software industry became increasingly geared to games production and adopted a structure akin to the record industry with latest releases, tie-ins with films and TV, and sequels to best-selling products. Game production moved from being a hobbyist endeavour to becoming routinized and continuous. Meanwhile, the magazine industry developed many new publications which were either devoted to games, or at least increasingly geared to games. These magazines provided the advertising space for games, as well as the reviews, top-ten charts and other forms of publicity. These developments in the production sphere in turn reinforced interest in games, whose fashions could now be 'followed'. In these ways, various producers themselves contributed to the changing identity of the micro.

Different circuits

The last factor to consider on the production side is the case where a product addresses several markets simultaneously. This is particularly well illustrated in the case of the BBC micro which sold into the educational sector and, even more unexpectedly, into the business market as well into the domestic one.

Again, we can trace some of the influences on product development to Acorn's interest in the educational market. The company's system for networking BBCs, 'Econet', was designed specifically with the school market in mind. This Local Area Network allowed different micros in the class to use a single, expensive, disk-drive. But the LANs were also introduced because of Acorn's vision of future classroom interaction — where the teacher's computer would communicate with micros on students' desks.

Apart from these design details, it is the interrelationship between the educational and home markets which is perhaps of most interest. Most of the main home computer manufacturers at some stage made an attempt to get into the education sector. This market not only had the potential to deliver extra sales, but companies foresaw positive repercussions on sales to the home. This process was supposed to work in two interrelated ways. The first, which was particularly clear in Acorn's philosophy from the start, was that if children became familiar with a brand of micro in school, they might well remain faithful to that familiar brand in purchasing a home machine, or later when they wished to use a machine in adult life. Secondly, the presence in the school market added educational respectability to the home machine. The self-referential conception had meant that many micros, and the BBC especially, were pitched at the public partly as machines for learning. Presence in the schools market added symbolic value in that it went a long way to enhancing that message in Acorn's case.

Consumption of technologies

This last section discusses the readings which consumers make of technologies and the place of these products in everyday life. The aim is to provide some examples of the types of issue which can be addressed in relation to this moment in the circuit.

One question simply concerns the initial popularity of the home micro. This is not to say that the home computer is by any means a 'dead' product now — as some accounts would have us believe. But in the early 1980s, home computers achieved a particularly high profile for some years, in terms of media coverage and in daily conversation. In this sense, the phenomenon of the 'boom' in home computers encompasses more than just the fast growth in sales figures shown in those years. So why did a particular technological product attract such a degree of attention for that period of time?

The answer lies beyond any narrow utilitarian assessment of the benefits which the micro could deliver. For those who looked at the 'market' in these terms, the popularity of the micro remained an enigma. While part of that popularity arose from the link with interactive games, the micro was also a very symbolic commodity. While all products are symbolic, the computer took on a particular resonance for many as a frontier technology. The micro provided both electronic enthusiasts and a wider audience with their first chance to acquire a product which crystallized a new generation of technologies promising to revolutionize our lives. The pundits held out the vision of future electronic cottages, greater leisure time and opportunities, and high-tech lifestyles. The more negative appeal to consumers rested on contemporary fears about the impact of IT on employment and education. Acquiring and learning about the microcomputer could be portrayed as a way to avoid being 'left behind' by 'progress'.

While we can examine producer efforts to create such meanings, we also have to ask why the micro was accepted in these terms by users and by the parents who eventually bought machines for their children.[5] Such inquiries lead to further issues concerning how the acquisition and presence of the micro was negotiated within households — or in some cases resisted. The point is that it is as important to explain consumer 'acceptance' of a product as to explain either the rejection of such products or the appropriation of technologies for new purposes.

A related question concerns why particular social groups — including those drawn from electronics enthusiasts, computer programmers, and school teachers — should have embraced micros in the early stages of their appearance. These groups appear to have played in important role in establishing a market for computers before it achieved wider acceptance. But again, why should the micro have had a special salience for these audiences? (Haddon, 1988a)

Of relevance for the link between the home and the school experience of microcomputers is the wider autodidactic tradition to which producers appealed. The process of exploring implied by the self-referential machine meant that people learnt in their own way, at their own pace. From talking to school students I found that this whole process was felt to clash with much of the computing in schools. While some teaching approaches encourage individual experimentation, the classes geared to eventual computer examinations were often far more formally organized. Some writers discuss the home-school link in terms of whether possession of micros gives some pupils an 'advantage' at school. Yet, we could equally well view the micro as providing an instance where 'school knowledge' can be at odds with other forms of 'learning'.

Lastly, this hobbyist approach to micros also provides an example of the construction and maintenance of expertise. People define and build up expertise in all walks of life, and computer clubs were probably not so different from any other gatherings where people sharing a common interest compare and demonstrate their knowledge. But, in the case of computing, we have an example of an expertise which achieved considerable value amongst a wider community once micros became more popular. There were new audiences for the self-taught experts. Arguably, this situation is of particular interest in the school context, where students who invested effort in learning about micros not only developed a speciality which was legitimized among peers because of wider public interest. That expertise was sometimes greater or equal to that of many school staff, which constituted an unusual case threatening to subvert the normal pupil-teacher relationship. Under conditions where teachers were increasingly expected to become familiar with micros, some pupils' knowledge of computing carried more potential weight than their expertise in fields such as pop music or motor bikes.

We can appreciate further the possible dimensions of cultural studies issues by noting that any of these inquiries about the readings and use of micros could be formulated specifically in terms of a social relation such as gender. For example, if the promise of the micro referred partly to future labour markets, to what extent and in what ways was this felt to be of different relevance to men and women? And if the micro was for the children's future, is there any pattern to the role of mothers and fathers in instigating this purchase and supporting or controlling later usage of the micro?

When turning to computer hobbyists, greater male interest is explained partly in terms of the masculinity implied in representing artefacts as 'high' technology and as being at a technological frontier. But, in addition, studies of gender and leisure would suggest that in terms of such considerations as money, time and space, males were in a much better position to develop this particular interest (Haddon, 1988a).

Finally, feminist writers have already drawn attention to the role played by the notion of 'expertise' in power relations — especially 'technological' expertise (McNeil, 1987; Cockburn, 1985). Hence, there would be an interest in the way in which computer expertise is constructed and utilized in the school, clubs and social networks, and even within families.

This brief list of examples is intended to provide some indication of the types of issue which might well be of interest to Cultural Studies analysts and hence of how this approach may extend our understanding of technology. Two areas will now be outlined in a little more depth. Given that many writers discuss the impact of technologies on the social world, it is useful to provide illustrations of the ways in which consumers can construct meanings and patterns of use which were not totally anticipated by producers.

The first example concerns the rise of games-playing on the computer. This usage dominated to such an extent that the home micro has often been identified as being mainly, or merely, a games machine. In the second case study, I examine some of the issues surrounding software hackers — who might for the moment be loosely defined as people breaking into software copyright protection for the very challenge of this activity.

The rise of computer games

Returning to our circuit of production, one of the influences on 'lived culture' is the experience of past products. This is particularly important when appreciating the rise of games-playing on home micros in general. In this case, we need to trace the lineage of interactive games, and so to appreciate the circuits of cultural production involving these game forms.

Computer games originated before micros. The first arcade-type games were developed on minicomputers in the 1960s and 1970s as one of the first tools to investigate the potential of real-time 'interactive' computing. Later, they found their way onto micros. The key point is that games proved acceptable to the hobbyist-orientated computer communities as a way of demonstrating and exploring the micro's capabilities. Thus, hobbyists provided not only initial consumers for computer games products but also a core of people willing to produce these programs.

But it was the lineage through arcade and home video games which was probably more significant for the later popularity of computer games. When interactive games were transferred from computer centres to coin-operated machines, they eventually became a replacement for pinball. In the public space of the arcade, male youth in particular not only became familiar with games-playing, but the product became embedded in social processes already established in these venues — including the rituals of admiring the prowess of achieving high scores and watching and discussing tactics.

This set the scene for later home video games and for computer games, where swapping software could now be added to the patterns of interaction which had built up around games. It was the original social location of the arcade product and its role for this particular group which continued to influence the content and style of game products and later played a major part in encouraging greater young male interest in games on the microcomputer (Haddon, 1988a, 1988c).

Software hackers

The term 'hacker' has covered a range of different notions. Indeed, we might say that that the concept and role of the hacker has experienced a 'career', evolving through different but related forms over time. Hacking has at various moments referred to breaking into telecommunications systems, to infiltrating distant mainframe computers, or to removing the copyright protection from software. More generally, it has referred to a rather intense preoccupation with exploring systems in general and computers in particular (Levy, 1984). In all these cases, the supposed key to the 'hacker ethic' is that the motive is the challenge of mastering the system and, in most of the above instances, defeating technological defences. Other considerations are secondary. In keeping with this ethic, it was clear from my own interviews that some of those who amassed software collections by hacking, though breaking the copyright protection, had no time to actually use much of what they had assembled.

So how can a Cultural Studies approach address hacking? First, we have issues which have been addressed in earlier Cultural Studies work on subcultures — for example, on the lives and views of 'motor-bike boys' and their relation to their machines (Willis, 1978). How do computer users draw upon and use this past history of the hacker in terms of constructing their own subjectivities, their own sense of self? And McNeil raises a range of questions about the gender implications of this: about the relationships of hackers with others, and about the nature of their relationship with technology (McNeil, 1989). But we should also learn from one criticism of early subculture research. The complaint was that these studies focused too narrowly on a closed, core group for whom membership was a central part of their identity — rather than looking at how subculture diffused to a less committed, but nevertheless interested, wider audience (Clarke, 1982). So perhaps we should not be asking simply about self-styled hackers. In what ways does a broader group of computer users relate to this character with its varied imagery of a social rebel yet virtuoso performer who is dedicated to technology?

Hacking, especially breaking into mainframes, has received considerable media coverage given the limited number of people involved. TV, newspapers and even films seem to find the whole area fascinating.[6] These media locate hackers at the frontier of expertise, as the individual (young) male defeating the massive resources of large corporations — with no harm done since it was all in fun (although this may soon change with the recent coverage of computer viruses). The hacker has become something of a folk hero, albeit an ambiguous one at times when portrayed as someone 'too' obsessed with machines. Even on the smaller scale of software hacking, peers can admire the prowess of breaking copyright protection with much the same sentiment as their mainframe-infiltrating counterparts.

Yet those whose computer systems or products are hacked regard the matter as serious. Certainly, concern is shown within the computer trade press about security and assumed loss of software sales. At stake is control of technologies as these consumers have gone further than the role expected of them. Most significantly, hackers challenge the principle of authors' and publishers' property rights to their products, refusing to recognize breaking into software protection as in any sense 'stealing' revenue. The problem for software producers, and for others whose products are broken into, is that hacking has at the moment achieved the status of respectable deviance which it is problematic to thoroughly criminalize. Thus, the idea of the hacker is a highly symbolic construct, though lived out by actual people, and it is worthy of study as a cultural phenomenon in its own right.

Technology-related studies

This paper has focused on technological artefacts. However, Cultural Studies analysts have a potentially broader interest in technology. For example, public discussions of technology and institutional change relating to technology could equally well be studied as cultural phenomena or objects in their own right.

In her outline of potential cultural issues relating to IT, McNeil notes how we could examine images of, and debates about, Information Technology in general. This might involve examining various futurological texts, science fiction, media coverage or international reports (McNeil, 1989).

Alternatively, the focus might be the specific discourses about IT in Britain. This could involve exploring the pronouncements of the Government and Opposition, or tracing the development of state-organized initiatives based around Information Technology — such as IT Year, IT for the disabled, IT for business, etc. McNeil also draws attention to the historical processes which brought debates about Information Technology to the public eye — such as the appearance of the home computer itself (McNeil, 1989).

More narrowly, we might study the introduction of IT into the education system. This might encompass particular reference to the entry into schools of computer technology (Linn, in this volume), but also examine ideas about using technology for distance learning or introducing a greater technological orientation onto the curriculum (Robins and Webster, 1987).

In other words, there are many dimensions of technology which can be examined by Cultural Studies, only one of which is the development of particular technological commodities. In any particular piece of research, some of the aspects are inevitably rendered as background considerations, to which others take centre stage. For example, in the study of the home micro's history on which this chapter is based, some of the wider discussions of IT futures are discussed only as part of the context for specific product developments, whereas another writer might well change the emphasis and discuss the way in which a particular product such as the micro contributed to broad futurological visions.

The last proviso to bear in mind is that most Cultural Studies research focuses on particular issues when 'interrogating' an area of study. For example, the history of the microcomputer might be examined in terms of gender issues, especially since several writers had referred to this commodity as a 'masculine technology' (Cockburn, 1985; Zimmerman, 1986). However, as McNeil notes, it would also be possible to ask about the male-orientatedness of the more futurological visions, to explore the gendered images of IT in Britain, or to analyze the implementation of IT in schools in terms of its implications for male and female staff and students. Hence, focusing on any one of these dimensions — such as gender and the home micro — provides only a contribution to what is a wider set of processes.

Summary

This discussion has not attempted to encompass all aspects of Cultural Studies analysis of technology. I have not tried to provide a history of writings in the field — which might well be taken to start with Williams' social history of television (Williams, 1974). Nor has there been any attempt to examine some strands such as the more psychoanalytically based analyses or to broach the issue of how artefacts are conceptualized as 'technologies' at all. However, an outline of some of the main concerns of this intellectual field indicate how the approaches of Cultural Studies can contribute to an understanding of technology.

The chapter started by noting that it is problematic even to define a

'Cultural Studies' discipline. Johnson's outline of a circuit of cultural production provides one useful overview, even though he only refers to technology by way of illustrating broader points. We saw some of the ways in which this schema can be elaborated when applied specifically to the area of technology.

The example of the BBC microcomputer was used both to illustrate the types of analysis which Cultural Studies might undertake and to further refine Johnson's schema for this particular area. This entailed discussions of:

(a) how we need to consider the development of micros in general as well as that of particular brands
(b) the role of other agencies besides the manufacturers
(c) the influence of interrelated products
(d) the different markets and hence circuits of production, in which the same product may be involved.

In this section, we saw the range of elements which constitute a 'technological product' and how these were shaped in the case of the BBC.

Next, we turned to the 'consumption' of technologies — a shorthand for the remaining elements in Johnston's circuit. The research here is less developed. So, the aim was to provide some illustrations from the history of the micros concerning the kinds of issues where Cultural Studies can broaden our understanding of technology. The outline of the rise of games and of software hackers provided more detailed examples of how we might formulate both the research issues and the types of analysis.

Although this chapter has dealt with the analysis of technological products, the final section aims to put such studies into context. Other technology-related cultural objects could also become relevant objects of study. Previously, we had seen how the social construction of the 'hacker' could be a project in its own right. Hence, Cultural Studies approaches have the potential to develop a broad range of insights pertaining to technology, despite the fact that the discipline has only engaged with this field of study to a limited extent so far.

Notes

1 Television (and for that matter cinema and radio) provide complex examples here since we have to simultaneously consider how people relate to and use both the technology and the texts (i.e., programmes) carried by that technology. Analyses of the control of TV and video technologies within families and how they are fitted into everyday life are provided in Morley (1986) and Gray (1987).
2 Current research on such producer conceptions of consumers is being conducted by A. Cawson, L. Haddon and I. Miles in the 'Delivering IT into the Home' project at Sussex University.
3 This same philosophy has influenced the design of the planned Keyline home

shopping being developed by the company of one of Acorn's founders, Chris Curry.
4 Curry continued this interest after he had left Acorn with his 'Red Box' home control system.
5 This is currently being investigated by D. Skinner and a PICT project at CRICT, Brunel University.
6 See, for example, the film 'Wargames'.

References

CLARKE, G. (1982) *Defending Ski-jumpers: A Critique of Theories of Youth Sub-Culture*, Stencilled paper, No. 71, Birmingham, Centre for Contemporary Cultural Studies.

COCKBURN, C. (1985) *Machinery of Dominance: Women, Men and Technical Know-how*, London, Pluto Press.

FORTY, A. (1986) *Objects of Desire: Design and Society 1750–1980*, London, Thames and Hudson.

FRY, T. (1982) 'Unpacking the typewriter', *Block*, 7, pp. 36–47, Polytechnic of Central London.

GOODALL, P. (1983) 'Design and gender', *Block*, 9, pp. 50–61, Polytechnic of Central London.

GRAY, A. (1987) 'Women and video', in BAEHR, H. and DYER, G. (Eds) *Boxed In: Woman On and In Television*, London, Routledge and Kegan Paul.

GRIFFIN, C. (1985) *Typical Girls: Young Women from School to the Job Market*, London, Routledge and Kegan Paul.

HADDON, L. (1988a) 'The Roots and Early History of the UK Home Computer Market: Origins of the Masculine Micro', PhD thesis, London, Imperial College, University of London.

HADDON, L. (1988b) 'The home computer: the making of a consumer electronic', *Science as Culture* 2, pp. 7–51, London, Free Association Books.

HADDON, L. (1988c) 'Electronic and computer games: the history of an interactive medium', *Screen*, 29, 21, pp. 52–73.

HALL, S. and JEFFERSON, T. (Eds) (1976) *Resistance Through Rituals: Youth Subcultures in Post-war Britain*, London, Hutchinson.

HALL, S. *et al.* (1978) *Policing the Crisis: Mugging, the State and Law and Order*, London, Macmillan.

HEBDIGE, D. (1979) *Subculture: The Meaning of Style*, New York, Methuen.

HOBSON, D. (1982) *Crossroads: Drama of a Soap Opera*, London, Methuen.

JOHNSON, R. (1983) *What is Cultural Studies Anyway?*, stencilled paper No. 74, Birmingham, Centre for Contemporary Cultural Studies, University of Birmingham.

JOHNSON, R. (1986) 'The story so far: and further transformations?', in PUNTER, D. (Ed.) *Introduction to Contemporary Cultural Studies*, Marlow, Longman.

LEVY, S. (1984) *Hackers: Heros of the Revolution*, Garden City, Doubleday.

MCNEIL, M. (1987) *Gender and Expertise*, London, Free Association Books.

MCNEIL, M. (1989) 'Turing's Men, Cyborgs and Wise Women: Information Technology, Gender and Culture', paper given at the PICT Gender and IT workshop, Eastbourne, May.

MORLEY, D. (1980) *The Nationwide Audience*, London, BFI.

MORLEY, D. (1986) *Family Television*, London, Comedia.

MURDOCK, G. and GOLDING, P. (1974) 'For a political economy of mass communications', in MILIBAND, R. and SAVILLE, J. (Eds) *The Socialist Register 1973*, London, Merlin Press.

ROBINS, K. and WEBSTER, F. (1987) 'Dangers of information technology and responsibilities of education', in FINNEGAN, R. *et al.* (Eds) *Information Technology: Social Issues*, Sevenoaks, Hodder and Stoughton.

SKINNER, D., ongoing PhD, CRICT, Brunel University, Uxbridge.

WILLIAMS, R. (1974) *Television Technology and Cultural Form*, Glasgow, Fontana/Collins.

WILLIS, P. (1978) *Profane Culture*, London, Routledge and Kegan Paul.

WILLIS, P. (1980) *Learning to Labour*, Farnborough, Gower.

ZIMMERMAN, J. (1986) *Once Upon a Time: A Woman's Guide to Tomorrow's Technology*, New York, Pandora.

Chapter 8

A Dialectics of Determinism: Deconstructing Information Technology[1]

Paul Dowling

> John Stuart Mill says in his *Principles of Political Economy*: 'It is questionable if all the mechanical inventions yet made have lightened the day's toil of any human being.' (Marx, 1976, p. 492)

In his book *Turing's Man*, David Bolter (1984) proposes that, in various historical conjunctures, particular key technologies — the potter's wheel, the clock — have lent a certain cultural unity to their respective societies, and have thus acquired the status of 'defining technologies'. Bolter considers that the place of defining technology in our current era has been taken by the computer, hence the title of the book.[2] Reflecting upon my own activities as an academic within the field of education, Bolter's image is not without appeal: in an area which, perhaps, would not immediately be thought of as high-tech, I nevertheless perform much of my work with the 'assistance' of a computer (one in my office, one at home and a laptop in case I'm somewhere in between) and would be most reluctant to do away with these 'labour-saving' devices. Furthermore, computers have entered the content of my work through, for example, penetration by models of 'artificial' intelligence as paradigms for the ways in which people think and learn (see, for example, Davis, 1984; Lawler, 1985; Minsky, 1987). In a study which extends a little beyond my everyday experience, Lazerson *et al.* place the spotlight clearly on computer technology.

> Computers are likely to alter our lives. They are already dramatically affecting the workplace, changing the number and kinds of jobs available. They are affecting our home and our leisure activities. They are modifying the ways we receive and store information and how we define problems and communicate. They may affect the distribution of power and authority. (Lazerson *et al.*, 1985, p. 84)

An unremarkable statement, perhaps; except that it actually makes better sense if we replace the word 'computers' with a term indicating a person or a group of people: 'the *new management* are likely to alter our lives ...', for example. The authors of this statement are attributing to 'computers' the sort of agency that sits happier with human beings. It is *computers* that are going to change the number and kinds of jobs that are available, presumably by substituting themselves for human workers (changing the number of jobs) and by reorganizing various aspects of the labour process (changing the kinds of jobs). By their excision of the human agent, Lazerson and his colleagues are engaging in *technological determinism* which, in this conception, comprises the attribution to technology of two kinds of agency: firstly, the potential to substitute for human labour; and secondly, the ability to *preconceptualize*[3] the mode of working.

That which at first appeared to be an unremarkable statement now becomes remarkable indeed, but how can such a statement be made? How is it that we can so calmly attribute transformative agency to an inanimate object? Indeed, how is it that we can talk about 'computers' or 'computer technology' or — especially, perhaps — 'Information Technology' as if these constituted a unity? In addressing these questions, I shall attempt to move towards a dialectical analysis of technological determinism in its dual aspects of substitution and preconceptualization. I want to examine these firstly with respect to strictly economic activity, and then within the context of schooling, the latter constituting a major site of ideological reproduction; finally, and in keeping with the dialectical nature of this analysis, I want to offer some tentative suggestions in terms of action for those of us who operate within the educational system.

Substitution and the division of labour

There is clearly a sense in which technology can be understood as potentially substituting for human labour: it may, for example, take three adults to raise a heavy weight working only with their own physical strength whilst a single individual might achieve the same result with the aid of a pulley system and rope, these having thereby 'substituted for' two of the adults. Paul Olson points to the sort of concerns that he feels we should have regarding such 'gains in productivity':

> ... this euphemism practically means substituting capital for labor; or substituting cheap labor for expensive labor. In practice this takes several forms. First, industrial processes are automated or mechanized when technology such as robotics and integrated assembly lines can make them more productive. Second, substituting capital for labor is a vital strategy in the rapidly growing service sector, where work now done by secretaries and file clerks will be eventually done by office

technology (word processing, automated filing, answering services, etc.). (Olson, 1987, p. 189)

Thus Olson proposes that an effect of the introduction of technology is a reduction in the production and clerical workforces, and indeed we can find this in the United States: production and related workers in manufacturing reducing from 13.2 per cent to 10.4 per cent of the total active labour between 1980 and 1987, and clerical and related workers in the same sector reducing from 2.6 per cent to 2.0 per cent over the same period.[4] In addition, Olson argues that new technology enables use to be made of cheap 'Third World'[5] labour through such devices as teleports. But what Olson's analysis ignores is that the very machinery that is used to substitute for file clerks or to make production workers more efficient, indeed the pulley and rope in my earlier example, are themselves the products of labour, what Marx referred to as *dead* labour which, like any other product, must be continually reproduced. Furthermore, it is the circumstances of the production and reproduction of this dead labour that gives the lie to the notion of substitution.

Firstly, the technology which is dead labour is the product of an international 'cooperation'. The design engineers (including programmers, in the case of computer technology), producers of raw materials (smelters of iron ore, oil refiners, etc.), workers involved in mining and other extraction industries, and agricultural workers (the others must all be fed) are distributed globally and remunerated at rates structured on the basis of a metropolitan-periphery division (in which the 'metropolis' consists of the US and Canada, most of Europe, Australia, etc.) and, within this division, on gender, race and class lines. The overall effect of this division of labour is the locating of the bulk of the efforts in the production of technology in the poorer parts of the world where they are provided by the poorer individuals in those areas, and the distribution of the bulk of the rewards to the richer individuals in the richer countries: in terms of surplus value, it need not be only the capitalist who benefits.[6]

Secondly, however, such a complex and widespread division of labour must be organized and, as Robins and Webster (1989) have argued, this organization is predicated on the development of sophisticated information-handling systems which allow, for example, the decentralization of production on a global basis; this, of course, constitutes a further development of the international division of labour. We might think of the development of Information Technology within a kind of *qawwali*[7] between the forces and the relations of production: the former arising from the oppressive cooperation of a developing division of labour, and facilitating ever more expansion and subdivisions within the latter; the computer emerges as simply a crescendo of the *qawwali*.

In other words, the Computer-Numerical-Control (CNC) machine that adumbrates redundancy on the shop floor is nothing, in itself, nothing but a signifier that the labour process is now moving (partially, at least) outside the factory and into the mines, fields, oil-rigs, research laboratories, etc., of the world at large. How is it, then, that we can come to understand it as a thing in itself, let alone something that is substituting itself for human beings? I suggest that the answer lies, once again, in the division of labour — that which is signified by the machine — the machine, in fact, becomes a text which is differentiated by and for the division of labour. Very simply, the different groups of workers that produce and reproduce the machine (and thus the 'labour' it performs on their behalf) are necessarily confronted by the machine in forms which relate to their respective contributions to it. For many workers — agricultural and mining workers, for example — the CNC machine must appear as something that is completely alien to the immediate products of their labour (it is difficult to imagine a sack of wheat or a lump of iron ore as part of a computer); for such workers, 'the computer' signifies something *other* than their labour. Assembly workers must have some partial knowledge of the physical arrangement of the machine, and operators must have a limited knowledge of its controls, thus Robins and Webster, citing Michael Donaldson *et al.*, point out that:

> Employers agreed that many of the lower ranks would be using IT in their work, but were confident that they could provide any necessary training on site, not least because the 'few at the top of the pyramid [would] make IT user-friendly and idiot-proof for those on the shop-floor'. (Robins and Webster, 1989, p. 178)

Both assembly workers and operators will receive some 'shop-floor' training focusing directly on the machine itself which appears as an object under construction (assembly) or as a tool (operation). Design engineers and other technical workers will see the machine as a site of problem-solving, and managers, accountants, etc., will imagine it as capital. The machine thus confronts workers within each cell of the division of labour as a signifier for a *technological text* which is specific to that cell,[8] as a synecdoche for the division of labour itself. The resulting system of texts constitutes a cultural division which corresponds to the division of labour and which cuts across other cultural groupings such as those referred to by Max Weber (1948) as 'status groups'. These culturally specific texts will both sustain the technology as a thing (the 'universal' signifier) and act to maintain the boundaries within the division of labour itself. It is being proposed here that this necessary correspondence of the cultural division with the division of labour is the mechanism which connects material production — the economic — with cultural and social reproduction in, for example, the school; I shall return to this later in this chapter.

Insofar as Information Technology is a requisite of the effective control of a highly complex international division of labour — as is suggested by Robins and Webster's analysis (1989) — then so is its dissemination; or, at least, its dissemination will be assured in competition between producers of such technology.[9] Furthermore, competition to gain more effective control of international labour will combine with the fruits of such enhanced control to develop the technology in an accelerating upward spiral: computer technology must become more and more powerful and more and more readily available within the metropolitan societies in which control is centrally located. It is here, I suggest, that we might look for signs of contradiction, and we find this in a challenge to the whole notion of property.[10]

A concept of 'property' remains universal within the general field of technological production. Each technology has to be defined in relation to property rights. Thus I can go and make a drawing of a bridge and keep or even sell the drawing; I cannot, however, build an identical bridge without infringing the property rights of the civil engineer who designed it. I can do my utmost to make an exact copy of Leonardo's *La Gloconda* and sell the result, as long as I don't pretend that I'm selling the actual canvas that Leonardo's (or his students') brushes traversed. Information Technology — expanded to include written, printed and recorded material — has, perhaps, the most stringent interdictions relating to property. As I understand it, you need special permission (or a license) even to copy out this book by hand. Computer hardware is very often specifically designed to allow you to copy programs so that the copies are just as good as the originals, and yet to do so is very often to lay you open to possible litigation proceedings; never has the whole notion of 'property' been so invitingly opened up for deconstruction. I shall return to a discussion of this contradiction later, but I want first to consider the second kind of agency which is attributed to technology by technological determinism.

Preconceptualization and the cultural and social shaping of technology

Clearly, there is some relationship between a given technological form and the practices in which it is embedded. Wallis (1971) reports that following[11] a dispute over a calculation of safety margins in testing an aircraft engine (in which Wallis was, empirically, proved to be correct), s/he constructed a data-sheet for the *Draughtsman's Handbook* which 'enabled anyone to predict "safe" distances merely by being able to read English'.[12] Presuming that Wallis's data-sheet became widely used, we might assume that it partially replaced the slide-rule in helping to decide where to stand when testing an aero-engine. This simple piece of 'Information Technology' was thus involved in a change in practice. However, firstly, it would have been Wallis her/himself, the publishers of the *Draughtsman's Handbook*, and the users of this volume (in terms of the trust invested in it) who would have been the principle movers in this transformation, not the technology itself. Secondly, Wallis's assertion that her/his work 'effectively inhibited thought' by moving a particular aspect of the 'design act' from the 'problem' category to the 'immediately answerable' category is, itself a simplification. Whilst we may accept that such technologies became part of the commonsense of design practices and, as such, tended to go unquestioned, we might suppose that the failure of anyone to produce such a simple piece of technology before was, in part, a result of a commonsense acceptance of a certain level of risk in testing aircraft. It is the commonsense status of accepted practices, not the level of technology involved in those practices, that inhibits creative thought.

So what is being rejected is any simplistic notion of preconceptualization in which practice is understood to be *determined* by specific forms of technology. It has been argued above that forms of Information Technology develop in a dialogical relationship with the division of labour as both the requirement and facility for more sophisticated levels of control increase; the actual context in which dead labour is brought to life has not been considered in this analysis. Much of the available work in this area has tended to focus on the shaping of the form of the technology — the signifier — rather than on the social contexts which provide it with meaning — the signified. Thus David Noble (in this volume) argues that the adoption of Numerical Control technology — which operates on the basis of a program — rather than record-playback machines — which need to be 'taught' by skilled workers — was influenced by the potential of the former to achieve greater control over the workforce by replacing skilled machinists with 'tractable "button-pushers"' and by regulating and pacing manufacturing operations. This was also intended to centralize control over design and thus reduce the possibility of espionage — crucial in the 'intensely anti-Communist 1950s'; furthermore, it 'dovetailed nicely with larger efforts to computerize company operations'. The 'de-skilling' processes associated with Taylorism and Fordism are also discussed at some length by Braverman (1974).

A rather different example is given by Langdon Winner in relation to civil engineering:

> It turns out ... that the two hundred or so low-hanging overpasses on Long Island were deliberately designed to achieve a particular social effect. Robert Moses, the master builder of roads, parks, bridges, and other public works from the 1920s to the 1970s in New York, had these overpasses built to specifications that would discourage the presence of buses on his parkways. According to evidence provided by Robert A. Caro in his biography of Moses, the reasons reflect Moses's social-class bias and racial prejudice. Automobile-owning whites of 'upper' and 'comfortable middle' classes, as he called them, would be free to use the parkways for recreation and commuting. Poor people and blacks, who normally used public transit, were kept off the roads because the twelve-foot tall buses could not get through the overpasses. (Winner, 1985, p. 28)

The tacit assumption in such work is that the form of control that is being sought after is actually achieved, that there is a hegemony in the signification of the technology, that is, technology preconceptualizes practice. Jane Barker and Hazel Downing (1985) attempt to make a similar argument with respect to the introduction of word-processors into offices. They suggest that the organization of the traditional office allows considerable space for women to control their own activities; the technology of the typewriter, for instance, can be exploited for resistance purposes:

> Because conventional typewriters rely on the control of the typist, she [sic] can adopt any number of methods to break the routine of typing: she can sit on her work and pretend to look busy to have a chat, she can drop a paper clip in the basket of her typewriter and wait around for the mechanic to come, she can run out of stationery and then with an excuse for being out of the office, go and visit someone in another office.... If the work is late then 'the ribbon got stuck' or she had to phone a company to get Mr So-and-So's correct title and 'it took ages getting through'. In addition, those activities which are auxiliary to typing, such as filing, or even photocopying, enable her not to be tied to the typewriter all day — thus she has a certain amount of control over her space and movements. (Barker and Downing, 1985, p. 149)

Barker and Downing propose that the introduction of computer technology, on the other hand, facilitates electronic monitoring and allocation of work, and fragments the work of the typist by, for example, separating printing and, possibly, final editing from typing, thus reducing her/his[13] control over the final product of her/his work. But is it the technology that is effecting the transformation, or is its introduction being used as an excuse to alter labour relationships? After all, we don't need electronic technology to effect tight monitoring of people's work; such monitoring has existed in school class-rooms for years with no more than pencil and paper technology. Further-more, as Barker and Downing realize, coffee split on an electronic keyboard is at least as effective as a paper clip in a typewriter. Neither is the fragmenta-tion of labour processes a function of technology but of management culture; Charles Babbage, writing in the latter part of the last century, points out that:

> the master manufacturer, by dividing the work to be executed into different processes, each requiring different degrees of skill or of force, can purchase exactly that precise quantity of both which is necessary for each process; whereas, if the whole work were executed by one workman [sic], that person must possess sufficient skill to perform the most difficult, and sufficient strength to execute the most

laborious, of the operations into which the art is divided. (quoted in Braverman, 1974, pp. 79–80)

Adam Smith's famous example of pinmaking illustrates this fragmentation:

One man [sic] draws out the wire, another straightens it, a third cuts it, a fourth points it, a fifth grinds it at the top for receiving the head; to make the head requires two or three distinct operations; to put it on, is a peculiar business, to whiten the pins is another; it is even a trade by itself to put them into the paper; and the important business of making a pin is, in this manner, divided into about eighteen distinct operations, which, in some manufactories, are all performed by distinct hands, though in others the same man will sometimes perform two or three of them. (quoted in Braverman, 1974, p. 77)

Word-processors *allow* keying and printing to be separated, but so does the linotype machine. Furthermore, this separation enables *me* to have much greater flexibility in my writing because I can experiment, cut and paste, even produce graphics before committing the final result to paper; the same feature of word-processing technology is oppressive to the typist, but liberating to me; in each case, the technology is given its signification only within the context of the cultural practices within which it is embedded. Furthermore, electronic monitoring is far from being the only method of replacing direct and constant supervision by a human supervisor.[14] Piecework methods of payment have been around for a very long time in factories, and are usual where typists are working from home. The fact that piecework has not yet been introduced in many offices is certainly a cultural rather than a techno-logical feature.

There is thus the possibility of a tension between, on the one hand, technological texts as features of the *de règle* division of labour (there exist typists, machine operators, designers, etc., with respective *nominal* rela-tionships to technology) and, on the other, the *de facto* culturally generated texts. The resulting dual signification of technologies allows space for resist-ance, but it may be that this resistance is, itself, part of the motor which is accelerating technological development in the quest for more effective con-trol; it does not consitute a contradiction so much as a spur.

Whatever its effectivity, it is clear that new forms of technology are introduced within the context of intended transformations in working prac-tices. The ensuing processes of training and the development of resistance strategies contribute to a focusing on the machine itself as determining these new working practices, and it is this focusing, I suggest, which facilitates the myth of preconceptualization. Having constructed links between the econo-mic and the cultural (which were only ever separated analytically) in terms of technological texts, I shall now consider the context of the school as a site for ideological (cultural) reproduction.

Schooling and social and cultural reproduction

> Insofar as productive capacities are brought to the foreground in discussions of the use of computers in the schools ... a proportion of teachers could possibly be seen as expendable — for with greater efficiency through the utilization of technological devices, presumably less human personnel would be required. This in fact has been foreshadowed by Fenton Sharpe, Director of Studies for the New South Wales Education Department who has been quoted as stating that 'Any teacher who can be replaced by a computer deserves to be'. (White, 1985, pp. 218–19)

The current situation in the UK combines a serious shortage in the supply of teachers (particularly in some scientific and technical areas) with a general interest (inside and outside of government) in the development of Information Technology within schools (and teacher education). Nevertheless, no one seems to be suggesting that we might cover third year maths by installing a few extra PCs in the local comprehensive. On the contrary, the response from government has been the introduction of 'licensed' and 'articled' teacher schemes which constitutes an easing in the training requirements for teachers:[15] an intervention on the supply side rather than on demand. However, as I have argued above, behind the myth of substitution lies a highly complex division of labour to which necessarily corresponds a division in terms of technological texts. It is this essential correspondence[16] which, I suggest, provides the link enabling the division of labour to be effective within the school curriculum.[17]

The division of technological texts within schooling is distinct from that within the economic sphere in two important ways. Firstly, it is necessarily greatly simplified, the school's responsibilities lying with the provision of generic rather than specific knowledges. Nevertheless, a division is present, as illustrated by Paul Olson:

> In middle-class schools, the number of computers relative to students is greater in contact hours, teacher support, etc. The curriculum form in such schools also tends to be general, emphasizing cognate skills, industry, generalizability, and language and programming skills. The usage tends to be specific in addressing the full technical content of a program but it also tends to have transferability across content. The use of computers in working-class schools, by contrast, tends to be rote and is either based on mechanical skills or involves operations of games. (Olson, 1987, p. 195 — referencing surveys of US data)

Secondly, since the school is officially concerned with the transmission of knowledge, it cannot openly adopt a curricular route aiming at ignorance. Thus the virtually empty texts of operators, assembly workers, etc., are recontextualized within the school as 'computer literacy' courses, many of which would be more accurately described as 'computer *illiteracy* courses'. The essential division is between Information Technology as an object of academic study in areas such as computer science, Information Technology as providing tools for specific activities — word-processing in office studies courses, computer-aided design in design and technology — and Information Technology as a theme within a non-specialist, low-level course (computer literacy); Information Technology also penetrates more traditional areas of the curriculum, and this is considered below. It is suggested that this division arises out of the dialogical relationship between the field of education and the economic field through the public development of curricula (for example, the Technical and Vocational Education Initiative and the National Curriculum). Furthermore, because the school texts are already class- and gender-specific (that is, they correspond to the division of labour), student positions are defined in terms of both courses and class/gender before the courses even start;[18] Michel Foucault makes this point in a more general context:

> Although education may well be, by right, the instrument thanks to which any individual in a society like ours can have access to any kind of discourse whatever, this does not prevent it from following, as is well known, in its distribution, in what it allows and what it prevents, the lines marked out by social distances, oppositions and struggles. Any system of education is a political way of maintaining or modifying the appropriation of discourses, along with the knowledges and powers which they carry. (Foucault, 1981, p. 64)

It is through this mechanism that cultural divisions — generated through the division of labour — facilitate the reproduction of the social divisions which sustain the form of the division of labour itself. In addition, the high visibility of 'technology' as a curricular 'subject' facilitates the separation of this signifier from its conditions of existence (the division of labour) and so provides further sustenance for the myth of substitution.

Joseph Weizenbaum understands a 'tool' as the instrument for its own reproduction:

> A tool is also a model for its own reproduction and a script for the reenactment of the skill it symbolizes. That is the sense in which it is a pedagogic instrument, a vehicle for instructing men [sic] in other times and places in culturally acquired modes of thought and action. The tool as a symbol in all these respects thus transcends its role as a practical means towards certain ends. (Weizenbaum, 1976, p. 18)

This is precisely the expectation of preconceptualization that I have discussed above. If this is an adequate description of the result of introducing particular forms of technology into the classroom then we would expect to see the transformation of the practices of teaching and learning, a transformation which, furthermore, derives from the specific technology, rather than from other sources. R.D. White (1985), for example, notes that much educational software — in particular, Computer Assisted Instruction (CAI) — is predicated on a 'banking' concept of learning and on behaviour modification techniques, and this is expected to influence pedagogic action. However, the reduction of education to the level of a technical problem, which is an aspect of behaviourist approaches, is not specific to computer technology. Indeed, the new National Curriculum in mathematics in the UK is very substantially informed by such an approach in its undue emphasis on assessment (see Dowling and Noss, 1990); furthermore, behaviour modification techniques are central to the control strategies of many teachers.

The point that I want to stress is that computer technology will tend to be constructed by teachers and students within classrooms in accordance with the cultural practices that obtain there. Some time ago, I visited a mathematics classroom in which the single RML 480Z was used simply to engage two members of the group, giving the teacher more time with the others — no attention was paid to the specific activities that the computer users were carrying out, and there was no evidence of any involvement on the part of the teacher; the machine was being understood as a placebo. Looking around this particular classroom, it appeared that the principal objective of the teacher was to get all of the children doing something under conditions that would pass for order; the use of the computer was entirely consistent with this classroom culture, and neither added to nor subtracted from this culture.

In another classroom, two students were running a 'Secondary Mathematics Individual Learning Experience' (SMILE) program in which they had to locate a hidden 'elephant' by guessing its coordinates, the machine responded to each guess by marking the point that it had been given, and stating its distance from the elephant. The students' strategy appeared to be a simple guess each time, with no regard to the additional information given by the program; students sometimes 'guessed' the same point more than once; one pair took 83 guesses to locate the elephant — there were only 81 points available on the integral grid. Again, looking at the rest of the class, the students were working diligently on their SMILE cards, but in a very mechanical way, there was no attempt to get them to formulate their own problems, or even to generate strategies for answering the questions on the cards; the assumption seemed to be that simply doing the activities would result in learning.[19]

In other classrooms that I have visited, every student in the room is sat in front of a computer keyboard and screen; communication between students is kept to a minimum. Such a scene is not really any different from the classroom in which each students is sat at their desk, working from their textbook, or the classroom in which thirty students are working separately in their respective SMILE cards or 'School Mathematics Project' booklets. In each case, the assumption is that students need to be insulated from each other, communication between student and teacher is strictly regulated, and communication between student and student is seen as disruptive. The computer fits into this culture, it does not cause or alter it. The computer, the SMILE card, or the textbook are instruments of oppression, but not because that is what they really are; rather, they are defined in this way by the culture in which they are embedded.

Evidence on how computers are generally used in schools appears to be in short supply, but my experience suggests that the two most common uses are the single machine being used for demonstration purposes to the whole class and the machine being dedicated to use by an individual, or sometimes a pair of students, for a block of time. If this is indeed the case, then it would hardly be surprising, because certainly the most common forms of classroom activity are a teacher expounding and students working alone or, when resources are limited, in pairs. The use of the computer is again defined by a pre-existing pedagogic culture.

Karen Sheingold *et al.* (1984) describe another image of the computer in the classroom, a situation in which two primary-school students are negotiating their respective roles in working with the machine and one is heard to say to the other 'I'm the thinkist, you're the typist'. Such a statement is, or course, a superb encapsulation of the notion of 'ability differentials' that is absolutely fundamental to most classrooms. The assumption that people have different abilities which they are born with or which become an indelible part of their character in very early family life has its roots in the eugenicist movement which began in the nineteenth century with Francis Galton. This assumption underlies almost every aspect of pedagogic culture, and gives meaning to expressions such as 'setting', 'mixed ability', 'special needs', 'low attainers', etc. Typing is regarded as a lower status activity than thinking (which is, apparently, unnecessary for typists); the subject of the thinkist/typist statement is asserting her/his superior ability. But again, this is an outgrowth of educational culture, and certainly not specific to computer technology. In another classroom that I visited recently, where two students were trying to solve a sort of three-dimensional tangram, one said to the other words to the effect of 'You just hold these pieces, I'll sort out the problem'; in other words, 'I'm the problem-solver, you're the problem-solver's mate'.

Dreyfus and Dreyfus (1984) argue that the computer in the role of a tutee, the role it fulfils in logo programming, for example, preconceptualizes children's learning by restricting them to the divination of rules. Expertise, they suggest, does not operate on the basis of rules, and so the computer actually prevents children from attaining higher orders of proficiency. However, the Dreyfuses are guilty of ignoring the diverse ways in which computers are actually used in classrooms. It is, in a sense, as ludicrous to suggest that using computers is limiting because there are things that they cannot do, as it is to make the same argument about pencils. The question is not about what computers can or cannot do, but about what teachers and students do. A traditional maths lesson is precisely about learning rules; a lesson based on Polya's heuristics is about learning rules; Sherry Turkle's 'soft masters', on the other hand, certainly aren't learning rules.

Conclusion

I have argued that the concept of Information Technology — 'the computer' — is reified in the spiralling dialogue between the means and relations of production through the separation of the machine itself from that which it signifies, that is, a highly complex, international division of labour. This signified is replaced by technological texts which are specific to particular cells in the division of labour. The introduction of a new technological signifier is necessarily associated with an attempted transformation of local relations of production, but this does not imply preconceptualization as much as an invitation to resistance, the latter being consistent with pre-existing practices. In turn, resistance strategies may constitute local invitations to develop the forces of production, corresponding to the global invitation that is the demand for control in the increasing complexity of the international division of labour. These technological resistance texts constitute a synecdochic reification of the signifier — 'the computer' — and so facilitate the myths of substitution and preconceptualization.

Technological texts relating to the division of labour are reproduced (in a modified form) in schooling through the dialogue between education and the economic in the public determination of the curriculum; because of their grounding within the division of labour they embody subject positions which are stratified according to class and gender. This, together with the objectification of technology within the school curriculum, ensures the reproduction of social and cultural stratification. I have also suggested that computer technology can no more preconceptualize the work of students and teachers than it can production workers, but that the practical signification of the machine will be consistent with a pre-existing classroom culture (which may, itself, already be under transformation).

The question which must now be addressed is 'what is an appropriate and possible response?' The dangers attendant on attempting to make pragmatic inferences from theoretical constructions are probably responsible for the common tendency of such issues to be left until the last chapter or paragraph, and I certainly make no claim to be offering a template for action. Nevertheless, it seems to me that there are two possibilities which are worth some consideration. Firstly, there is the tension that I have proposed between technological and resistance texts: to what extent might it be beneficial to concentrate on the production of more powerful forms of resistance? As I have suggested, it seems likely that this area is of importance in the generation of technological escalation and, therefore, the development of a more highly complex and oppressive division of labour; resistance at this point is tantamount to engagement in a cold war.

On the other hand, technological development has, as I have illustrated, produced a contradictory challenge on the status of property, and it may be that it is here that efforts should be directed. The increasing dissemination of Information Technology means that it is more and more readily available as the tool of its own deconstruction. It is beginning to become possible for teachers and students in schools to carry out important and meaningful research and develop their own understandings of the international division of labour that are independent of the artificially constructed documentaries of the mass media.

Naturally, neither teachers nor school students are yet trained in such uses of technology, but there is no reason why this should continue to be the case if the division of labour between schools, on the one hand, and universities and polytechnics, on the other, can be weakened. Cooperation between schools and higher education (both under threat from the current government) will facilitate the interrogation and interpretation of databases which have been in the public domain for years but which have remained refractory to the technologies of the slide-rule and pocket calculator. The abolition of the elitism of the university through its extension into all domains of education will massively expand the base for critical action in fields which are already attracting public interest — green issues, health care, taxation, issues of social inequality, criminal and civil law, etc., all issues which are sensible of the division of labour. Information Technology can only control when it is controlled, that is, when it is restricted. The education system which, as a major site for the reproduction of ideology, is also a potential site for its deconstruction, is suffering under the rigidity of its own division of labour.

There is, here, no Luddite advocacy of a 'return' to some utopian state in which there is only one subject position and no division of labour. It is *forced* division of labour, not division of labour *per se*, that is being opposed.[20] Dowling and Noss (in press) have argued (in relation to academic subject specialisms) that oppositional strategies can be more effective within a form of division of labour which is cooperative and dynamic. Such cooperation can only come about through the development of a form of praxis which is predicated on autocritique. Information Technology does not *embody* capitalist relations of production, it *signifies* them; in order to deconstruct this signification those of us within the education system must look to our own technological and resistance texts. In a footnote to his use of John Stuart Mill's aphorism (quoted at the head of this chapter) Marx adds the following qualification:

> Mill should have said, 'of any human being not fed by other people's labour', for there is no doubt that machinery has greatly increased the number of distinguished idlers. (Marx, 1976, p. 492fn)

To whom might he have been referring?

Paul Dowling

Acknowledgments

I am very grateful for the critical comments made by Andrew Brown and Parlin Bahl on an earlier draft of this paper.

Notes

1 It is consistent with the argument that is developed in this paper that there is no ontic distinction to be made between 'Information Technology' and 'technology'; these terms — and the term '(the) computer' — are therefore used throughout the paper as seems appropriate to the specific context; I have capitalized the initals of 'Information Technology' to underline its locutionary nature.

2 The sexist nature of this title is perhaps appropriate given the patriarchal nature of society; it is not clear that Bolter intended this particular correspondence.

3 This term was coined by Mike Hales (1980).

4 Information calculated from International Labour Organisation (ILO), *Year Book of Labour Statistics*, 1988.

5 I want to distance myself from the use of such terms which imply a leadership in terms of human development by 'First' and 'Second' World countries; it is consistent with the argument being made in this paper that such 'development' as may have occurred within these latter nations has only been possible at the expense of those societies that they are supposed to be leading.

6 Incidentally, the same division of labour enables me to spend hours writing this paper whilst not having to worry unduly about where my next meal is coming from.

7 A dialogical and improvisational form of Indian/Pakistani singing, sometimes competitive (*muqabla-e-qawwali*).

8 That is, as defined by the differentiation in the immediate context of production: 'cell' and 'technological text' thus delimit each other, although they are analytically separable, since their respective contents may vary independently when, for example, a new machine is to be assembled within an existing labour structure.

9 Evidence of the *de facto* dissemination of technology as both physical and discursive resources is apparent in the examples offered in the first paragraph of this chapter. It is suggested that competition will result in such dissemination as capitalists seek to maximize return on technological development through the construction of new markets (what Robins and Webster refer to as 'Sloanism').

10 This is not, of course, to maintain that this is the sole point of contradiction: the serious (and increasingly apparent) threats to global physical resources that accompany developments in the forces of production are clearly important examples.

11 Wallis states: 'A long time after ...' (*op. cit*; 17).

12 Wallis is, perhaps, unduly optimistic in the use of 'anyone'; presumably the individual would have to be a trained 'draughtsman' [sic].

13 It is interesting to note that Barker and Downing do not use a gender-neutral pronoun for typists; are there actually no men holding such positions?

14 This suggests that the mapping of signifier onto signified is not simply a one-to-many relation (multiple signification by any given signifier) but also a many-to-one relation (multiple signification of any given signified). This might encourage us to abandon Saussure's (1972 edition — this edition translates *significant* and *signifié* as 'signal' and 'signification' respectively; I have employed the rather more common 'signifier' and 'signified') biplanar model of language in favour of an image of the cultural domain as a single level of elements which combine according to different functions to generate distinct cultural contexts.

15 In the case of the 'licensed teacher scheme', this is a reduction of the requirements in level of qualification, effectively an ending of the 'graduate status' of the teaching profession.

16 This is to be distinguished from the unexplained correspondences in the work of Bowles and Gintis (1976).

17 This link is implicit in Bernstein's (1982) theoretical construction.

18 The definition of subject positions in this way is similar to the way in which Walkerdine *et al.* (1989) describe girls as being defined as irrational and nurturing irrespective of (and in advance of) their actual behaviour. In terms of the construction of subjectivity, Althusser's (1971) notion of 'interpellation' provides a useful metaphor.

19 This was presumably the hope of the Department of Education and Science and the Department of Industry in their 'Microelectronics Programme' of the early 1980s; the programme involved providing every primary and secondary school with a single microcomputer.

20 Nor is the kind of division of labour that is envisaged in any sense equivalent to Durkheim's (1984) telos of an 'organic' division of labour, which is a more static conception, lacking, it seems, any space for praxis.

References

ALTHUSSER, L. (1971) *Lenin and Philosophy*, London, New Left Books.

BARKER, J. and DOWNING, H. (1985) 'Word processing and the transformation of patriarchal relations of control in the office', in MACKENZIE D. and WAJCMAN, J. (Eds) *The Social Shaping of Technology*, Milton Keynes, Open University Press.

BERNSTEIN, B. (1982) 'Codes, modalities and the process of cultural reproduction', in APPLE, M.W. (Ed.) *Cultural and Economic Reproduction in Education*, London, Routledge and Kegan Paul.

BOLTER, D. (1984) *Turing's Man*, Harmondsworth, Penguin.

BOWLES, S. and GINTIS, H. (1976) *Schooling in Capitalist America*, London, Routledge and Kegan Paul.

BRAVERMAN, H. (1974) *Labor and Monopoly Capital: The Degradation of Work in the Twentieth Century*, New York, Monthly Review Press.

DAVIS, R.B. (1984) *Learning Mathematics*, London, Croom Helm.

DOWLING, P.C. and NOSS, R. (Eds) (1990) *Mathematics Versus the National Curriculum*, Basingstoke, Falmer Press.

DREYFUS, H.L. and DREYFUS, S.E. (1984) 'Putting computers in their proper place: analysis versus intuition in the classroom', *Teachers' College Record*, 85.

DURKHEIM, E. (1984) *The Division of Labour in Society*, Basingstoke, Macmillan.

FOUCAULT, M. (1981) 'The order of discourse', in YOUNG, R. (Ed.) *Untying the Text: A Poststructuralist Reader*, London, Routledge and Kegan Paul.

HALES, M. (1980) *Living Thinkwork: Where Do Labour Processes Come From?*, London, CSE Books.

LAWLER, R.W. (1985) *Computer Experience and Cognitive Development: A Child's Learning in a Computer Culture*, Chichester, Ellis Horwood.

LAZERSON, M. *et al.* (1985) *An Education of Value: The Purposes and Practices of Schools*, Cambridge, Cambridge University Press.

MARX, K. (1976) *Capital, Vol. 1*, Harmondsworth, Penguin.

MINSKY, M. (1987) *The Society of Mind*, London, Heinemann.

OLSON, C.P. (1987) 'Who computes?', in LIVINGSTONE, D.W. *et al.*, (Eds) *Critical Pedagogy and Cultural Power*, Massachusetts, Bergin and Garvey.

ROBINS, K. and WEBSTER, F. (1989) *The Technical Fix: Education, Computers and Industry*, Basingstoke, Macmillan.

SAUSSURE, F. de (1972 edition) *Course in General Linguistics*, London, Duckworth.

SHEINGOLD, K. *et al.* (1984) ' "I'm the thinkist, you're the typist": the interaction of technology and the social life of classrooms', *Journal of Social Issues*, 40, 3.

TURKLE, S. (1984) *The Second Self: Computers and the Human Spirit*, London, Granada.

WALKERDINE, V. *et al.* (1989) *Counting Girls Out*, London, Virago.

WALLIS, B.W. (1971) 'How is mathematics used', *Mathematics Teaching*, 56.

WEBER, M. (1948) *From Max Weber: Essays in Sociology* (edited by Gerth, H.H. and MILLS, C.W.) London, Routledge and Kegan Paul.

WEIZENBAUM, J. (1976) *Computer Power and Human Reason*, San Francisco, W.H. Freeman and Co.

WHITE, R.D. (1985) 'Australian teachers and the impact of computerization', in LAWN, M. (Ed.) *The Politics of Teacher Unionism: International Perspectives*, London, Croom Helm.

WINNER, L. (1985) 'Do artifacts have politics?', in MACKENZIE, D. and WAJCMAN, J. (Eds) *The Social Shaping of Technology*, Milton Keynes, Open University Press.

Chapter 9

Microcomputers in Education: Dead and Living Labour

Pam Linn

The present govermental consensus representing microelectronics and computing as 'a good thing' stands in marked contrast to the uncertainties of new-technology policy and practice. I shall try to show that Marx's notion of labour process can be used to overcome the conceptual and political paralysis, the lack of serious critique, surrounding new technology. This attempt will be expressed in relation to one particular set of computer-related work processes: microcomputer use in schools.

With the arch-capitalist of new technology, Sir Clive Sinclair, scratching around for venture funds, we can safely assume that the consumer bubble in microcomputers has burst. Acorn and other microcomputer manufacturers are in serious trouble, and a number of high-street retailing chains are contracting. The worldwide volatility and present slump in chip demand echoes these trends in domestic consumption.

Given the extravagance of early claims, it is hardly surprising that the home microcomputer bubble has burst. Sinclair may go the way of the hula hoop and the skateboard. Yet at the rhetorical level there persists a remarkable consensus on the economic necessity of new technology in general and its educational significance in particular:

> Rapid technological change will affect most, if not all, of Britain's workforce. That is why our future prosperity depends on education and training of a high standard to meet new and unforeseen circumstances. We must seize the immense economic opportunities contained in advanced technologies by producing 'high-tech' goods and services. That means making a much bigger investment in high-tech education and training at all levels — covering qualified scientists, engineers and technicians. (TUC/Labour Party, 1984, para. 44)

That comes from the Labour Party, but it could as easily have come from the other side of the political divide.

Rhetorical representations of new technology as necessary for economic survival are blandly unspecific: they yield an undifferentiated view of microelectronics and computing and mask the contradictory tensions in technology-related work, in schools as elsewhere. Furthermore, the glossy language of automation — robotics, fifth-generation computing, expert- and knowledge-based systems and the like — obscures the workaday practices of producing and consuming new technology.

Dead labour and living labour

Marx's account of the labour process is our starting-point. Marx's concept of this transforming process embodies three elements:

> (1) purposeful activity, that is, work itself;
> (2) the object on which that work is performed; and
> (3) the instruments of that work (Marx, 1954, p. 174).

Each constituent, including the living worker, is, in turn, the product of past labour processes:

> Although a use-value emerges from the labour process, in the form of a product, other use-values, products of previous labour, enter into it as a means of production. The same use-value is both product of previous process and a means of production in a later process. Products are therefore not only results of labour but also its essential conditions. (p. 176)

Thus Marx points to the symbiotic relationship between production and consumption; to the productive links between past and present work; and to the technical, historical and social relationships between diverse groups of workers. Despite the recent wealth of literature addressing the Marxian conception of labour process, the *relation* between past and present labour — dead and living labour, as Marx distinguished it — has been almost entirely neglected.

The labour process debate[1] appears to have three significant silences relating to human labour and its products. First, insufficient weight has been given to the uniqueness, agency and centrality of human consciousness in the process of production. Second, labour process literature has inadequately recognized the extent to which dead labour embodies not only the living labour of the past, but also the contradictions, differing purposes, tensions and compromises of those past workplaces. Third, and most important, most labour process accounts have employed a technicist or deterministic view of the way in which past labour structures the possibilities of living labour in the paid and unpaid workplace.

This last feature is particularly serious. Braverman — the instigator of the labour process debate — suggested that technology is an extension of managerial authority, to the degradation and ultimate redundancy of the worker. Subsequent labour process writers have applied this analysis to the recent rapid development, convergence and introduction of microelectronic, computing and telecommunication technologies into workplaces. As a result, these particular technologies have largely been seen as a managerial advance rather than as specific products with their own histories, use-values and embodied contradictions.

The industrial relations emphasis of Braverman-inspired debates has focused attention on paid work and, as it relates to technology, on male paid work. But Marx's combination of materials, tools and purposive living labour in useful production has application beyond narrowly defined commodity production. Marx's analysis, applied to the introduction of new technology into education and training, serves to reaffirm that dead labour alone is inert, that it is the addition of purposive living labour which unlocks the use-value of technology, and that putting dead labour to productive use is never easy; there is always some area of intractability between the rigidities of the dead labour and the variable particulars of the present task.

Marx is able to offer a sense of social process, at once transforming and transformative; without this sense, one may neglect the vitality and variability of human labour embodied in technology. We may be so dazzled by the glamour of representations of automation, so seduced by the lure of technological infallibility, that critical scepticism is either suspended or seen as 'backward-looking' or (inaccurately) as 'Luddite'. A neglect of the social relations of production may cause us to ignore the irregularities and limitations of specific technologies and to treat technology as a homogeneous category. Particular technologies perform particular functions, providing both constraint *and* utility for living labour.

Governmental focus on the economic aspects of technological change, and labour process focus on paid labour contexts, has led to a relative neglect of non-waged sites of technological consumption. There are two further silences in Marxian literature on new technology: the gendered constitution of technological practices in paid and unpaid contexts; and the ideological representations of new technology, especially the anthropomorphism associated with computers (a practice which materially influences policy and purchasing decisions).

Computer-based forms of automation exert a siren attraction. These most powerful expressions of expertise may lead us to blur the central distinction between human consciousness and the inert physical and intellectual products of human labour. I believe the computer to be yet another example of a technicist inversion, a set of practices which attribute consciousness to machines and mechanism to human labour power.

The technicist inversion

Treating machines as people, and people as machines, is not new. Commodity labour and commodity technology are often treated as interchangeable, depending solely on cost considerations. I am pointing to something other than this.

Two processes are simultaneously at work. First, technology design, particularly computer design, has become so *dedicated*, so geared to a precise set of functions, that users appear to have little choice, only restricted opportunities to exercise their uniquely human characteristics. In the processes of consumption, users become more like machines. Second, machines, particularly computer technologies, are accorded *super*-human powers. These extend beyond mammoth data-handling facilities to language, problem-solving, expertise, and other forms of intellectual creativity. The elitist exclusions of computer science and technology, in the absence of a socialist critique of computer technology, help to perpetuate this Frankenstein myth. These combined tendencies seem to me to be a major source of the commonly expressed deference towards computers and, paradoxically, may also explain the obsessional enthusiasm which they excite.

There are commonplace examples of these processes in patterns of home computer promotion and consumption. At the height of the microcomputer boom in the early 1980s, the UK had the highest saturation of home personal computers in the world. Whilst the bulk of these were low-cost Sinclair products, there was evident popular interest in this relatively inscrutable technology. The high sales have now crumbled, but the moment of microcomputer popularity remains as a curious cultural phenomenon.

Home computers have been promoted as an intellectual toy. The sell has been aimed at parents who are ambitious for their children, who are alarmed at high levels of youth unemployment, and who believe the rhetoric that new technology equals new jobs. The association of computing with cleverness and knowledge and power made for a seductive sell. (After several years many purchasers are still wondering what on earth to do with the product — beyond playing repetitious games.)

There is a similar association of computing with knowledge and power in the promotion of desk-top micros for management. The association provides a stark example of the technicist inversion, of a confusion between living and dead labour.

Knowledge-based systems, *information* technology, *intelligent* terminals, and *expert* systems are more than the anthropomorphic use of language; such labels represent a belief that a computer assumes human powers over knowledge and information. Yet computers simply manipulate data. Data is inert, dead labour. Data, like marks on a printed page, is not power — but knowledge can be. Knowledge inheres in people, in the purposes of living labour. By confusing data with knowledge, we ascribe the power of consciousness to computers. At the same time human judgment is denied full expression in computer use and devalued for its wilful unpredictability.

Standardization through dead labour

Capitalism turns differences in kind to differences in quantity — Karl Marx

To catalogue the ramifications of the historical shift from tools to machinery to modern industry is also to chart the history of increasing regularity, uniformity and standardization in both products and processes of production. Standardization enters paid and unpaid labour processes in a number of ways: through the restricted choice of instruments of production imposed by mass production; through managerial attempts to Taylorize the technology of paid production; and most particularly through the consumption of systematized automated processes. Dead labour brings with it regularity. Marx points to the distinctive features of machinery, *size* and *constancy*.

> Increase in the size of the machine, and in the number of its working tools, calls for a more massive mechanism to drive it; and this mechanism requires, in order to overcome its resistance, a mightier moving power than that of man, apart from the fact that man is a very imperfect instrument for producing uniform continued motion. (Marx, 1954, p. 355)

Uniformity of motion and economy of effort — the very characteristics which the hirer of labour power would seek to achieve in modern industry — were already becoming identified with the technology of production. Marx continues the passage:

> In the same way the irregularity caused by the motive power in mills that were put in motion by pushing and pulling a lever, led to the theory, and the application, of the fly-wheel, which afterwards plays so important a part in Modern Industry. (1954, p. 356)

The fly-wheel, the storer or regulator of the motion of machinery, could well be the leitmotif of technological developments in the processes of production.

Whilst Marx is clearly concerned with physical size, in computing terms this may be interpreted as more data, faster processing, more rapid output, and the like. (The hardware of computing tends to decrease in size with each new model, accompanied by corresponding increases in software complexity and lines of code.) Similarly, the constancy of motion can be seen in terms of the step-by-step process through a program, and the repeatability of those procedures.

Machines are attractive to capital because they appear more reliable, more controllable, in their motion. Turning that motion into a productive process is the difficult part. The precise regularities of mechanical movement do not interface easily with the ambiguity and variability of human labour processes. And yet, as Marx outlines, the value of the dead labour of technology can only be realized through the action of living labour.

Standardizing living labour

There are two reciprocal problems here for the capitalist in modern industry. First, how to construct the labour process, including the technological component, so that the act of working compels the worker to accept the discipline of the machine-regulated labour process (i.e., how to make the worker assume the relentless drive of the machine). Second, how to construct the labour process, including the technological component, so that the accumulated experience of the living worker becomes objectified in the machine (i.e., how to make the machine assume the experience and variety of living labour).

The first side of this problem involves managerial control over the precise process of production by means which Braverman has elaborated. That mode of control derives not from the *efficiency* of technology, but from the purposeful design of commodity technology to meet the productive needs of paying consumers — in this case, managements. Technological products designed for domestic consumption are similarly designed to appeal to paying consumers, whose labour is not only regulated, but 'saved' by the incorporation of technological dead labour.

But the regulatory effects of technological dead labour are more pervasive than that: uniformity comes not only by design but from the *inflexibility* of design objectified into artefacts. No matter how 'automatic' or 'intelligent' or 'user-friendly' the product, it has a fixed number of operations — embodied, prescripted. Thus the characteristics of dead labour provide a structuring effect on subsequent labour processes.

The obverse of the capitalist's problem — how to make machines resemble people — has two aspects. First, it is extremely difficult, both 'technically' and socially, to capture experience in dead labour. In the case of computer technology, anthropomorphic language, falsely ascribing purposes to the artefact, conceals the banality of the processes executed. Second, experienced labour, in its collective form skilled labour, resists debasement by automation; even when skilled groups are technologically usurped, they may be at least partially replaced by other sets of skilled workers, for instance system designers or electronic engineers. These workers, too, present a labour-control problem to capital.

Producers of commodity technology try to convert worker experience into dead labour. But to concretize expertise, and put it under the control of the owner (capital), implies that the social complexity of the already existing process of production is accurately mapped. Dead labour can, of course, be constructed to imitate specified aspects of human labour — to saw wood, weld metal, add numbers, file text. The distinguishing characteristic of carpenters, metalworkers, accountants and secretaries is that they perform these tasks to realize specific purposes. So when these workers are frustrated in their intentions, they resourcefully attempt to achieve their purpose by other means. Imitative automatic processes cannot have conscious purposes; so when they are confronted with the irregularities of a social world, they — for example — make sawing motions even when the wood fails to arrive, make welding actions over a non-existent car body, endlessly cast preposterous (to us) numbers which have been entered in error, rearrange and print text which is evidently nonsensical.

It is, of course, possible to construct automatic processes which have an element of adaptation, which, for example, stop sawing when the wood is absent or inappropriately positioned. But that circumstance has to be specified and quantified in advance. There can be no context where all eventualities are accurately predicted and regularized because there are no contexts where history does not enter.

As the objectified product of past labour, technology must embody the contradictory purposes and irregularities of those past workplaces — so technology can never be wholly reliable, any more than people can be entirely predictable. Further, as the objectified product of past labour, technology must embody in its design some conception of future use. Designers (and the many other workers who contribute to the final shape of a product) must envisage the purposes for which consumers will want to use the product and *literally* incorporate those ideas. Nowhere is this more so than in the design and manufacture of computer hardware and software. Yet the variability of use outstrips these embodied projections. The experience of frustration at the immutability of a tool or a machine is commonplace in domestic settings. When did you last gnash your teeth over a lost car key? — a case where design for security is not rapidly changed to design for forgetfulness. Why should anyone be seduced into thinking that high-tech is any different? Stored-up labour can amplify living labour in glorious ways; but those ways are, necessarily, fairly narrowly prescribed.

Microcomputer technology in schools

From its inception, state schooling has been recognized as a significant terrain for class struggle; educational innovation has always been debated, contested, negotiated and compromised. More recently debates have encompassed race and gender divisions as well. Protracted debates bear witness to the class character of the struggle — over progressivism, comprehensivization, secondary certification, and the determinants of the curriculum. Such debates have started from a concern for societal or industrial needs, or personal development, or the characteristics of objective knowledge.

The introduction of microcomputers into state schools has not had this contested character. The *desirability* of computer-related learning is taken for granted. No such unexamined assumptions were in force in the shift from fountain pens to ballpoints, or from slide-rules to calculators: these were debated. But where educational computing is concerned, technicist assumptions substitute for educational debate. The Council for Educational Technology (CET), for instance, establish the importance of school microcomputing in a few words:

> Microelectronics — very cheap, very small, highly complex electronic control circuits on a wafer of silicon — are now accepted as being a potential agent of social and economic change comparable with the development of new sources of power which brought about the industrial revolution. (CET, 1978, p. 1)

Adopting an equally apocalyptic tone, Professor William Gosling (1981) adds a biblical warning:

> from sand is the silicon microcircuit created, from sand the optical fibre. The most common and worthless material about us, available in inexhaustible quantities, suddenly is transformed to be the key to all our futures, in a world so different from the one we know that merely to turn our minds to it stuns our imagination. The task of education in helping our kind to make the transition to a new lifestyle is one which will demand all our skills, insights, flexibility. Yet the role of education is central, for it is in the mind of man that the revolution to come will be fought. In the Kingdom of Sand all things become possible, and only imagination rules.

Thus the technical director of Plessey Electronics Ltd, and former head of the School of Electrical Engineering at the University of Bath, intones his vision of educational computing: one that appears to have a closer relation to science fiction than technological practice, closer to shifting sand.

Ahistorical celebrations of new technology are not hard to find (such as those criticized by Robins and Webster, 1985). We are asked to wonder at the powers of this unique phenomenon, which is apparently unrelated to other technologies, the commodity form, or the labours of those who produced it. When such enthusiasm substitutes for educational argument, then the glamorous sci-fi associations of the new technology become dangerous.

It is difficult to think of another technology, or another commodity, which would warrant major initiatives from the Department of Education and Science (DES) and the Department of Trade and Industry (DoI); the establishing of around 150 Information Technology Centres (ITeCs) by the Manpower Services Commission; the production of a string of discussion and policy documents from the Further Education Unit; the provision of an array of in-service courses for teachers, and resource commitment for computer hardware; and a burgeoning literature. Will bio-engineering, similarly praised for its wealth-making potential, attract a comparable response? What would mark out any particular technology as being educationally relevant? Birth control, refrigeration, electric power, and polyfibres could all be regarded, by those most affected, as the most significant technical development of this century — yet they have not generated an educational bandwagon.

Microelectronics and computing are presented as economically indispensable, yet the criterion slips — economic utility is portrayed as educational usefulness. Thus, the new technology promoted by the state and by industry as one panacea for economic recession becomes, in the context of schooling, a necessary part of teaching and learning. The economic arguments for the wholesale support of Information Technology are crude; the educational arguments fallacious. This slippage, from a technological and economic determinist commentary on new technology in society to the necessity for computers in schools, is evident in a number of contexts — most particularly where curriculum design reflects the presumed needs of the economy.

In the next sections I chart some of the practical implications of the new-technology fantasy. There are two parts to the argument. First, I outline the ways in which the introduction of computing into state schools can be understood in terms of the *limitations* of commodified dead labour. Second, I discuss ways in which the educational use of personal computers may be conceptualized in terms of the relation between living and dead labour.

Micros and schools: a technical matter?

First, I draw attention to the pervasive technicism that rushed computers into schools and colleges as if it were a matter of hardware, and indicate the wealth of *social* arrangements implied by school computing. I point to the implications of commodification in school computing. All these aspects contribute to the imperative to use computers in schools and colleges.

An unexamined technological determinism is a commonplace in social analyses — Marxian and non-Marxian alike. Within technological determinist accounts, the labours of technological production are rendered invisible, the labour of technological consumption is seen one-dimensionally as a take-it-or-leave-it choice. This neglect of past producers and present consumers has serious immobilizing effects, particularly in the face of changing computer technology. I shall argue here for a more social account.

Pam Linn

State policy: the 1976–79 Labour administration

Our competitors — a warning:
> Unless the UK does all it can to accelerate its own microelectro-
> nics revolution, it will be subjected to even fiercer international
> competition in the home market, and will also fail to win large new
> overseas markets for related products. Although developments in
> many areas are not yet as dramatic as some commentators have been
> claiming, it is of the utmost importance that the UK be ahead of its
> competitors in benefiting [sic] from the productivity increases which
> the application of microelectronics will make possible. Internationally
> it will be a case of the devil take the hindmost. (CPRS, 1978)

Thus in November 1978 the Central Policy Review Staff set the mood: the train was leaving the station, jump on or be left behind.

The panic was confirmed and consolidated by, of all things, a TV programme. The BBC *Horizon* film 'Now the Chips Are Down', which signalled the beginning of the new-technology media event, was broadcast on 30 March 1978. Shortly afterwards, the DoI began to set up the various strands of the Microelectronics Application Programme (MAP) to disseminate information, training, and consultancy in order to insert microelectronics into the processes and products of British industry. At the same time the National Enterprise Board similarly capitalized initiative and enterprise in the micro-electronics industry to set up three costly ventures: INMOS (chip manufacture), NEXOS (office systems), and INSAC (computer software).

At that time a remarkable torrent of literature — research findings, analysis, speculation and millenarianism — began to flow from diverse sources. Trailing at the back of the field, in March 1979 the DES produced the £12.5m *Microelectronics in Education: A Development Programme for Schools and Colleges*. This document outlined a loosely defined programme of microelectronics-related educational activities, concerned with staff development and software production. The purchase of hardware, microcomputers, was *not* included in the proposal. A masterpiece of vacillation, this paper managed to be quite clear about keeping some things intact. First, it was thought appropriate that the majority of pupils should retain their technical mystification and be schooled merely in using, not in understanding:

> The programme will be concerned primarily with the applications of
> the new technology rather than with its science. It will not cover
> specialist training in microelectronics, for which arrangements are
> being studied separately, since neither the schools nor the majority of
> FE courses need to be concerned with how microprocessors are made
> or the detail of how they work. (DES, 1979, para. 7)

Second, the boundaries of the science and technology curriculum went un-challenged. No encouragement was given to set awareness or familiarization activities in their social context:

> Nor will it [the programme] be concerned with promoting studies of the wider long-term implications of microelectronics for society — for example on employment and leisure patterns or on re-training and the general provision of adult education.

Third, the preservation of privilege was assumed by proposing

> the development of courses with a high microelectronics content for pupils showing exceptional ability in this area.

Ripples of concern reached the highest echelons of the education community. In March 1979 the DES had issued its first development programme, and by May the Committee of ViceChancellors and Principals had prepared their response to the government on the programme for schools and colleges. Each document echoed a fatalistic acceptance of economic necessity.

> The development of microelectronics is of major importance to our industrial future. The Government's view is that there is no time to lose if we are to make successful use of the new technology....
>
> Education, together with training, has a major part to play in producing the skills and qualifications to enable the new technology to be exploited to best advantage; and in preparing society for its full consequences. (DES, 1979, paras 1–2)

> The 'revitalisation' of industry requires that more of the most able young people are encouraged to seek careers in engineering and with knowledge of microelectronics. (Committee of Vice-Chancellors and Principals, 1979, para. 1)

The economic assumptions that underpin competitive 'necessity' concern international trade. Microelectronics and computing represent a range of new products for governmental, industrial, commercial and domestic consumption. The 'rapid rate of change' repeatedly associated with these new products (deriving from high levels of research and development funding and not from any inherent technological determination) adds additional urgency to the necessity to develop new products. The DES and Vice-Chancellors here both take this commercial urgency in *international* trade and uncritically transfer these market forces to the use of computers in schools. Neither body give any indication of the educational purposes or practice of the new technologies.

Thus, a curious philosophy of education, coupled with our unexamined notion of learning, emerges.

After forty years of liberal state education, the purposes of schooling are assumed to be chiefly commercial; after eighty years of educational psychologies, learning is assumed to derive from exposure to hardware. The implicit assumption is that the incorporation of computing into the practice of schooling will, somehow, transform familiarity into ability: technological proximity will translate into entrepreneurial success.

The Vice-Chancellors' response to the DES may be uncritical about the notion of microelectronics as economic transfusion but does have highly predictable views on other aspects of microelectronics in education. Such views recur in other educational commentary; class divisions, for instance, are treated as fixed whilst gender divisions are fashionably broached (although 'femininity' is not challenged):

> A nationally co-ordinated programme should therefore include the following objectives:
> (a) to give a general education in the uses of microelectronics and computers to all children so that they have an appropriate basis which will enable them to adapt to the technological world in which they will grow up;
> (b) to encourage more of the most able students including girls to take subjects leading to careers in industry and technology. Microelectronics and computing provide a very suitable basis for careers for women, as does professional engineering, but only one in 500 girls in the UK enter the engineering profession compared to 1 in 50 in France. (Committee of Vice-Chancellors and Principals, 1979, para. 4)

In their asocial 'technological world' the Vice-Chancellors are not alone in seeing microelectronics as intrinsically suitable for women workers — as if any technology could have any inherent properties at all, as if appropriateness could be judged separately from workplace relations or particular (in this case, class-specific) definitions of women. The Vice-Chancellors confirmed the elitist assumptions of their vocationalism:

> Much of the science and technology of microelectronics is naturally best taught in depth at the higher education level but it is essential, if more of the most able young people are to be encouraged to seek careers in the general field of electronics and its applications, that a good basic education is provided at school in mathematics and the physical sciences. (para. 6)

A purist, highly research-oriented view of new technology is suggested here. Mathematics and the physical sciences are seen as fundamental and necessary

— but would be of little use in systems programming, analysis or design. Interestingly, there is no corresponding necessity to understand the social world to ensure appropriateness of 'applications'.

And, finally, the Vice-Chancellors gave the DES's Microelectronics in Education Programme a characteristically technical focus:

> Since the programme is to be concerned primarily with the applications of the new technology rather than with its science, it is suggested that it would be advisable to involve applied scientists and professional engineers rather than relying too heavily on computer scientists in many of the activities envisaged. (para. 4)

University Departments of Education do not seem to have been considered.

Whilst other voices in education have taken up new technology in characteristic ways, a number of familiar themes recur: the *evocation* of rapid social and technical change as a substitute for educational debate; the deployment of a new-technology terrain to reaffirm social divisions in education; the seduction of dead labour as a duplicate living labour.

In sum these themes contribute to the technicist inversion that characterizes educational computing: while the human processes of teaching, learning and knowledge production are cast in mechanical terms, human or super-human powers are ascribed to computer technology. The following sections attempt to indicate the specificities of this tendency. In each case the celebration of technological features serves to reproduce and sustain existing social divisions, and to diminish the unique capabilities of human consciousness by an emphasis on mechanical criteria of excellence.

State policy: the 1979–83 Conservative administration

The change to a Conservative government intent on cutting public spending put the DES programme proposals in abeyance. However, the Microelectronics Awareness Programme (MAP) gathered momentum throughout 1979, despite the change in government. The reports of the campaign are impressive, as Maddison details from DoI figures:

> The sharp end of the awareness campaign had been a series of 140 'workshops' held from May to July, 1979, at centres throughout the country for 'the top 2,000 decision-makers in a cross-section of the leading 1,000 companies' ... Other activities ... included 'presentations' to major institutions, forms of plant, and exhibitions, the most important of these being the Science Museum exhibition. By 31 July the DoI and the NCC (National Computing Centre) had approved 79 additional courses from universities, polytechnics, further and higher education institutions, research associations, semi-conductor

and software houses and individual course providers. By February 1980, the 'awareness' programme had covered over 120,000 'key decision-makers' and the number of training places for engineers had increased by a factor of 15. (Maddison, 1983, p. 63)

By March 1980, the DoI had spent £10.165m supporting the microelectronics industry through a number of schemes.[2] The same month, March 1980, the DES announced a cut-back version of the original programme.

In response to a parliamentary question in the House of Commons, Mr Neil Macfarlane, Parliamentary Under-Secretary of State at the DES, not only indicated a shift in the orientation of the Microelectronics in Education Programme (MEP) away from an educational thrust and towards industrial and economic ends, but also restated the common rhetoric that new technology is an economic saviour.

The programme will serve the needs of education and industry by helping schools and colleges to make better use of microelectronics as a teaching resource and to equip young people with the skills which are required to exploit the economic potential of the 'new technology'. Much innovation is already taking place and the programme will only be successful if local education authorities take up the ideas and activities which prove to be effective. It is designed to stimulate and support local initiatives and not to replace them. (*CET News*, No. 9, March 1980)

It was now proposed that £9m be spent, over four years, on a number of coordinated projects, especially those concerned with curriculum development, with the development of material for teacher training courses, and with arrangements to make more and better software available for schools and colleges. Attention was to be focused on subjects such as science, mathematics, design and technology, business studies and technician studies. Special education also received a mention. Purchase of hardware, computers, was explicitly excluded from the programme.[3] Since nearly all computer programs are machine-dependent — that is, they are written for particular computers and even particular models — this appeared to be a bizarre decision. Having programs and no microcomputer is like having a film and no projector. And, unlike film, microcomputer program design is not limited to two formats (8mm and 16mm in the case of school film). Usually, programs will only run easily on one make of computer; if no school knew when and where their next microcomputer was coming from, then the costly process of software development could be a hit-or-miss affair.

Alongside the fruitless policies and belated practice of the DES, the DoI fostered the spirit of competitiveness by organizing an essay competition which offered 100 microcomputer systems, each worth £2,000, to winning schools. Secondary school pupils were asked to submit a project describing how their school would best use a microcomputer. Possibly with an eye to the publicity gains, it was announced that projects outside the science and maths areas would be 'especially welcome'. Judging took place during August 1980.

As a measure of DES activity in the area of microelectronics and computing, it is interesting to note that:

Seven short courses organised by Her Majesty's Inspectorate were planned for 1980; two of these were specifically on microelectronics (use in schools and in science teaching), the remaining five short courses being on other subjects but said to deal with microelectronics. The number of places planned for teachers for these courses was about 400 in all. (Maddison, 1983, p. 64)

As Maddison points out, at the time there were over half a million serving teachers and eleven million pupils in 38,000 schools in Britain.

Meanwhile, with extraordinary slowness and indeterminacy, the DES Microelectronics in Education Programme was launched. After the first year, during which time £1.2m had been allocated, the director of the programme took up his post. Richard Fothergill, biology teacher turned educational technologist, although appointed in July was not released until November; thus other central staff were not interviewed until after Christmas for an April release from existing teaching commitments. Thus *Microelectronics Education Programme: The Strategy* did not appear until 6 April 1981. It did not represent any new thinking:

The aim of the Programme is to help schools to prepare children for life in a society in which devices and systems based on microelectronics are commonplace and pervasive. These technologies are likely to alter the relationships between one individual and another and between individuals and their work; and people will need to be aware that the speed of change is accelerating and that their future careers may well include many restraining stages as they adjust to new technological developments. (DES, 1981)

Dead labour, even that in a microcomputer, does not have agency. On its own it cannot 'alter' relationships. 'New technological developments' do not happen from some autonomous inner volition. This first paragraph of the strategy document sets up the framework of technological determinism within which the rest of the paper is conceived. Chiefly *The Strategy* is remarkable because it focuses a whole policy around a particular device, the microcomputer, and this fails to give primacy to questions about the quality of learning and the active role of the learner (a point I will develop later). In addition, an interesting shift has occurred: from an explicit disavowal of concern for 'the wider long-term implications of microelectronics for society' in 1979 to a concern in 1981 for 'life in a society in which devices and systems based on microelectronics are commonplace'.

Here, as elsewhere, technological determinism was evoked as an obvious justification for educational change. Here, as elsewhere, the *use* of microcomputers in schools is assumed to provide educationally worthwhile familiarization experiences.

In developing a strategy for the Programme it has been assumed that:
. . .
(ii) with the dual aim of enriching the study of individual subjects and of familiarising pupils with the use of the microcomputer itself, methods of teaching and learning should make use of the microcomputer and other equipment using microprocessors. This may be expected to add new and rewarding dimensions to the relationship between teacher and class or teacher and pupil. (*ibid.*, para. 2)

The computer is placed at the centre of the educational enterprise. For example, under 'Curriculum Development':

New materials for teaching and learning are needed to meet the following needs:
(i) materials which make use of microcomputers and other devices based on microprocessors to assist with the teaching of 'traditional' subjects. (*ibid.*, para. 8)

The curious assumption that the existence of microcomputing *generates* educational need is reproduced in the fabric of the whole programme. Conventional educational criteria are subordinated to the demands of programme management: technical compatability and the diffusion of software and computing skills. New technologies apparently have 'needs' which inform curriculum development, which in turn provides the direction for teacher traning:

Teachers require both information about microelectronics and professional skills to apply the technology effectively in the classroom. The training of teachers, both in-service and pre-service, must therefore be organised in such a way as to support the curriculum changes envisaged . . . above. (*ibid.*, para. 22)

The DoI Micros in Schools scheme was announced at the same time as the strategy document appeared. Under the scheme, secondary school teachers had to choose either an RML 380Z or a BBC Acorn microcomputer. The RML 380Z is difficult to move around and thus not easily suited to flexible educational use, whilst the BBC model was unavailable at that time (and did not become generally available until spring 1982). This selection of microcomputers was justified on the grounds of their British manufacture. Yet the microcomputer chips, the single most indispensable component in a microcomputer, are produced in the USA,[4] by Zilog, a branch of Exxon, and by Rockwell.[5] Other vital integrated circuitry is largely produced by Japanese and US companies, like National Semiconductor, Nippon Electric Company, Fairchilds and ITT.[6]

At the time of the DoI offer to secondary schools, the RML 380Z was already becoming the local authority *de facto* standard. It had been adopted by the Inner London Education Authority, Havering, Birmingham, and other local authorities. These choices were already under way by the time the Regional Information Centres were set up under MEP. The whole programme had therefore to adapt its activities to the microcomputers already in schools and to those for which schools could obtain funding. Consequently, MEP software support and in-service training programmes have focused heavily on the 380Z. The primary school subsidy scheme echoed this by including the 380Z-compatible RML 480Z.

This emphasis on a particular machine has had important consequences for the development of microcomputer-related work in schools. For whilst there are other means by which schools can obtain a microcomputer (say, through a parent-teacher association, through capitation, or grants from industry), there are fewer ways of obtaining the three essential back-up services: a range of programs and program development, staff training and technical support. This limitation on machine choice and associated dependency on central services has implications for both teachers and headteachers, with or without some microcomputer background. Such dependency applies not only to schools, but also to staff in Teachers' Centres and to Computer Advisors. It is not at all surprising that most schools have opted for one of the recommended machines. ILEA Computer Education Inspectorate have unequivocally recommended the RML machine to primary headteachers. It is interesting to speculate upon which group of people would have a sufficiently sound knowledge of both microcomputing and of primary education to make such a recommendation.

In October 1982, primary school headteachers heard that they were to be included in the Micros in Schools Scheme set up by Kenneth Baker, Minister for Information Technology at the DoI. The £9m subsidy scheme enabled primary schools to obtain a microcomputer at half price. There are a number of revealing aspects to this generous offer. Both in terms of state initiatives and implied views of microcomputer education, the offer represents a stale rehearsal of what has gone before.

If the DoI made an offer to subsidize paintbrushes, Wendy Houses or reading schemes, eyebrows would be raised, questions asked. Yet the present relative poverty of many school budgets provides as good a case for funding those tools as for a microcomputer. If the DoI were to offer to subsidize the acquisition of workcards, blackboards, calculators or drawing blocks, suspicions and hackles would rise; there would be jokes about industriousness and increasing pupil productivity. Yet, as currently used, the microcomputer in school is nothing but an electronic workcard, blackboard, calculator or drawing block. At the same time, it did not seem remarkable that the Department of *Industry* should be concerned to place so much emphasis on one particular piece of *educational* technology. Yet, why should the department think the microcomputer so special or so different?

It may well be that the scheme can be justified by the DoI in terms of bolstering domestic industry and creating markets for computer products (both in schools and through pupil demands for a home computer). That intention is unrelated to the institutional consequences of the scheme. Under the leadership of Kenneth Baker, the DoI has been quick to fill the gaps left by the characteristic tardiness of the DES. The school activities of the DoI signal a significant shift in state policy and funding. Administratively, in terms of organization and philosophy, the DES may be more resistant to the harsh realities of the present Tory government; policy and practice get bogged down in the different local education authorities and their machinery. The DoI, on the other hand, provides a far more direct means of influencing educational practice.

Thus the DoI set events in train, the RML 380Z and BBC computers achieved significant domination in educational markets and this shaped subsequent teacher training. With considerable *élan* the DoI has successfully organized and managed the distribution of microcomputing equipment to schools. Similarly, the MEP has organized a significant teacher-awareness programme. By focusing on the distributive aspects, both the DES and the DoI have structured subsequent *educational* experiences for teachers and pupils.

The RML became the *de facto* educational standard in many primary and secondary schools by the overdetermined means I have outlined. Children's educational experiences of computers were similarly prescribed. Any particular objectified design inevitably enables the user to do some things and not others. The typewriter I am presently using allows me to indent lines but not quotations — the design is for business rather than essay writing. The RML 380Z has its designed omissions. It is, for instance, difficult for beginners to get the machine running at all (the language processors have to be loaded separately) and difficult for experts to follow the manual. Colour, graphics, disk-drive and standard programs (e.g., a text editor) allow you to do clever things — but are very expensive extras. These are not 'design faults' readily rectified in the next model. They are characteristics of the RML processes of production and represent rigidities in the physical and marketing composition of the 380Z.

Schools as consumers of the microcomputer product

As we have seen, the Micros in Schools Scheme offered schools a choice of hardware — RML 380Z and BBC for secondary schools — which was later amended to RML 480Z, BBC, and Sinclair Spectrum for primary schools. All these products are assembled in the UK. Of the 109 local education authorities in England and Wales, twelve strongly recommended RML as the preferred machine, fifty authorities gave some choice — RML or BBC — and no authority recommended the Spectrum. The twelve authorities underwriting the RML option included the metropolitan authorities and those that offer significant computing support. Authorities favouring BBC hardware were more likely to look to commercially produced BBC materials, including television programmes, for staff development and support.

The Inner London Education Authority (ILEA), by far the biggest and (at that time) the best-resourced authority in the country, put considerable pressure on headteachers to adopt RML as authority standard. Announcing the primary stage of the DoI scheme, and outlining the results of a pilot study, Bryan Weaver, ILEA Inspector for Computer Education, concluded:

> *As a result of these studies, the machine recommended for ILEA Primary Schools is the Research Machines 480Z.* (Weaver, 1982 — original emphasis)

This advice was given some force in the following paragraphs:

1. The resources required adequately to support schools are enormous, and the ILEA, along with virtually every other Authority, needs to standardise on a small range of equipment in order to use more effectively the resources available. Any funding available in the future will be allocated in accordance with this policy.

   The Inner London Educational Computing Centre (ILECC) currently supports fully the Research Machines 380Z (at present installed in all secondary schools and colleges, and the pilot primary schools) and its sibling 480Z.

2. The cost of computer equipment is only one part of the cost to a school or Authority. To this cost must be added that of such items as maintenance, software provision and in-service training. Moreover, comparisons of cost between different computers are often misleading, since very rarely is like being compared with like. In addition, factors such as the reliability of the equipment, the availability of support from the suppliers, and the reliability of the company are impossible to quantitify.

   The initial cost of the hardware is therefore only one factor to be considered.

3. The need for assistance to be made available to schools in terms of technical support and the maintenance of equipment is great, particularly considering the absence of relevant skills in most schools. The BBC machine has not yet proved sufficiently reliable or robust,

and is currently not supported by DMEE (Division of Mechanical and Electrical Engineers) for maintenance purposes. Any school which purchases this machine will need to arrange its own maintenance agreements, the cost of which must be met by the school. (Weaver, 1982)

Thus, by reference to funding for support services and appeals to expert knowledge, the ILEA inspectorate justified its adoption of the Research Machines microcomputers. Whilst an authority standard may be administratively neat, and technically 'necessary' because of the difficulties of converting software to run on another machine, there are educational issues at stake in these apparently technical arguments which remain unaddressed by the Inspector for Computer Education.

A headteacher of a London primary school, writing to the ILEA journal *Contact* in January 1982, questioned ILEA's policy. He argued that standardizing on one machine restricted the range of facilities available to teachers, that it was a mistake to concentrate on Basic as a common language, that for many computer-related educational tasks the computer was quite redundant, that there are serious educational limitations if the focus is on computers rather than the broader questions raised by Information Technology in everyday life, and that organizing the distribution and dissemination of computer-based learning along hierarchical lines served to increase teachers' dependency on experts. He concluded:

The two point whatever million pounds being invested by ILEA would be better spent in opening up, not closing the discussion about microchips; in providing the facilities for local initiatives to be developed, not in dismissing them; and in encouraging the crossflow of ideas, not blocking them. At present we have the enthusiasm of interested teachers being dampened, the needs of schools being ignored and the experience of schooling being further removed from the real life of our children.

Two years later the debate reopened in *Contact* when the Computing Inspectorate again defended the 480Z. Another primary headteacher, and his chair of governors, expressed reservations about the ILEA policy. On this occasion the writers separately drew attention to the benefits of the Sinclair Spectrum over the authorities' preferred Research Machines 480Z. The correspondents testified to the sustained reliability of the Spectrum, the adequacy and cheapness of Spectrum software compared to the poor choice of Research Machines software, and the ease of use of the Sinclair. The Governor pointed out that the 480Z costs six times as much as the Spectrum. (The 480Z was already half the price of the 380Z.) He said, 'ILEA should realize they are dealing with computers for schools, not men to the moon or storing the London telephone directory.'

The headteacher poured some realism onto the debate by emphasizing the social and economic constraints of computer-based learning:

> It seems a little fatuous to talk of 'computer curriculum objectives in the classroom' when a school has only one £600 computer. How do we hump the thing around a three- or four-decker building? ... Our recently ordered batch of Spectrums arrived within a week, but now we have to wait for ILEA-approved TVs. The last one took seven months to arrive, and I gather this is not an uncommon experience. (ILEA, *Contact*, letter, 4 May 1984)

The relative advantages of Research Machines and Sinclair cannot be reduced to a *Which*?-type consumer survey, where price and reliability are given so many stars. Any evaluation of these microcomputers has to derive from *educational* purposes and criteria.

ILEA's decision to support the RML 380Z microcomputer was taken some time before the MEP was instituted. The decision was made by reference to technical criteria, but was to have a significant educational consequence. Like any other consumers of computer products, ILEA had entered a symbiotic relation with Research Machines.

When ILEA opted for the 380Z microcomputer it cost between £1,200 and £1,500. At that time the Commodore Pet, with roughly equivalent power, cost about £450. The price difference was justified — by both ILEA and Research Machines — in terms of the superior robustness of the 380Z. With falling component costs, a variety of cheaper, more powerful microcomputer products was developed and directed at the home market. To retain their credibility in the market, Research Machines had to lower their price and increase the performance of their next model, the 480Z. Unlike their competitors, RM had to design their product with upwards compatibility: this placed severe constraints on the facilities of the 480Z. Like other manufacturers, RM found that their dominance in the market (in this case the educational market) provided both advantages and disadvantages.

From the point of view of the marketing activities of the manufacturer, upwards compatibility provides a strong selling-point: customers who have purchased or developed software can be more easily persuaded to trade up if their existing software will retain its utility. This attractive feature masks a high element of customer control, which IBM, for example, have employed to great effect. If a company decides to change its computer system, a great deal of upheaval is entailed, with associated high risks and costs. Programs go wrong in quite subtle ways and it may take years to sort out a range of operating difficulties. Thus the promise of a computer that is faster and bigger and yet will run existing programs is very attractive. IBM offer software facilities that customers want, but that usually requires more hardware — memory, disks, or a faster central processing unit.

Those computer-manufacturing companies which make IBM-compatible machines are trading on the same desire for a more powerful system with minimum upheaval. In the case of the IBM lookalike products, that desire is always tinged with doubt about whether the cheaper imitation will run both existing programs and any future IBM software products. Thus producers can construct and confirm their market position with existing customers. Customers, then, can maximize the usefulness of their existing relations of production at the cost of even greater involvement with the economic durability and design decisions of the computer company.

But producers, too, are caught in a dilemma. They can exploit past sales success and accept the design constraints of compatibility. Or they can abandon previous design criteria, take advantage of research work, and build a product at the so-called 'state-of-the-art'. RM took the former option, retained the Z80 chip and thus were limited to a maximum 64K memory size on the RM 480Z. The new model was repackaged to look less industrial and more like the BBC product.

The latter option — start again from scratch — was taken by Sinclair in the design of their QL microcomputer. Previous Sinclair products had been based on the Zylog Z80 chip, which has 8-bit data flows. The QL is based on the Motorola 68000 chip, which handles data in 32-bit chunks. Significant improvements in performance are made possible by this means, even though the QL is incompatible with all previous Sinclair products. When Sinclair announced the QL, 32-bit data channels were in the vanguard of computer design. The company has managed to minimize the effect of uncertainties and costs associated with new components by using a hybrid 68000 chip — the 68008. This enables the data to be entered by 8-bit channels (although manipulated in 32-bit formation). Thus Sinclair can take advantage of all the tried, tested and cheap 8-bit support chips which control the memory, visual display and keyboard.

Other computer manufacturers tackle this problem of compatibility by providing an upward path — usually a free software package that enables the new machine to *emulate* the old machine and thus enables existing programs to be utilized. Such emulation is achieved by slow, cumbersome software. Thus, the consumer avoids the risks and costs of changing data records, work procedures — at the high cost of time and efficiency of machine use.

This all may seem like a very obvious restatement of continuities in the computer commodity workplace. No different, for example, from considerations which influence the choice of a new car or a piece of furniture: the purchase has to offer something extra whilst still being in harmony with existing arrangements. My point is that educational consumers, like other commercial enterprises, are bound in a dependency relationship to computer companies, and that dependency derives its power from previous labour processes.

For the manufacturer, that dependency derives from the heritage of past sales success. For the consumer, that dependency derives from investment in staff training and development, in the integration of the computer system into the *process* of productive work. The education referent of dependency is the commitment of people and plant to school computing: the growth of the Computer Inspectorate, MEP, the creation of posts of responsibility, and related acquisitions of hardware and materials.

The rigidities and immutabilities of these embedded status-related decisions and hierarchies of expertise constitute, if not a determinism, then a kind of embodiment or immanence. Ironically, this social pressure comes about not because a particular design path is so *good* (as the technological determinists argue) but because computer systems achieve nothing without a wide circuit of supportive social arrangements in the processes of production and consumption. A number of factors thus came together to structure and limit the modes of educational computing available to London teachers: a market-focused administration which associates new technology with economic growth; DES ineptitude; hardware-focused DoI policies more appropriate to the distribution of machinery to competitive industry; the narrowly technical criteria upon which hardware choices were made; and a staff and software development programme based upon the hardware decision to standardize. As a result, London teachers were largely limited to RM products, with a costly 480Z and an obsolete 380Z. Nor can many schools afford to risk the other option: to buy much cheaper Sinclair machines without technical and staff support.

The relation between producer and consumer, between past and present labour, extends beyond the most obvious makers and users. Production is not confined to work directly on the technical commodity, any more than consumption is limited to domestic sites. The mutual dependencies are a feature of all commodity relations. Such relations are not merely expressive of strengths and weaknesses in the market-place. They are also expressions of the ways in which labour processes interpenetrate. The washing machine, or this typewriter, or the Sinclair Spectrum arrive as inert packaged goods. Such goods have a history, a history of constitutive labour processes which make matter a cultural product. In the case of school computers, that constitutive labour structures teaching and learning possibilities. The living labour of teaching and learning is not constrained by the *technical* detail of the computer configuration, but by the labour process of both production and consumption. *Technical* detail is abstract knowledge, abstracted from the connections and conjunctions of everyday life. Abstraction excludes. To know that a car does 0–60 in 15 seconds is not much use if the vehicle does not have an MOT certificate of roadworthiness. Culturally, to have a car, one to use, means to have a car with an MOT certificate.

The Metropolitan Police in London recently discovered the worldliness of computer technology. In 1985 they contracted Plessey to design a £7m data network for their Command and Control operations, even though their previous system had only been completed in 1984. The Metropolitan police found it prudent to make this expensive revision because the cost of the necessary private telephone lines had risen from £330,000 to £1m per annum. The Met wanted a system which used cheaper British Telecom telephone lines (*Computer Weekly*, 1 August 1985, p. 2). The technical detail of the old system remained adequate, but irrelevant.

Similarly, technical adequacy does not suffice as a basis for choosing computers, which likewise are cultural products. The financial uncertainties around both Sinclair and Acorn diminish the use-value of their computer products. Although each has a large user base, there is no guarantee that technical support would continue if the companies were to fold. And it is unlikely, in the present climate, that other companies would market new software or peripherals for these machines.

Technological immanence

I began this section by suggesting that technicism, particularly technological determinism, has immobilizing effects. After illustrating the series of embedded events which led to the adoption, in London and elsewhere, of a particular microcomputer design, I would like to return to the notion of technological immanence.

When I first bought an automatic washing machine I threw away the spin drier, rearranged the kitchen, plumbed in the new toy, bought automatic washing powder and started noticing those wash numbers on our clothes. I also rearranged the way we collected up dirty clothes so that we could wash all the same numbers together. Since the machine is noisy, I got into the habit of washing late at night when we could leave the kitchen. Only when it broke down did I realize the changed processes of production that this commodity had encouraged. Only when it resisted repair did I realize the measure of dependency that had grown up around the machine. We had no other soap powder, no other means of wringing out the water, and no knickers for the next day. In commercial contexts, that dependency is just as apparent. The accommodation and integration of dead labour into present productive processes happens, over a period of time, as the utility and limitations of the machine are explored. It happens with computer technology, and in educational settings as much as commercial and domestic ones.

After all the fuss (and cost) of installation and changing the routine, the new machine didn't live up to all its promises. This happened not simply because of mechanical failure but because of the conditions of washing-machine design endemic in the circumstances and relations of production of this technology. I didn't get to look like the woman in the ads, and there was still a lot of work attached to getting clean clothes. Managers of larger enterprises have their disappointments: they too are subjected to the ideological assault of microelectronic wizardry, they too are disappointed, and surprised, by the amount of living labour still necessary. A recent survey of senior banking managements in twenty-six countries found that bankers were disappointed with the results of their multi-million-dollar investments in computing:

> the results of our interviews and research strongly show that senior executives of banks generally are disappointed in the return on their technology investment in terms of:
> Inability to use technology to achieve lasting competitive advantages *vis-à-vis* their principal competitors.
> 'Failure to achieve expected economic returns through reduced operating costs and/or inability to be adequately compensated for providing additional services. (Touche Ross International, 1985)

'Failure to achieve ... reduced operating costs' is bankspeak for 'we still need to employ large numbers of people'.

When a machine is acquired, it already has a particular design. A whole pattern of social interaction of use develops in accordance with the perceived limitations of this design. A particular way of achieving results intricately comes into being. In the case of school computers, those modes of working are becoming inscribed in training programmes, staff-support facilities, technical back-up services and a whole array of curricular practices.

Technological determinism attributes power to dead labour by suggesting that technology itself changes things. By recognizing the close interrelationship of dead and living labour, we can grasp the *immanence* of technological change by social and historical means. Most significantly, the centrality of living labour to this process suggests possibilities for political action rather than fatalistic acceptance. What appears to be inexpert dependency on immutable computer technology can then be seen as more to do with familiar aspects of the social relations of schooling — still not easy to change, but not fixed either.

The user-friendly computer: the relation between past and present labour

The thing about machines, about technological dead labour, is that they appear fixed, immutable. To some people in some circumstances, this may be an attractive feature — unambiguous, certain, cut and dried. In other circumstances, the apparent immutability of technological artefacts is frustrating and oppressive. Microcomputer technology too can be both precise *and* inflexible, despite the attempts of advertisers to present the micro as scientific power with a human face: a 'user-friendly' computer.

This common descriptor of computer programs embraces a peculiar anthropomorphism. Who would think of describing an ergonomically designed car-seat as 'user-friendly'? Yet many programs *are* described in this way, deriving chiefly from the fact that computer programs are sometimes difficult and frustrating to use. A programmer has to try to envisage every possible contingency and circumstance and to embody this range of possibilities within the structure of the objectified labour, the program. Features of 'unfriendly' programs which exasperate the user include: having to remember a long list of difficult commands; inconsistencies like entering 'H' for 'HELP' but 'K' for 'REPEAT'; getting into a loop of instructions from which escape is impossible without restarting; programs which do not allow the user to go back and correct something; programs with non-mnemonic, meaningless command names which — like 'GREP' in the Unix program — make it difficult to remember what they signify.

User frustration derives from the unpredictable variety of responses which users make and the purposes they pursue, set against the rigidity of the dead labour of computer software. Against the common experience of irritation, the claim to 'user-friendliness' has great attraction, most especially in educational settings. Friendliness suggests an absence of frustrating features and usually implies the incorporation in the program of a 'HELP' facility, perhaps a menu to make user choice easier, or some personalized, chatty dialogue.

In practice, 'user-friendly' means that the programmer has adopted a deficiency model of the user's competence and has encoded another layer of instructions to present a quasi-human appearance to the language which confronts the program user. In practice 'user-friendliness' makes a program easy to use *at the cost* of understanding how the program actually achieves its effects. Thus ease of use is related to powerlessness, rather than to control.[7]

But 'understanding' and 'control' are not straightforward, either in themselves or in relation to each other. When pupils use a lathe in the metal workshop, or use an oven in the domestic science room, or see a video in humanities, or run a program on the school microcomputer, there are several ways in which they can be helped to understand those technological artefacts. They can instrumentally learn the procedures for use, in the same way that consumers of domestic appliances find out where the switch is, what attachments to use, and the telephone number of the service centre. This kind of understanding sits entirely within the dependency relationship determined by manufacturers.

Pupils can be given an explanation, guided towards an understanding based on the disciplines of physics or electrical and electronic engineering. Given the tight framing of those subject areas, it is difficult to see how knowledge of electrons, say, would help a user baffled by the instructions of an educational computer program.

Or pupils may be given a heuristic or metaphor to help the process of conceptualization, to help users to *imagine* (and the word is appropriately concerned with fantasy) what the technology is doing. This is a device employed by manufacturers of computers for business use. On the Apple LISA and the Rank Xerox STAR, the 'desk-top' metaphor is heavily underlined: the screen is dark grey, as a desk, an in-tray is pictured and so is an 'icon' of a wastepaper-basket. Users are then alerted to incoming messages by an 'item' appearing in the tray. This they can then process and move to the waste-bin by quasi-physical means with the use of a 'mouse', or screen pointer. 'Filing cabinets' for databases and 'recipes' for programs are other commonly used metaphors to describe computing processes.

In any case, there are two distinct modes of understanding at issue here. In an educational setting there is the explicit *content*: turning, cooking, criticizing the topic of the video, spelling or word-processing on the microcomputer, say. There is also the *means*, or tools, of teaching that content: the lathe, the oven, and so on. Through neglect, schools overwhelmingly mystify these means of educational production.

Even book production may be similarly mystified. Readers may presume expert authors and objective facts, until we meet the writers or recognize their political position. But books do not have the ideological resonance of computer technology, although they may have carried similarly exclusive meanings at one stage. The association of the technicist notion of automation with computing makes an added case for understanding both topic and tool where school computing is concerned.

If pupils do not understand the means by which screen-displayed data is generated, across a range of labour processes, they have no way of resisting its objective authority. With strong media suggestions that computers are 'intelligent', pupils need some means of situating computer output if it is not to assume a super-human or magical quality. What are required are ways of using dead labour which deconstruct its givenness, but that cannot be achieved by deference to a scientific or technical account — nor, indeed, *solely* by the sympathetic examination of the constituent labour processes of the artefact: cooker, micro, video recorder, or whatever.

Some pedagogic approaches do appear to give children the experience of control and mastery, a sense of expressing themselves *through* the dead labour. Bricks, sand tray, paintbrushes and dressing-up clothes are bent to the productive purposes of infant school children. Such pedagogy demands, firstly, that children's purposes are given central importance, and, secondly, that the tools of teaching and learning have limited structuring effect on the mode of consumption.

To what extent does microcomputer-related teaching restrict the range of purposes that children may pursue? Conversely, to what extent can microcomputer use assume the broad variability, provide the rich possibilities for invention and exploration of these traditional and highly mutable forms of dead labour? And the broader questions: how do people work on dead labour? How is computer technology incorporated into human purposive work? What are the sources of fascination, deference and intimidation that computer technology engenders?

Of the growing literature on the use of microcomputers in schools, there is little that transcends the traditional educational technology genre, where technology is treated as given, neutral and difficult — requiring much technical advice on its use but little consideration of the purposes of use. There are very few attempts to develop a conception of computer use which goes beyond this tradition and to place human users at the centre of the analysis. The most notable has been Sherry Turkle's *The Second Self: Computers and the Human Spirit*. I shall turn now to a brief discussion of this book and its related themes as a way of considering the questions above. Be warned: there are no answers here, merely an attempt to formulate some useful questions.

Sherry Turkle examines the ways in which particular groups of people use computers: young children with microelectronic toys, child programmers in school, video games enthusiasts, personal computer hobbyists, computer hackers, and Artificial Intelligence workers in academia. Each group is considered in turn. Each adds to Turkle's notion of 'the subjective computer. This is the machine that enters into social life and psychological development, the computer as it affects the way that we think, especially the way we think about ourselves' (1984, p. 3). I will focus here chiefly on Turkle's analysis of two groups of users: children in school and personal computer hobbyists.

School computing

Describing young children in a computer-rich experimental environment at Austen School, Turkle discerns differing styles of computer use: hard masters and soft masters.

> Hard mastery is the imposition of will over the machine through the implementation of a plan. A program is the instrument of premeditated control. Getting the program to work is more like getting 'to say one's piece' than allowing ideas to emerge in the give-and-take of conversation. The details of the specific program obviously need to be 'debugged' — there has to be room for change, for some degree of flexibility in order to get it right — but the goal is always getting the program to realise the plan.
>
> Soft mastery is more interactive. Kevin is like a painter who stands back between brushstrokes, looks at the canvas, and only from this contemplation decides what to do next. Hard mastery is the mastery of the planner, the engineer; soft mastery is the mastery of the artist: try this, wait for a response, try something else, let the overall shape emerge from an interaction with the medium. It is more like a conversation than a monologue. (p. 103)

Turkle sketches the computing styles of four girls and six boys: of these, one is black, one pointedly underprivileged, one a star athlete and school success, two are computer whizzes.

Turkle assumes that differences in programming style reflect differences in personality: 'What makes the [Austen] community most special is that it includes children with a wide range of personalities, interests, and learning styles who express their differences through their styles of programming' (p. 98). Thumbnail sketches serve to illustrate these differing styles:

Jeff, a fourth-grader, has a reputation as one of the school's computer experts. He is meticulous in his study habits, does superlative work in all subjects. His teachers were not surprised to see him excelling in programming. Jeff approaches the machine with determination and the need to be in control, the way he approaches both his schoolwork and his extracurricular activities. He likes to be, and often is, chairman of student committees. At the moment, his preoccupation with computers is intense: 'They're the biggest thing in my life right now.' He speaks very fast and when he talks about his programs he speaks even faster, tending to monologue. He answers a question about what his program does by tossing off lines of computer code that for him seem to come as naturally as English. (p. 98)

Kevin is a very different sort of child. Where Jeff is precise in all of his actions, Kevin is dreamy and impressionistic. Where Jeff tends to try to impose his ideas on other children, Kevin's warmth, easygoing nature, and interest in others make him popular. Meetings with Kevin are often interrupted by his being called out to rehearse for a school play. The play was *Cinderella*, and he had been given the role of Prince Charming. Kevin comes from a military family; his father and grandfather were both in the Air Force. But Kevin has no intention of following in their footsteps. 'I don't want to be an army man. I don't want to be a fighting man. You can get killed.' (p. 99)

Other pupils exemplify other conventional views of childhood. The barely literate girl who treated 'her' computer as a person and used it to overcome the obstacle of messy handwriting; and the artistic girl who programs by putting herself into the space of the birds she is designing on the screen. 'Her method of manipulating screens and birds allows her to feel that these objects are close, not distant and untouchable things that need designation by variables' (p. 114).

The account of Ronnie makes Turkle's assumptions particularly explicit:

Many of us know mathematics only as an alien world designed by and for people different from us. The story of a third-grader named Ronnie may be a portent of how computers in children's lives can serve as a bridge across what we have come to accept as a two-culture divide. For Ronnie, as for the soft masters Anne and Kevin, building this bridge depends on the ability to identify physically with the sprites on the computer screen. The accessibility of the formal system depended on its having hooks in the world of the sensual.

Ronnie is eight years old and black; his family has recently moved to Boston from a rural town in South Carolina. He comes to school with a radio and dances to its beat. He climbs all over my colleague as he works with him at the computer. Ronnie is filled with stories — stories about his father's adventures as a policeman, about visits to his grandmother's farm down South, about the personalities of the baby chicks in his classroom ... Ronnie is bright and energetic but is doing badly in school. He has trouble with mathematics, with grammar, with spelling, with everything that smacks of being a formal system.' (p. 119)

The account details how Ronnie constructed a computer display — a 'pulsating dance of colour, to which Ronnie responds by dancing, too' (p. 119).

Yet there is nothing particularly sensual about a computer screen, nothing that particularly lends itself to physical identification, nothing in the electronic certainties of computerized data manipulation that provides a bridge between the formal and the affective. Similarly, the account holds no evidence which suggests ways of changing a division of labour where maths is designed 'by and for people different from us'. The story of Ronnie rests on Turkle's exaggerated view of computer uniqueness and on her narrowly Piagetian definitions of learning.[8]

I find all these stereotypes implausibly cute, and the Ronnie example particularly crude. Here, as elsewhere in the book, Turkle appears to do violence to computer users. She abstracts these school children from the cultural context of school and presents them solely as psychological entities. Here, as for other groups, Turkle sets up an analysis of duality — hard or soft masters — and fits her examples into that framework. These, and the curious language of affect which her respondents consistently adopt when describing their computing activities, are serious methodological worries.

But my central concern here is to work towards a labour process analysis of computer consumption. And, obliquely, there is something to be learned from Sherry Turkle. At a simple level we can learn that you do not need to be Fairchild or a computer expert to discuss the educational use of computers. Turkle, like Seymour Papert, demonstrates that. Both discuss computer use from outside the technical ghetto. More specifically, we can learn from Turkle's treatment of computer technology.

Turkle is impressed by the power of computers. She does not explore this enthusiasm, she takes it for granted:

When you play a video game you enter into the world of the programmers who made it. You have to do more than identify with a character on the screen. You must act for it. Identification through action has a special kind of hold. Like playing a sport, it puts people into a highly focused, and highly charged state of mind. For many people, what is being pursued in the video game is not just a score, but an altered state. (p. 79)

It's difficult to remember the tiresome banality of Space Invaders after that. Turkle assumes that children will be gripped; she does not comment on those who are bored by or uninterested in computer technology. Given the popular image of computing, the turned-off group are equally interesting.

It would, of course, be a quite valid psychological enterprise to investigate the uses which children make of computers — in the same way that Lego, bricks, inflatables or felt-tip pens might be addressed. Such an investigation would embrace particular learning theories and would probably touch on educational resourcing, classroom interaction and institutional organization as well. But Sherry Turkle wants to do more than this: she wants to introduce the computer as actor whilst ignoring the cultural context within which the real actors operate.

The following two examples are drawn from Turkle's analysis of child programmers in school.

Consider Robin, a four-year-old with blond hair and a pinafore, standing in front of a computer console, typing at its keyboard. She is a student at a nursery school that is introducing computers to very young children. She is playing a game that allows her to build stick figures by commanding the computer to make components appear and move into a desired position. The machine responds to Robin's commands and tells her when it does not understand an instruction. Many people find this scene disturbing. First, Robin is 'plugged into' a machine. We speak of television as a 'plug-in drug', but perhaps the very passivity of what we do with television reassures us. We are concerned about children glued to screens, but, despite what we have heard of Marshall McLuhan and the idea that 'the medium is the message', the passivity of television encourages many of us to situate our sense of its impact at the level of the content of television programming. Is it violent or sexually suggestive? Is it educational? But Robin is not 'watching' anything on the computer. She is manipulating — perhaps more problematic, *interacting with* — a complex technological medium. And the degree and intensity of her involvement suggest that (like the children and the video games) it is the medium itself and not the content of a particular program that produces the more powerful effect. (p. 90)

We see at Austen not only a model of the male model that characterizes 'official science', but a model of how women, when given a chance, can find another way to think and talk about the mastery not

simply of machines but of formal systems. And here the computer may have a special role. It provides an entry to formal systems that is more accessible to women. It can be negotiated with, it can be responded to, it can be psychologized.

The computer sits on many borders; it is a formal system that can be taken up in a way that is not separate from the experience of the self. As such, it may evoke unconscious memories of objects that lie for the child in the uncertain zone between self and not-self. These are the objects, like Linus' baby blanket, the tattered rag doll, or the bit of silk from a first pillow, to which children remain attached even as they embark on the exploration of the world beyond the nursery. (pp. 117–18)

Turkle here attributes significant intrinsic power to the computer — a power that appears to sit outside the cultural context of the school and outside the hype of media representations about computing. It is difficult to remember that these children are in *school*, where specific teaching and learning purposes are pursued. The analysis reduces pedagogic purposes to psychic ones. Turkle suggests that the computer has unique educationally liberating properties; in so doing she takes the technology outside history and outside the varying purposes and contexts of consumption. To suggest that computer hardware itself occupies a space between quantitative and qualitative work is to deny property rights, divisions of labour, the exclusions of technological practices.

Turkle's construction of hard and soft masters (tellingly not wet and dry) appears as a device to avoid discussing gender differences. She includes examples of hard girls and soft boys but acknowledges they are exceptions. She presents differences in programming style as differences of individual psychology. Yet gender differences — particularly the gendered exclusiveness of maths, science and technology — are collective expressions; Turkle's individualism prevents her from addressing this. Sadly, the computer — complex product of gender-differentiated, hi-tech workplaces across the globe — cannot itself redistribute the gendered power of scientific and technical expertise.

Turkle focuses her attention on the ways in which school children appropriate computer technology for their psychological purposes. In doing this she presumes these singular properties of the computer. But computers in schools need no special appraisal, other than that which teachers routinely extend to other curriculum materials. Given the deference which popularly surrounds microelectronic technology, it is particularly important to regularize these curriculum products along with the rest, and to ask the usual questions. What are the ground assumptions of the authors/producers? How closely do they correspond with my own? What bits can I use? What is relevant to what we have done and the lives of learners? How much does it cost? How can I bend it to my style of working? Yet Turkle never gets to see the computer as one device in the battery of educational techniques. For her, it remains unique.

Computer hobbyists

Sherry Turkle presents a second view of computer use in her analysis of hobbyists. Here she again focuses upon the emotional satisfaction which personal computer users find.

Turkle details the sense of power and identity which users obtain from working on their computers. She argues that hobbyists gain a sense of control lacking to them at work; enhance their sense of identity when this had seemed to them inadequate; and computers provide the opportunity for mind-stretching exploration within a 'safe environment of my own creation' (p. 173); and give users control and understanding where the everyday world is experienced as chaotic and determining. Typically, Turkle's respondents express some sense of inadequacy and powerlessness. She contrasts collective worker experience with hobbyist work:

At work, when something goes wrong with the system, it is usually the fault of an intermediary person, one of the many 'somebody elses' who deals with the machine.... At home the hobbyists feel themselves as working directly with the CPU, in complete and direct control of the machine's power. And when something does blow up, the situation has a special immediacy. It is between them and the bare machine. (p. 187)

In addition to powerlessness, respondents spoke of their exclusion from the legitimating power of science and mathematics:

Alan: After Sputnik, when I was in grade school and then in Junior High, there was all that fuss, all the kids who were good at maths got to be in special classes. Rockets were going up ... men trying to go to the moon. Decisions about things. Scientists seemed to be in charge of all that. (p. 170)

Barry went to college for two years, hoping to be an engineer, then he dropped out and went to technical school. He has a job calibrating and repairing electronic equipment for a large research laboratory, and he likes his job because it gives him 'a chance to work on a lot of different machines'. But he came to it with the feeling of having failed, of not being 'analytic or theoretical': 'I always had a great difficulty with mathematics in college, which is why I never became an engineer. I just could not seem to discipline my mind enough to break mathematics down to its component parts, and then put it all together. I could never grasp what was really important in science.' Five years before I met him, Barry bought a programmable calculator and started 'fooling around with it and with numbers the way I had never been able to fool around before'. He says that 'it seemed natural to start to work with computers as soon as I could'. To hear him tell it, numbers stopped being 'theoretical', they became concrete, practical, and playful, something at which he could tinker. (p. 171)

Turkle here leaves Barry's analysis of his own success and failure unchallenged. Failure is seen as an individual phenomenon. She presents Barry's account not only as ethnography but as fact, because she wants to support the case for computer technology as an unblocker of learning failure — whilst *not* addressing the race, class, gender and age constituents of institutionally orchestrated student failure. It is here that Turkle's gullibility and enthusiasm for computing is at its most dangerous. She assumes an individualized account of learning; she implies that, if students fail, they can recoup their position with Piaget-compatible computers. But what are we to think of those who fail even after exposure to the magic technology?

For Turkle the computer not only offers exceptional learning opportunities, but also provides a terrain for psychological sensation. Thus she presents computer technology as a compelling tension between local simplicity and global complexity:

> Depending on how the programmer brings local simplicity and global complexity into focus, he or she will have a view of the machine as completely understandable and under control or as mysterious and unpredictable, even fraught with risk. By concentrating on the global, you see control slip away and can then feel the exhilaration of bringing it back. (p. 179)

Turkle argues for the irreducibility of computation:

> saying that a computer 'decided to move the [chess] Queen by adding' is a little bit like saying that Picasso 'created *Guernica* by making brushstrokes'. Reducing things to this level of localness gives no satisfying way to grasp the whole. Just as in theoretical psychology there is a tension between the Gestalt and the atomic, so too in computation there is a pervasive tension between the local simplicity of the individual acts that comprise a program or a computation, and what one might call the 'global complexity' that can emerge when it is run. (p. 283)

Turkle needs to retain a holistic notion of computing in order to argue for the microcomputer as 'an object of projective processes'. But the comparison of computer chess with *Guernica* is mischievous. The *computer* does not create the whole chess strategy, while Picasso moved from conception (intensely integrated human experience) to execution, through the medium of the brush. *Guernica* was not achieved with a painting-by-numbers kit.

In grasping the whole, Turkle simultaneously mystifies the whole. In any case, the Gestalt analogy does not hold up. In computing there is a complete account of the whole in terms of the parts that can be made explicit and public by those engaged in the relevant engineering disciplines. *Guernica* was not made by rules that can be made explicit and public — even if Picasso wanted to explain how he had done it.

However, this representation of the microcomputer as 'local simplicity', as transparent and knowable, goes beyond debates within the philosophy of mind, since transparency and simplicity deny the high complexity of divisions of labour which constitute the microcomputer. Of course, the highly specialized skills which are embodied in the microcomputer are not transparent at all; they are rendered highly *opaque* (although potentially knowable) — both by the commodity form and by the diversity of contributors. Divisions of labour (and narrowly cast theories of divisions of labour) mitigate against intelligibility, except in the broadest terms. Turkle confuses complexity and rapidity (or, more accurately, her respondents do and she fails to examine their responses). The speed of computer processing can easily fool the eye. No one would suppose the chess Queen's move to be magic if it were accompanied by a stream of numbers on the screen and a lengthy response time.

One of the few other people to comment in *educational* terms on children's use of computers is Trevor Pateman. In his 1981 paper, 'Communicating with Computer Programs', Pateman argues that using a computer program can provide opportunities for 'play which does not risk going wrong'. He argues that the very impersonality of computer software has liberating potential: the user can explore ideas without the relationship difficulties associated with learning from another living person. On this model of use, the computer has something exceptional to offer the enterprise of learning that is unavailable by other means.

Despite the seriousness of Pateman's attempt to understand the processes of user enthusiasm and machine-generated dialogue (more accurately, variable monologue), his careful argument does not entirely dispel the suspicion that he has been caught up in the glamour industry which surrounds computing. Any attempt to understand the subjective dimensions of computer use must necessarily confront this difficulty. In a world where computers are uncritically regarded as intelligent, where vast amounts of otherwise living labour can happen 'automatically', 'at the touch of a button', it is difficult to apprehend computer use outside this cultural ether of enthusiasm and/or gullibility. And assumptions about automation and the quantum leap that microelectronics is supposed to represent are not confined to research subjects, to *Tomorrow's World*, to child programmers or computer hackers; those who attempt to *analyze* computer use are also susceptible to computer dazzle. And, equally, it is not easy to find language which renders the computer ordinary, as another piece of frustrating machinery for which we are often grateful.

In fact, one of the most telling aspects of *The Second Self* is as an exemplar of the technicist phenomenon of computer dazzle. Turkle claims to have written an ethnographic account:

> The style of inquiry of this work is ethnographic. Like the anthropologist who lives in an isolated village in a far-off place to get to know its inhabitants, their ways of seeing and doing things, their myths and rituals, their economy and artifacts, I lived in worlds new to me, tried to understand what they are about, and tried to write about my understandings so that the worlds I studied could come alive for others ... I came to the job with training and experience as both a sociologist and a clinical psychologist. I considered myself a member of the 'culture' of humanists; I had never touched a computer. Thus, this book is a product of something that anthropologists call *dépaysement*, which refers to the dislocation and change of perspective that

makes being a stranger in a foreign place both difficult and exciting.
(p. 328)

Turkle has attempted to investigate the subjective and subcultural dimension
of computer use, yet one of the most marked phenomena of computer use —
seduction by the machine — is not seen as strange. Surely that itself *is* strange.
Turkle claims to be rendering the computer world strange, yet suspends her
critique before the getting to the computer. In short, she affirms claims to
the uniqueness of computing. Thus Turkle reproduces the sense of magical
possibility around computers and programming by dismissing the social
constituents of computer use; by refusing to recognize the many labours of
computer production; by ignoring the cultural definitions of particular user
groups (*how* products are consumed is framed by the purposes of that
workplace — what does a reading group do but change the context and
purposes of reading?); and by failing to critique the exaggeration of computer
power in popular representation.

These are all matters of sociological method. Yet the popularity of
Turkle's book is some testimony to the pervasive suspension of social concerns and critical debate which surrounds the topic of computer technology.
Had she written in such an ahistorical and asocial manner about the educational use of film, there would be no such deference.

Context and content

While social theorists bracket off technology from critical scrutiny and fail to
challenge the power that computers mediate, the criteria of automation are
increasingly used to evaluate human affairs, including the learning process.
People will need to understand educational computing for particular purposes: teachers to fight for less prescribed syllabuses; learners to increase their
autonomy and to lessen the oppressive authority of the screen; parents to
empower themselves as customers; and social theorists to understand the
computer as a particular expression of domination. These areas of analysis all
derive from the central argument of this chapter: technology is not a thing but
a set of practices. I have tried to present the view that some version of a
labour process analysis is useful in understanding those practices. Within such
an analysis, the constitutive practices of technology are embodied in dead
labour (in computers, school buildings, timetables, authority structures,
established forms of classroom interaction, and curriculum organization) and
include the living labour of all those involved in the project of schooling.

Like other curriculum materials — like any other teaching technique or
technology — microcomputers embody particular pedagogic assumptions
about the subject area, about learning, and about classroom relations. (The
materials of teaching often embody assumptions about profit-making too.)
The school also has its embedded features. The possibilities and limitations of

microcomputer hardware and software are, in part, structured by the school context, and beyond the school by the local education authority and the government. School computer consumption is structured, for instance, by how much money is spent on equipment and staff development, by the status ascribed to computing, and by the legitimating activities of examining bodies and the DES. In addition to these already existing features of school practice, living labour also shapes the character of school computing as a technological practice. The purposes of living workers — teachers, learners and those in authority positions at local, regional and ministerial levels — are all significant in any attempt to realize particular use-values of computer technology.

Many differing workplaces contribute to the production of school computer equipment. Technical, geographic and gendered divisions of labour are as evident here as in any other workplace. Specific analysis of computer-related workplace divisions goes part-way to historicizing those products, part-way to subverting the awesome givenness of the commodity product. Where computing is concerned, it is often particularly illuminating to explore the work of marketing departments. To understand, for instance, the continued and escalating customer dependency which is often designed into computer products, helps to put alienating technology into a clearer social perspective. Or to recognize the diverse purposes of hardware and software production — military, industrial, commercial — whose products are then adapted for educational use, gives some leverage on the sources of rigidity and prescription in the technology. But in addition to the physical constitution of microcomputer technology, other workers, in more representative capacities, contribute to the ideological framing within which school computing occurs. Most noticeable here is the use of computers — in films, graphics and journalism — as a symbol of modernity, super-humanness, and transcendence of the known constraints of the present. The interrelatedness of workplaces, waged and unwaged, is emphasized by an examination of the labour processes of representational workers. They don't collude with computer manufacturers, they live in symbiosis with them.

And infusing all these workplaces is a pervasive technicism, an objectified and ahistorical view of computer technology. For example, Turkle describes machines with the powers of teachers, and learners with predictable learning patterns. Other writers and other practices more explicitly invert human consciousness and machine regularity; examples here are computer-marked assignments which prioritize the capability of the computer, or 'learn-at-your-own-pace' instructional software which requires the user to go through a series of rigidly predetermined steps. I do not want to suggest that the social world is made up solely of complex contingencies: that way lies liberalism. I do want to assert the social and historical character of technology, and move towards providing the means by which social theorists can assist in dethroning the computer idol. In our everyday lives most of us either defer to computers or distrust them as another expression of capital; why not analyze them?

Notes

1 See, for example, Braverman (1974), CSE (1980), Nichols (1980), Thompson (1983), Wood (1982) and Zimbalist (1979).
2 Microelectronics Support Scheme (£6.579m), Electronics Component Industry Scheme (£318,000), Microelectronics Industry Support Programme (£1.168m), Computers, Systems and Electronics Requirement Board (£1.75m), Advanced Computer Techniques Project (£350,000). This is all *additional* to funds allocated by the National Research Development Corporation and the NEB.
3 See the *Times Education Supplement*, 27 February 1981, for debates around this.
4 Designing, marketing and profit-taking take place in the USA; much of the labour-intensive part of chip production is done by cheap labour in the Free Enterprise Zones of the Third World.
5 Zylog make the Z80 chip used in the RML and Sinclair microcomputers. Motorola make the 6502 chip used in the Acorn.
6 For instance, in the Sinclair Spectrum, the following microchips are to be found: three important integrated circuits (ICs) from Zylog, Ferranti and NEC; eight chips from Texas Instruments, six from Motorola, eight from NEC, Ireland; the regulator comes from Singapore, and the video/board interface from the Philippines.
7 Photography provides an everyday example of this. Point-and-click cameras, in their very convenience, represent a real loss of choice and user autonomy; lost is the choice, for example, to take a grainy or darkly atmospheric picture, or to shoot in a range of 'non-standard' conditions. A 'deficiency model' conception of the domestic photographer means that, for particular purposes, users inevitably find it frustrating *not* to be able to alter the variables. It is not logically possible to build many choices into an 'automatic' or point-and-click camera. So design of the product is geared to the use of the most common, stereotypically conceived consumer of the product.
8 Piaget's model sees learning as an ordered, staged process in which mental development corresponds to the structure of knowledge. Turkle defers to Papert's acceptance of Piaget: 'The child programs the computer. In "teaching" the machine, the child learns to speak its language and manipulate formal and mathematical systems. Papert calls this kind of natural learning "Piagetian" learning — learning that happens spontaneously when people are in contact with the right materials' (p. 95).

References

BRAVERMAN, H. (1974) *Labour and Monopoly Capital: The Degradation of Work in the Twentieth Century*, New York, Monthly Review Press.
CET (1978) *Microelectronics: Their Implications for Education and Training*.
COMMITTEE OF VICE-CHANCELLORS AND PRINCIPALS (1979) *Microelectronics*, May.
CPRS (Central Policy Review Staff) (1978) *Social and Employment Implications of Microelectronics*, NEDC, November.

CSE Microelectronics Group (1980) *Microelectronics: Capitalist Technology and the Working Class*, CSE Books.

DES (Department of Education and Science) (1979) *Microelectronics in Education: A Development Programme for Schools and Colleges*, March.

DES (1981) *Microelectronics Education Programme: The Strategy*, April.

Gosling, W. (1981) *The Kingdom of Sand*, CET Occasional Paper No. 9.

Maddison, J. (1983) *Education in the Microelectronics Era*, Oxford University Press.

Marx, Karl (1954) *Capital, Vol. I*, Lawrence and Wishart.

Nichols, T. (1980) *Capital and Labour*, Glasgow, Fontana.

Pateman, T. (1981) 'Communicating with Computer Programs', *Language and Communication*, I.

Robins, K. and Webster, F. (1985) 'Higher education, high tech, high rhetoric', in Solomonides, T. and Levidow, L. (Eds) *Compulsive Technology: Computers as Culture*, London, Free Association Books.

Thompson, P. (1983) *The Nature of Work*, Macmillan.

Times Education Supplement, 27 February 1981.

Touche Ross International (1985) *The Impact of New Technology on Banking*, World Summary.

TUC/Labour Party (1984) *A Plan for Training*.

Turkle, S. (1984) *The Second Self: Computers and the Human Spirit*, Granada.

Weaver, B. (1982) 'Document C: the DoI offer — advice by ILEA', 14 October.

Wood, S. (Ed.) (1982) *The Degradation of Work? Skill, De-skilling and the Labour Process*, Hutchinson.

Zimbalist, A. (Ed.) (1979) *Case studies in the Labour Process*, Monthly Review Press; see also essay review in *Radical Science Journal* 11 (1981), pp. 111–22.

Technology as an Educational Issue: Why it is so Difficult and Why it is so Important

Michael Young

Introduction

Discussions about technology in education are characterized by abstractness and extreme diversity of focus. They are frequently polarized between the perceptions of two groups who understand little of each other. These are the specialists, often but not always in electronics or computing, and the rest who have little concrete knowledge of either (or any other) technologies. For the specialists, attempts to question the purposes of a new technological artefact are likely to demonstrate the questioner's lack of specialist knowledge. On the other hand, the non-specialist will be dismayed at the way the enthusiasm of technical specialists so easily excludes wider questions of educational and social purpose.

This book aims to be a contribution to overcoming this impasse. It argues that technology is an educational issue of great immediacy and importance for both specialists and non-specialists. As a part of any society's culture and of how it produces its livelihood, technology is the most human of phenomena and is intimately involved in all spheres of social life. Although in the past it may have been reasonable to leave technological decisions to the specialists, for economic, ecological and political reasons this is no longer true. It is simply not possible today for a democratic society to allow its citizens to remain ignorant of how technological decisions shape and are shaped by social purposes. This is, at least in principle, recognized by the proposals to include technology as a foundation subject in the National Curriculum. It means that there is a possibility, for the first time in a mass education system, for some systematic understanding of the significance of technology in our lives to be part of the experience of all students.

This chapter aims to be a contribution to the principles that might guide a programme of technological literacy. It starts with the assumption that as teachers are going to have to interpret the National Curriculum Council guidelines, the beliefs they have about the purposes of teaching technology are of crucial importance. The chapter therefore is not concerned with the National Curriculum itself but with some of the ideas that will be brought to making sense of its guidelines on technology. It has two parts:

- A brief review of the ways the teaching of technology may be shaped by school subject traditions and recent attempts to 'vocationalize' the secondary curriculum.
- Technology as a 'social phenomenon' and its possible implications for developing an approach to technological literacy.

I shall argue that how we understand and how we use technology and therefore how it becomes part of the curriculum will determine not only the form of our education system but also the kind of society we create for the next century.

The cultural and educational shaping of school technology

Technology has no unambiguous meaning except with reference to specific technologies, though it has powerful rhetorical and ideological connotations. It subsumes and is often equated with a whole range of notions such as being modern, progressive, practical, politically neutral, economically relevant, productive, efficient, quick, reliable, accurate.

Invariably, then, the potentialities of a particular artefact, machine or gadget are compared with the burdens of the same tasks being being carried out by people. Though our actual experience of using technological artefacts maybe at odds with the general claims made, we do not find it easy to use that experience to challenge the assumptions of technology's effectiveness. It is all too easy for anyone who wants to question this rhetoric to be labelled a modern Luddite.

This difficulty that we have in thinking about the place of technology in the curriculum reflects something much wider about how it has been treated in English culture. To a much greater extent than in other European cultures, technology, and even to some extent science, has been excluded from wider discussions about culture and the school curriculum. This may reflect the perpetuation of landed aristocratic values that tend to denigrate trade and manufacture and thereby anything associated with practical skills.

Discussions of culture and its basis in the curriculum, whether from the Right or Left, have been rare in this country. Such discussions as there have been have largely originated in debates about the teaching of literature. There has been no framework outside the rather rarefied debates about modernism and post-modernism within which the meaning of technology as a cultural phenomenon with enormous ramifications in every field of life could be explored.

So long as technology in the curriculum was restricted either to specialized aspects of engineering or to the skills associated with craft apprenticeships, this absence was not directly apparent, at least to educational policy makers. The separation of technology as something of significance only for those wanting to specialize meant that in effect it was not treated as part of the culture at all.

The last ten years have begun to change this, largely as a result of anxieties about the economy and the failure of our system of vocational education and training. We have in this period seen a number of attempts to broaden access to technological knowledge in the 14–19 curriculum. This was initially through TVEI, a funding programme to enhance the secondary curriculum. Technology is also identified as part of the core element in a whole range of vocational programmes (e.g., YTS and CPVE as well as many BTEC courses). There is little research evidence to indicate the outcomes of these developments or the way they have interpreted technology. However they are all based on the assumption that a much higher proportion of employees than in the past are going to need to be familiar with technology in some form. Although technology is no longer only associated with specialist engineering it is far less clear what a broader notion of technological literacy might mean.

There have been a variety of schemes for integrating an understanding of technology into the curriculum as a whole, largely stimulated by TVEI. Some of the most imaginative have arisen out of whole school technology audits which have made explicit the range of subject areas in which technological issues are addressed in some way. However, given the history of neglect and the lack of a clear location for technology in either the culture or the curriculum, it is not surprising that such developments have been fragmented. They can be divided broadly into two kinds:

- Those arising out of the reform of existing subjects.
- Those concerned with cross-curricular issues such as bringing work and education closer together.

Technology and school subject teaching

What follows is no more than a list, but it serves to emphasize not only the way technology education has been so fragmented into different traditions which often know little about each other, but also the potential resources and experience available for a more coherent and integrated approach.

School Science

Secondary school science represents a most obvious resource for technology education. However, its single-subject tradition of physics, chemistry and biology has until recently cut school science off from any broader discussions about the relationship between science and technology. The Secondary Science Curriculum Review represented a significant shift away from this separate subject focus together with the greater role school science departments have played in the later phases of TVEI.

Craft and Design (CDT)

Craft and Design has not surprisingly been the main starting point for school technology, though it has had to overcome its narrow association with craft teaching. It was a major beneficiary of TVEI for both funding and resources and has been able to introduce various new combinations involving design and electronics.

Art

Changes in art teaching have given it a greater industrial design emphasis and sometimes provided an integrating basis for technology across the curriculum.

Business Studies

Changes in business studies have taken into account the impact of new technology on commercial and office organization.

Computer Studies

The shift in emphasis from computing as a separate school subject to IT across the curriculum is the most significant recent change.

These traditions represent considerable areas of specialist knowledge. What is lacking, even in the National Curriculum Council guidelines, is an overall sense of the educational purposes of teaching about technology that could give them a sense of coherence.

Technology and the vocationalization of the curriculum

The most significant new context for how technology has been introduced into schools and colleges and one that may offer the greatest possibilities for educational coherence may not be through separate subjects but through a reassessment of recent attempts to 'vocationalize' the curriculum. The link between technology and the 'world of work' was made explicit in the terms of reference of the *Technical and Vocational* Initiative. It is not surprising therefore that technology in TVEI (and elswhere) has been seen primarily in terms of its occupational relevance rather than its part in broadening general education. It has therefore frequently taken on the characteristic features of the other 'vocationalizing' innovations such as work experience and business studies. Like them it has been frequently associated with (a) low-level courses, (b) gender stereotyping and (c) narrow specialization.

TVEI has assumed that there is a link between understanding about the world of work and understanding technology, and that this refers not to occupational preparation but to a much broader concept of 'vocationalism'. However, that broader vocationalism and the nature of the link has never been made explicit. The result is that both the world of work and understanding technology, though often enthusiastically taken up by pupils and their teachers, have been taught quite separately from mainstream curriculum subjects like English, history and geography.

The implicit message of this curricular separation of technology is that, despite its inescapably human origins and consequences, it cannot be classified among the humanities. This reflects the view referred to earlier that technology is not a part of the culture and therefore that its history and the values and the purposes that it embodies are not of educational importance. Separated from the humanities and social sciences, technology becomes no more than a combination of artefacts and specialized knowledge.

For a broader notion of technology that goes beyond a definition in terms of artefacts and specialized knowledge we need to turn to the analyses that treat technology as a social phenomenon and explicitly link it to the organization of work.

Technology as a social phenomenon

Most approaches to technology as a social phenomenon that begin by making connections between technology and work have their roots in industrial sociology. They have been largely inspired by Braverman's (1974) account which led to a whole new research tradition known as 'labour process analysis'. In his book *Labor and Monopoly Capital*, Braverman graphically describes the process of deskilling of work under capitalism. He was not interested in technology *per se* but in how, in a wide range of industrial and commercial sectors, it has been used by managements to displace and deskill craft and skilled workers. The purposes of this chapter are not to review debates from industrial sociology but to consider the educational implications of this kind of analysis. Labour process analyses make two points which are important here:

- That despite its apparent neutrality and objectivity, technology is always designed for particular purposes.
- That technology needs to be understood in relation to people's work. It does not have purposes or effects of its own.

This approach is important in countering the influence of technological determinism and the tendency to view technology in terms of artefacts. It has, however, limitations for educational purposes which arise from its origins in industrial sociology with its narrow focus on particular kinds of workplaces.

In countering the technological determinism of much previous industrial sociology, Braverman and those who followed him stressed *management's* purposes rather than the complex combination of purposes likely to be involved in actual technological decisions. Similarly, in the way he links technology to work, the industrial emphasis leads to a concentration on (male) *waged* work rather than the variety of working contexts that may be involved in the shaping of technologies.

Another aspect of the narrowness of labour process analyses, at least as they have been applied to education, appears in the way they tend to assume that capitalist production always links technological investment to labour subordination and displacement. Educational critics of technology have so far neglected the possible implications of recent and more diversified accounts of management strategies that have been developed by industrial sociologists such as Friedman and Child.

Recent comparative studies (e.g., Lane, 1988) provide evidence of the very different ways in which technologies are becoming part of the production systems of capitalist firms in different countries, with deskilling and the subordination being only one strategy and often not that associated with the most successful companies. The possibility that the significance of technological innovation can be very different as it becomes part of quite different industrial strategies has profound implications for what might be meant by technology education. We are dealing not with technology as sets of artefacts or as part of an almost universal management strategy but as part of changing systems of production and wider changes in the culture. This raises questions about the appropriateness of the traditional division between academic and technical or vocational curricula as the framework for a broad based understanding of technology. This section therefore considers two questions:

1 What is the alternative to the existing academic curriculum?
2 What are the implications of changes in the organization of work and different industrial strategies for a broad approach to technology in education?

Michael Young

Technology and the liberal academic curriculum

Despite the subject-boundness of the National Curriculum and the government's refusal to reform 'A' levels, it is more and more widely recognized that the old academic curriculum of single subjects and sharp divisions between it and vocational courses will not work for a 'modern' society whatever the political character of its government. It does not produce enough people with enough of the kind of qualifications that a modern society needs if it is to avoid becoming dependent in the way 'Third World' countries find themselves today.

A modern curriculum will be more integrated, more technological, more informed about economics and the world of work, more multilingual and more oriented to learners' rather than teachers' needs, and will encourage far higher levels of participation. Such a curriculum will take many different forms, but these same general tendencies can be found in all the main continental European systems. It is the specific form that such a curriculum might take that will provide the context for any future discussions of technological literacy, not the increasingly outmoded academic curriculum of separate subjects clearly set apart from applied and vocational studies.

Technology and the end of mass production

As Robin Murray so well describes in his chapter in this book, the transformation of mass production in a whole variety of fields from media and communications to food and clothing is becoming possible. This is partly through changes in the balance of world trade and partly as a result of the unintended consequences of the US defence and space policies of the 1960s and 1970s. The electronics designed in the true spirit of Taylorism to provide the maximum of prediction and control to NASA and the Pentagon have been commercially exploited in quite unexpected ways. In particular, the possibilities of decentralizing decision-making without losing control has led to outcomes that are radically changing the organization of paid work in a growing number of sectors.

There are few signs yet of such developments in this country. However, in the car and consumer electronics industries in Japan and, increasingly, in West Germany, Scandanavia and other European countries (the Italian fashion industry for example), quite new approaches to technology, industrial relations and markets are being developed.

The consequences for education and training are no less vast though even less realized. Teamwork, quality control and shop-floor and office innovation are among the elements of a new mode of production which is emerging. This can lead to reskilling as well as deskilling, and to strategies for strengthening employee loyalty rather than displacing it. Investment in technology is seen as wasted without investment in employees, as private sector companies form networks of cooperation and work in close collaboration with public sector institutions. There are examples in West Germany of educational institutions being asked by the private sector to give the lead on appropriate curricula for company-based training. This is, of course, still capitalism, but it is a far cry from most British firms with their low priority on training and their tradition of adversarial industrial relations.

The features of this scenario for the end of mass production that are most immediately significant for the question of technology in education are:

1   Distinctions between mental and manual labour are becoming blurred as managements need to know more about practical skills and shop-floor employees need to have a grasp of the system as a whole to be able to respond to sudden problems and changes of demand. There are indications that, for example, the French government is aware of such developments in their plans for the new *Baccalaureate Professionale*.

2   Traditional sector divisions are also disappearing (e.g., service, manufacturing, etc.). As technologies enable old structures to be reorganized, these are likely to take on increasingly similar characteristics.

3   The importance is increasingly recognized of broadening the range of people with technical knowledge in order to encourage innovations from the shop floor or office rather than just those imposed from the top.

Each of these developments points to the need to rethink many traditional specialized programmes in engineering, their separation of craft skills from higher-level studies and the way they tend to be limited to particular occupational sectors.

The tendency still to view technology as artefacts, rather than as an integral part of the transformation of production, has been perpetuated by the publicity associated with electronics-based technologies. It has masked the extent to which the effective introduction of what Zuboff (1989) calls informating technologies necessitates radical changes in shop floors and managements with profound implications for educators.

If technology is viewed in the broad context of production decisions that involve many conflicting beliefs, purposes and interests, it is not technological knowledge in the old sense of specialist technical knowledge of machines that is going to need to be part of the modern curriculum. What will be needed will be knowledge about how technological choices are enmeshed in organizational, economic and political choices. For example, whether a machine tool is designed to limit the need for skilled operators or leads to demands that operators have a broader-based education and training depends more on management and design philosophy than on developments in metallurgy or control engineering (Noble, 1984).

Technologies have to be seen as systems, not machines, and the purposes associated with technological design are increasingly the responsibility of those involved in marketing and advertising as much as it is of those involved in engineering.

The changes in production that have been alluded to mean that the idea of technologies being shaped socially is becoming a practical issue for educators as well as for managers and Unionists, and not just an academic one. Current ideas and research on technology being shaped as a social phenomenon are still limited. References to the social shaping of, for example, machine tools (Rauner *et al.*, 1988) focus on the factory and do not incorporate the wider context within which design and investment decisions are made. Even Mathews' argument in his chapter in this book stays within the bounds of a fairly conventional view of production and its link to paid or waged work.

The tendency to equate technology with physical artefacts is deeply held and influences attempts to develop a more contextual view. It is perhaps not surprising, therefore, that the focus of research has been on decisions concerned directly with design and production. This emphasis on production is, however, part of our industrial history rather than something intrinsic to technology itself. In thinking about how design decisions may be influenced by forces outside the context of production, there are examples to draw on. Lessons need to be learnt both from the idea of feedback from consumers as pioneered by companies such as Benetton and from political initiatives to involve consumers such as the Technology Networks set up by the Greater London Council (both of which are discussed in the chapter by Robin Murray).

Conclusions — possibilities for technological literacy

The argument of this chapter has been that extending technology in education from the preparation of technological specialists to the idea of technological literacy for all raises fundamental questions not only for the curriculum but for English culture generally. I have argued that in order to develop a programme of technological literacy it is necessary to break away from current conceptions both of technology and of curriculum. It will need to go beyond a view of technology as 'artefact' and its narrow association with engineers and others with specialist knowledge and beyond a curriculum conceived in terms of divisions between academic and vocational programmes. What is needed is a concept of technology as a social phenomenon intimately bound up not only with changes in production but also with every area of social life, and a model of a unified model of the curriculum in which work in its broadest sense is an educational principle for all. It has been suggested that economic developments and some of the new production strategies that they give rise to can create the conditions for developing a much less exclusive view of technology and a less divided curriculum. Consideration of the educational implications of such developments have hardly begun.

What this book aims to do is to create to dialogue between the kinds of analyses that are included and the many teachers, both specialist technologists and others, who want to see technology as an integral part of a broad-based 14–19 curriculum for all.

Technology is difficult because it is hard to be precise about what we are talking about without falling in to the trap of thinking narrowly in terms of artefacts. Technology is important both on account of the enormous ideological power associated with technological expertise, and on account of the way technologies pervade more and more parts of our lives. If it is to become part of a more participative and democratic society, we have to find ways of making explicit how different purposes are involved in its design, its implementation and its use, and how at each stage there are potential choices and decisions to be made. This means a technologically literate population and an increasingly wide debate about the content and meaning of technological literacy.

References

BRAVERMAN, H. (1974) *Labor and Monopoly Capital: The Degradation of Work in the Twentieth Century*, New York, Monthly Review Press.

LANE, C. (1988) 'Industrial change in Europe: the pursuit of flexible specialization in Britain and West Germany', *Work, Employment and Society*, 2, 2.

NOBLE, D. (1984) *Forces of Production*, Alfred Knopf.

RAUNER, F., RASMUSSEN, L. and CORBETT, M. (1988) 'The social shaping of technology and work: human centred CIM systems', *Artificial Intelligence and Society*, 1, 2.

ZUBOFF, S. (1989) *In the Age of the Smart Machine*, Heinemann.

Note on Further Reading

Hughie Mackay

There is one edited volume which provides access to a broad range of the *social shaping of technology* literature (Mackenzie and Wajcman, 1985); it has stood the test of time in a rapidly developing field, and has a comprehensive postcript on 'other areas of study' and an extensive bibliography.

On *technology and the state*, Webster and Robins (1986) document with rigour the forces behind the promotion and acceptance of IT. Campbell and Connor (1986) provide a detailed account of the increasing capacity of the state, through its use of new technology, to know about its population. Ackroyd *et al.* (1980) detail the technologies used by the security forces in Northern Ireland, and predict their more widespread use elsewhere. Lyon, who contributes to this volume, is developing work in the area of surveillance (Lyon, 1990).

On the *social constructivist* approach to technology, Bijker, Hughes and Pinch (1987) is the best source; it has papers from the authors of the main variants of the perspective. A subsequent volume, of papers from the second Twente Conference, is to be published in 1990 (Bijker and Law). Latour and Woolgar (1986) constitutes a classic ethnographic study in the social constructivist tradition, applying in relation to science some of the ideas that have been translated and applied to technology.

On *technology at work* and the labour process, Braverman (1974) is the starting-point. The collections of papers from the annual Aston/UMIST Labour Process Conference provide access to the debates, and case studies of a range of industries, occupations, sectors and societies (Knights, Willmott and Collinson, 1985; Knights and Willmott, 1986a, 1987). The most recent of these volumes (Knights and Willmott, 1990) contains a number of papers which summarize the progress, scope and direction of work on the labour process. Thompson's book (1983) reviews the deskilling debate; and Wood's collection (1989) has some useful papers on technology, work organization and changing patterns of production.

One of the Labour Process Conference collections deals with *gender* and the labour process (Knights and Willmott, 1986b). Cockburn's work on print workers (1983) and technology generally (1985) is of enormous value. There are some excellent papers in Rothschild (1983), Faulkner and Arnold (1985), and Kramarae (1988). Most recently, Hacker's two books include discussion of how feminism can contribute to changing the role and impact of technology (1989, 1990).

The *Cultural Studies* approach is recent and growing fast. The journal *Science as Culture* (which has replaced *Radical Science*) has some useful work in this tradition — Keen's study of home video, for example (1987). Slack (1984) discusses how IT is ideological, and Stephen Hill (1988) develops arguments about technology as a cultural artefact and 'text'. Morley, well known for his work on television audiences (1980a, 1980b), is investigating the consumption of new domestic technologies (Morley and Silverstone, 1990).

Athanasiou (1985) reviews some of the main arguments against *artificial intelligence* (AI), and is critical of AI in education in particular. Weizenbaum (1976) is among those 'insiders' (to the AI community) who have provided useful critiques; and Searle (1984), a philosopher, addresses some of the arguments about the differences between mind and brain, and whether computers can think.

On the *possibilities of technology* there is some literature on socially useful production (SUP), much of it drawing on the experience of the Greater London Enterprise Board (GLEB) and other similar initiatives (Collective Design Projects, 1985). Cooley, a pivotal character in the Lucas Aerospace Corporate Plan, puts forward some of the arguments (1980) and is currently working on human-centred computer-integrated manufacturing.

On *education* the literature is conspicuously lacking — hence the rationale for the present volume. There is an enormous quantity of material which starts from an uncritical, often accolatory, approach to technology in education; Papert's advocacy of LOGO (1980) is probably the best work in this tradition; and there are vast numbers of publications from writers in the AI and cognitive psychology traditions (e.g., Rutkowska and Crook, 1987). There is a tradition of evaluation studies (e.g., London Mental Models Group, 1988), but all within a very narrow paradigm.

As we see it, there is a need for a widening of the research agenda. Educational researchers need to develop analyses which treat technology as a social phenomenon; and we need to build on the few works which take an educationalist approach to technology in education — Webster and Robins on higher education (1985) and education generally (Robins and Webster, 1987; Webster and Robins, 1989), and Apple (1986, 1987). Culley's work on gender and computing in schools (1986) provides us with one of the few works which link some of these debates with classroom practice; we would see ethnographic accounts of technology in classrooms as a most fruitful development. Finally, we need practical critical accounts, on the lines of the collection edited by Conlon and Cope (1989). As the National Curriculum emerges, more than ever before, we need accounts of the developments which teachers are making. We hope that this volume will be informing these.

Hughie Mackay

References

ACKROYD, C., MARGOLIS, K., ROSENHEAD., J and SHALLICE, T. (1980) *The Technology of Political Control*, 2nd ed., London, Pluto.
APPLE, M. (1986) *Teachers and Texts: A Political Economy of Class and Gender Relations in Education*, London, Routledge and Kegan Paul.
APPLE, M. (1987) 'Mandating computers: the impact of the new technology on the labour process, students and teachers', in WALKER, S. and BARTON, L. (Eds) *Changing Policies, Changing Schools: New Directions for Schooling?*, Milton Keynes, Open University Press.
ATHANASIOU, T. (1985) 'Artificial intelligence: cleverly disguised politics', *Radical Science*, 18, pp. 13–35.
BIJKER, W.E., HUGHES, T.P. and PINCH, T.J. (Eds) (1987) *The Social Construction of Technological Systems: New Directions in the Sociology and History of Technology*, Cambridge, Mass., MIT Press.
BIJKER, W.E. and LAW, J. (Eds) (1990) *Proceedings of the Second Twente Conference*, Cambridge, Mass., MIT Press.
BRAVERMAN, H. (1974) *Labor and Monopoly Capital: The Degradation of Work in the Twentieth Century*, New York, Monthly Review Press.
CAMPBELL, D. and CONNOR, S. (1986) *On the Record: Surveillance, Computers and Privacy*, London, Michael Joseph.
COCKBURN, C. (1983) *Brothers: Male Dominance and Technological Change*, London, Pluto.
COCKBURN, C. (1985) *Machinery of Dominance: Women, Men and Technical Know-how*, London, Pluto.
COLLECTIVE DESIGN PROJECTS (1985) *Very Nice Work If You Can Get It: The Socially Useful Production Debate*, Nottingham, Spokesman.
CONLON, T. and COPE, P. (Eds) (1989) *Computing in Scottish Education: The First Decade and Beyond*, Edinburgh, Edinburgh University Press.
COOLEY, M. (1980) (revised ed. 1987) *Architect or Bee? The Human Price of Technology*, London, Hogarth Press.
CULLEY, L. (1986) *Gender Differences and Computing in Secondary Schools*, Loughborough, Loughborough University of Technology Department of Education.
FAULKNER, W. and ARNOLD, E. (Eds) (1985) *Smothered by Invention: Technology in Women's Lives*, London, Pluto.
HACKER, S. (1989) *Pleasure, Power and Technology: Some Tales of Gender, Engineering and the Cooperative Workplace*, London, Unwin Hyman.
HACKER, S. (1990) *'Doing It the Hard Way': Investigations of Gender and Technology*, London, Unwin Hyman.
HILL, S. (1988) *The Tragedy of Technology*, London, Pluto.
KEEN, B. (1987) '"Play it again, Sony": the double life of home video technology', *Science as Culture*, 1, pp. 7–42.
KNIGHTS, D. and WILLMOTT, H. (Eds) (1986a) *Managing the Labour Process*, London, Macmillan.
KNIGHTS, D. and WILLMOTT, H. (Eds) (1986b) *Gender and the Labour Process*, Aldershot, Gower.
KNIGHTS, D. and WILLMOTT, H. (Eds) (1987) *New Technology and the Labour Process*, London, Macmillan.

KNIGHTS, D. and WILLMOTT, H. (Eds) (1990) *Labour Process Theory*, London, Macmillan.

KNIGHTS, D. WILLMOTT, H. and COLLINSON, D. (Eds) (1985) *Job Redesign: Critical Perspectives on the Labour Process*, Aldershot, Gower.

KRAMARAE, C. (Ed.) (1988) *Technology and Women's Voices: Keeping In Touch*, London, Routledge and Kegan Paul.

LATOUR, B. and WOOLGAR, S. (1986) *Laboratory Life: The Construction of Scientific Facts*, 2nd ed., Princetown, New Jersey, Princeton University Press.

LONDON MENTAL MODELS GROUP (1988) *Tools for Exploratory Learning*, ESRC InTER Paper 5/88, Lancaster, InTER (Department of Psychology, University of Lancaster).

LYON, D. (1990) 'The new surveillance: electronic technologies, power and social divisions', Paper presented to British Sociological Association Conference, University of Surrey, April.

MACKENZIE, D. and WAJCMAN, J. (Eds) (1985) *The Social Shaping of Technology*, Milton Keynes, Open University Press.

MORLEY, D. (1980a) *Family Television: Cultural Power and Domestic Leisure*, London Comedia.

MORLEY, D. (1980b) *The Nationwide Audience: Structuring and Decoding*, BFI TV Monograph No. 11, London, British Film Institute.

MORLEY, D. and SILVERSTONE, R. (1990) 'Domestic communication — technologies and meanings', *Media, Culture and Society*, 12, 1, pp. 31–55.

PAPERT, S. (1980) *Mindstorms: Children, Computers and Powerful Ideas*, Brighton, Harvester.

ROBINS, K. and WEBSTER, F. (1987) 'Dangers of information technology and responsibilities of education', in FINNEGAN, R., SALAMAN, G. and THOMPSON, K. (Eds) *Information Technology: Social Issues: A reader*, Sevenoaks, Hodder and Stoughton.

ROTHSCHILD, J. (Ed.) (1983) *Machina ex Dea: Feminist Perspectives on Technology*, Oxford, Pergamon.

RUTKOWSKA, J.C. and CROOK, C. (Eds) (1987) *Computers, Cognition and Development*, Chichester, Wiley.

SEARLE, J. (1984) *Minds, Brains and Science*, Harmondsworth, Penguin.

SLACK, J. (1984) 'The information revolution as ideology', *Media, Culture and Society*, 6, 3, pp. 247–56.

THOMPSON, T. (1983) *The Nature of Work: An Introduction to Debates on the Labour Process*, London, Macmillan.

WEBSTER, F. and ROBINS, K. (1985) 'Higher education, high tech, high rhetoric', *Radical Science*, 18, pp. 36–57.

WEBSTER, F. and ROBINS, K. (1986) *Information Technology: A Luddite Analysis*, New Jersey, Ablex.

WEBSTER, F. and ROBINS, K. (1989) *The Technical Fix: Education, Computers and Industry*, London, Macmillan.

WEIZENBAUM, J. (1976) *Computer Power and Human Reason: From Judgement To Calculation*, Harmondsworth, Penguin.

WOOD, S. (Ed.) (1989) *The Transformation of Work*, London, Unwin Hyman.

Notes on Contributors

John Beynon is Reader ank Course Tutor of the BA in Communication Studies and MA in Communication, Culture and Society at the Polytechnic of Wales. A former comprehensive school teacher and journalist, he has published extensively in the areas of classroom interaction and ethnographic methodology, notably *Initial Encounters in the Secondary School* (Falmer Press, 1985) and *Be a Man!* (Routledge and Kegan Paul, forthcoming).

Cynthia Cockburn is a Research Associate in the Department of Social Science and Humanities, City University. She is author of *Brothers — Male Dominance and Technological Change* (Pluto, 1983), *Machinery of Dominance: Women, Men and Technical Know-how* (Pluto, 1985), and *Two-track Training: Sex Inequalities and the YTS* (Macmillan, 1987).

Paul Dowling is a Lecturer in Mathematics Education in the Department of Mathematics, Statistics and Computing, Institute of Education, University of London. Recently he edited, with Richard Noss, *Mathematics versus the National Curriculum* (Falmer Press, 1990).

Leslie Haddon is a Research Assistant in the School of Social Sciences at the University of Sussex. He recently completed his PhD at Imperial College, University of London on the development of the home computer market (and has published a paper in *Science as Culture*, Vol. 2, on the subject), and currently is working on how other new technologies for the home are developed.

Pam Linn is Head of Continuing Education at Westminster College, Oxford, and is completing a PhD thesis in the sociology of technology.

David Lyon is a Senior Lecturer in Sociology at Bradford and Ilkley College, and Tutor for the Open University. He is author of *The Information Society: Issues and Illusions* (Polity, 1988), and is currently working on IT and community projects, and on state surveillance.

Hughie Mackay is Senior Lecturer in the Sociology of Technology at the Polytechnic of Wales. He has published work on headteachers, computer literacy and systems analysis.

John Mathews is Senior Lecturer in the School of Industrial Relations and Organizational Behaviour at the University of New South Wales, Australia. He has worked in the labour movement, and is author of *Tools of Change: New Technology and the Democratisation of Work* (Pluto Australia, 1989) and *Age of Democracy: The Politics of Post-Fordism* (Oxford, 1989).

Robin Murray is a Fellow at the Institute for Development Studies at the University of Sussex, and was Director of Economic Planning for the GLC.

David Noble is a Professor of History at Drexel University, Philadelphia. He is author of *America by Design: Science, Technology and the Rise of Corporate Capitalism* (Knopf, 1977) and *Forces of Production: A Social History of Industrial Automation* (Knopf, 1984), which is a fuller version of the paper in this volume.

Kevin Robins is a Research Associate at the Centre for Urban and Regional Development Studies at the University of Newcastle upon Tyne. He is author, with Frank Webster, of *Information Technology: A Luddite Analysis* (Ablex, 1986), *The Technical Fix: Education, Computers and Industry* (Macmillan, 1989) and is editor, with Les Levidow, of *Cyborg Worlds: The Military Information Society* (Free Association Books, 1989).

Frank Webster is a Professor of Sociology at Oxford Polytechnic. He is author, with Kevin Robins, of *Information Technology: A Luddite Analysis* (Ablex, 1986) and *The Technical Fix: Education, Computers and Industry* (Macmillan, 1989).

Michael Young is Senior Lecturer in the Sociology of Education and Co-ordinator of the Post 16 Education Centre at the Institute of Education, University of London. He has published widely in the sociology of education, notably *Knowledge and Control* (Collier Macmillan, 1971) and on vocational education and training.

Index